MULTICULTURAL EDUCATION SERIES

James A. Banks, Series Editor

Why Race and Culture Matter in Schools:
Closing the Achievement Gap in
America's Classrooms

TYRONE C. HOWARD

Culturally Responsive Teaching: Theory,
Research, and Practice, SECOND EDITION

GENEVA GAY

Diversity and Equity in Science Education:
Research, Policy, and Practice

OKHEE LEE AND CORY A. BUXTON

Forbidden Language: English Learners and
Restrictive Language Policies

PATRICIA GÁNDARA AND MEGAN HOPKINS, EDS.

The Light in Their Eyes:
Creating Multicultural Learning
Communities, 10TH ANNIVERSARY EDITION

SONIA NIETO

The Flat World and Education:
How America's Commitment to Equity Will
Determine Our Future

LINDA DARLING-HAMMOND

Teaching What *Really* Happened:
How to Avoid the Tyranny of Textbooks and
Get Students Excited About Doing History

JAMES W. LOEWEN

Diversity and the New Teacher:
Learning from Experience in Urban Schools

CATHERINE CORNBLETH

Frogs into Princes: Writings on School Reform

LARRY CUBAN

Educating Citizens in a Multicultural Society,
SECOND EDITION

JAMES A. BANKS

Culture, Literacy, and Learning:
Taking Bloom in the Midst of the Whirlwind

CAROL D. LEE

Facing Accountability in Education:
Democracy and Equity at Risk

CHRISTINE E. SLEETER, ED.

Talkin Black Talk:
Language, Education, and Social Change

H. SAMY ALIM AND JOHN BAUGH, EDS.

Improving Access to Mathematics:
Diversity and Equity in the Classroom

NA'ILAH SUAD NASIR AND PAUL COBB, EDS.

"To Remain an Indian":
Lessons in Democracy from a Century of
Native American Education

K. TSIANINA LOMAWAIMA AND
TERESA L. MCCARTY

Education Research in the Public Interest:
Social Justice, Action, and Policy

GLORIA LADSON-BILLINGS AND
WILLIAM F. TATE, EDS.

Multicultural Strategies for Education and
Social Change: Carriers of the Torch in the
United States and South Africa

ARNETHA F. BALL

We Can't Teach What We Don't Know:
White Teachers, Multiracial Schools,
SECOND EDITION

GARY R. HOWARD

Un-Standardizing Curriculum: Multicultural
Teaching in the Standards-Based Classroom

CHRISTINE E. SLEETER

Beyond the Big House: African American
Educators on Teacher Education

GLORIA LADSON-BILLINGS

Teaching and Learning in Two Languages:
Bilingualism and Schooling in the
United States

EUGENE E. GARCÍA

Improving Multicultural Education: Lessons
from the Intergroup Education Movement

CHERRY A. MCGEE BANKS

Education Programs for Improving Intergroup
Relations: Theory, Research, and Practice

WALTER G. STEPHAN AND W. PAUL VOGT, EDS.

Walking the Road: Race, Diversity, and Social
Justice in Teacher Education

MARILYN COCHRAN-SMITH

City Schools and the American Dream:
Reclaiming the Promise of Public Education

PEDRO A. NOGUERA

(continued)

Why Race and Culture Matter in Schools

Closing the Achievement Gap in America's Classrooms

TYRONE C. HOWARD

Foreword by Geneva Gay

Teachers College, Columbia University
New York and London

Published by Teachers College Press, 1234 Amsterdam Avenue, New York, NY 10027

Library of Congress Cataloging-in-Publication Data

Howard, Tyrone G.
  Why race and culture matter in schools : closing the achievement gap in America's classrooms / Tyrone G. Howard ; foreword by Geneva Gay.
      p. cm.—(Multicultural education series)
  Includes bibliographical references and index.
  ISBN 978-0-8077-5071-1 (pbk.)—ISBN 978-0-8077-5072-8 (hardcover)
  1. Educational equalization--United States. 2. Academic achievement—United States. 3. Minorities—Education--United States. I. Title.
  LC213.2.H67 2010
  379.2′60973—dc22

                                                              2009051102

ISBN 978-0-8077-5071-1 (paper)
ISBN 978-0-8077-5072-8 (hardcover)

Printed on acid-free paper
Manufactured in the United States of America

17   16   15   14   13   12   11   10   8   7   6   5   4   3

In memory of
Chip
(1958–2009)

Contents

Series Foreword

Explanations for disparities in the academic achievement of low-income, minority, and mainstream students have a long, complex, and contested history in the United States as well as in other nations (Banks, 2004; 2009). President Lyndon B. Johnson's War on Poverty, initiated by legislation introduced in 1964, focused attention on the nation's poor (Harrington, 1962), including vulnerable students in the schools. In the 1960s, the genetic explanation or paradigm, as Howard points out in this comprehensive, important, and engaging book, was an institutionalized explanation for the academic achievement of students from low-income and ethnic minority groups. Liberal social scientists and educators constructed the cultural deprivation paradigm to provide an alternative to the genetic explanation that was embedded and largely uncontested in American institutions, including the schools, colleges, and universities.

The cultural deprivation explanation—which must be understood within its historical, cultural, and political context—was constructed by progressive social scientists such as Benjamin C. Bloom, Allison Davis, and Robert Hess (1965), who were on the faculty of the highly esteemed education department at the University of Chicago. The cultural deprivation explanation, as Howard makes explicit, views the limited cultural capital in the home and communities of low-income and minority students as the major factor which explains their low academic achievement. It devotes little attention to other factors, such as the political economy of the larger society or the structures within the school. Consequently, the cultural deprivation paradigm, as Ryan (1971) cogently argues, was widely viewed as "blaming the victims" for their dismal educational status and structural exclusion.

Howard describes how the cultural deficit paradigm still casts a long shadow on the American educational landscape, is internalized by many teachers, and results in low teacher expectations and uninspiring teaching in many inner-city classrooms populated heavily by African American and Latino students. He gives appropriate and deserved respect and recognition to the pioneering scholars who constructed the cultural difference paradigm in the 1970s and 1980s to critique and provide an alternative to the cultural deficit paradigm. These scholars included Manuel Ramírez, Aflredo Castañeda (1974), Ronald Edmonds (1986), and A. Wade Boykin (1986).

The cultural difference explanation provided a significant antidote to the cultural deficit paradigm and reveals the strengths and resilience of the families, communities, and cultures of students from diverse racial, ethnic, and linguistic groups (Wang & Gordon, 1994). However, as Howard points out in one of the most sophisticated and nuanced discussions I have read on the role of culture in learning, cultural difference explanations—if they are not mediated by a deep understanding of the ways in which cultures are fluid, changing, multifaceted, contextual, and complex—can lead to stereotypic thinking about cultures and the essentialization of the cultures of students from diverse groups. The constructors of the cultural difference theories were acutely aware of this risk when their work was interpreted and implemented by school practitioners. In 1981, Cox and Ramírez described how the theory of field-sensitive and field-independent learning styles that Ramírez and Castañeda constructed had been misapplied:

> The concept of cognitive or learning styles of minority and other students is easily oversimplified and misunderstood or misinterpreted. Unfortunately, it has been used to stereotype minority students or to further label them rather than to identify individual differences that are educationally meaningful. (p. 61)

In his informative and insightful discussion of the teaching implication of culture, Howard presents an overview of the work of scholars who are conducting pioneering investigations on the instructional implications of culture, including research by Lee (2007) on teaching literacy skills to inner-city African American students; Nasir (2007) on using basketball to teach high school mathematics to African American students; Rogoff (2003) on how learning is embedded in communities, and research on culture and teaching by Gutiérrez and Rogoff (2003). Howard's authoritative and astute discussion of culture and teaching makes it explicit why teachers need to "move . . . beyond superficial, essentialized notions of student and group culture" that give little consideration to "student individuality or group variability."

Howard thinks that it is essential but not sufficient for teachers to acquire a sophisticated and deep understanding of culture and its teaching implications. He also believes that race still matters and influences teaching and learning in diverse schools in powerful ways.

Howard describes why an analysis and understanding of race is a critical part of school reform designed to narrow the achievement gap between students of color and mainstream students. He adduces empirical evidence by researchers such as Steele (2004), Polluck (2004), and Lewis (2003) to describe the ways in which race influences student and teacher expectations in significant ways, and yet is denied by educators who embrace a colorblind or colormute stance (Polluck). The student voices describing how their teachers discriminate against them because of their race is chilling.

Howard's book will help practicing educators deal effectively with the growing ethnic, cultural, and linguistic diversity within the nation and the schools. American classrooms are experiencing the largest influx of immigrant students since the beginning of the 20th century. About a million immigrants are making the United States their home each year (Martin & Midgley, 2006). Between 1997 and 2006, 9,105,162 immigrants entered the United States (U.S. Department of Homeland Security, 2007). Only 15% came from nations in Europe. Most came from nations in Asia, from Mexico, and from nations in Latin America, Central America, and the Caribbean (U.S. Department of Homeland Security, 2007). A large but undetermined number of undocumented immigrants also enter the United States each year. In 2007, *The New York Times* estimated that there were 12 million illegal immigrants in the United States (Immigration Sabotage, 2007). The influence of an increasingly ethnically diverse population on U.S. schools, colleges, and universities is and will continue to be enormous.

Schools in the United States are more diverse today than they have been since the early 1900s when a multitude of immigrants entered the United States from Southern, Central, and Eastern Europe. In the 34-year period between 1973 and 2007, the percentage of students of color in U.S. public schools increased from 22 to 55 percent (Dillon, 2006; National Center for Education Statistics, 2008). If current trends continue, students of color will equal or exceed the percentage of White students in U.S. public schools within one or two decades. In 2004, students of color exceeded the number of Whites students in six states: California, Hawaii, Louisiana, Mississippi, New Mexico, and Texas.

Language and religious diversity is also increasing in the U.S. student population. In 2000, about 20% of the school-age population spoke a language at home other than English (U.S. Census Bureau, 2003). The Progressive Policy Institute estimated that 50 million Americans (out of 300 million) spoke a language at home other than English in 2008. Harvard professor Diana L. Eck (2001) calls the United States the "most religiously diverse nation on earth" (p. 4). Islam is now the fastest-growing religion in the United States as well as in several European nations such as France, the United Kingdom, and The Netherlands (Banks, 2009; Cesari, 2004). Most teachers now in the classroom and in teacher education programs are likely to have students from diverse ethnic, racial, linguistic, and religious groups in their classrooms during their careers. This is true for both inner-city and suburban teachers in the United States as well as in many other Western nations (Banks, 2009).

The major purpose of the *Multicultural Education Series* is to provide preservice educators, practicing educators, graduate students, scholars, and policy makers with an interrelated and comprehensive set of books that summarizes and analyzes important research, theory, and practice related to the education of ethnic, racial, cultural, and linguistic groups in the United States and the education of mainstream students about diversity. The dimensions of multicultural education, developed by Banks (2004) and described in the *Handbook of Research on Multicultural Education,* provide the conceptual framework for the development of the publications in the *Series.* They are: *content integration, the knowledge construction process, prejudice reduction, an equity pedagogy,* and *an empowering school culture and social structure.*

The books in the *Series* provide research, theoretical, and practical knowledge about the behaviors and learning characteristics of students of color, language minority students, and low-income students. They also provide knowledge about ways to improve academic achievement and race relations in educational settings. Multicultural education is consequently as important for middle-class White suburban students as it is for students of color who live in the inner city. Multicultural education fosters the public good and the overarching goals of the commonwealth.

Teachers and other educators who read this engrossing, incisive, and informative book will gain a complex understanding of culture and teaching, and a knowledge of how race influences teaching and learning in diverse schools. They will also acquire, from the case studies of the four effective schools whose populations consist primarily of African American and Latino students, a knowledge of what exemplary schools look like and how to reform schools to make them more culturally responsive, intellectually challenging, and joyous places for students from diverse groups.

Howard, like an earlier generation of scholars such as Edmonds (1986), Sizemore (1987), and Levine and Lezotte (1995), identifies the characteristics of effective schools for low-income and minority students. Howard's characteristics are (1) visionary leadership; (2) teachers' effective practice; (3) intensive academic intervention; (4) the explicit acknowledgment of race; and (5) the engagement of parents and community. It is illuminating to juxtapose the characteristics of effective schools for low-income and minority students identified by Howard with those described by Levine and Lezotte in their 1995 research review. Most of the studies they reviewed were published in the 1970s and 1980s. This juxtaposition reveals both the continuity and changes in research on effective schools for low-income and minority students over several decades. Levine and Lezotte identified the most frequent characteristics of effective schools,

> [A] *safe and orderly environment, a shared faculty commitment to improving achievement, orientation focused on identifying and solving problems, high faculty cohesion, collaboration, and collegiality, high faculty input in decision making, and schoolwide emphasis on recognizing positive performance.* (pp. 525–526) [italics in original]

Howard enlivens this informative and insightful book with a human touch—he describes how the students in his inner-city fifth grade class actualized Mrs. Hazel Russell's high expectations for them, and how his son Jabari became a victim of cultural misunderstandings by his teacher and his successful intervention. A paramount goal of Howard's project is to complicate and deepen educators' understanding of culture and its implications for closing the achievement gap. He has achieved his goal admirably. His lucid and succinct writing style will captivate and endear teachers, curriculum specialists, educational administrators, and citizens concerned about improving schools. I hope this needed, heartfelt, and timely book will be read by scores of educators and will deeply affect their hearts, minds, and interactions with students.

James A. Banks

REFERENCES

Banks, J. A. (2004). Multicultural education: Historical development, dimensions, and practice. In J. A. Banks & C. A. M. Banks (Eds.). *Handbook of research on multicultural education* (2nd ed., pp. 3–29). San Francisco: Jossey-Bass.

Banks, J. A. (Ed.). (2009). *The Routledge international companion to multicultural education.* New York and London: Routledge.

Banks, J. A. & Banks, C. A. M. (Eds.) (2004). *Handbook of research on multicultural education* (2nd ed.). San Francisco: Jossey-Bass.

Bloom, B. S., Davis, A., & Hess, R. (1965). *Compensatory education for cultural deprivation*. New York: Holt.

Boykin, A. W. (1986). The triple quandary and the schooling of Afro-American children. In U. Neisser (Ed.), *The school achievement of minority children: New perspectives* (pp. 57–92). Hillside, NJ: Erlbaum.

Cesari, J. (2004). *When Islam and democracy meet: Muslims in Europe and the United States*. New York: Pelgrave Macmillan.

Cox, B. G. & Ramírez, M. III (1981). Cognitive styles: Implications for multiethnic education. In J. A. Banks (Ed.), *Education in the 80s: Multiethnic education* (pp. 61–71). Washington, DC: National Education Association.

Dillon, S. (2006, August 27). In schools across U. S., the melting pot overflows. *The New York Times*, vol. CLV [155] (no. 53,684), pp. A7 & 16.

Eck, D. L. (2001). *A new religious America: How a "Christian country" has become the world's most religiously diverse nation*. New York: HarperSanFrancisco.

Edmonds, R. (1986). Characteristics of effective schools. In U. Neisser (Ed.), *The school achievement of minority children: New perspectives* (pp. 93-104). Hillside, NJ: Erlbaum.

Gutiérrez, K. & Rogoff, B. (2003). Cultural ways of knowing: Individual traits or repertoires of practice. *Educational Researcher, 32* (5), 19-25.

Harrington, M. (1962). *The other America: Poverty in the United States*. New York: Macmillan.

Immigration sabotage [Editorial]. (2007, June 4). *New York Times*, p. A22.

Lee, C. D. (2007). *Culture, literacy, and learning: Taking bloom in the midst of the whirlwind*. New York: Teachers College Press.

Levine, D. U. & Lezotte, L. W. (1995). Effective schools research. In J. A. Banks & C. A. M. Banks (Eds.), *Handbook of research on multicultural education* (pp. 525–547). New York: Macmillan.

Lewis, A. E. (2003). *Race in the schoolyard: Negotiating the color line in classrooms and communities*. New Brunswick, NJ: Rutgers University Press.

Martin, P. & Midgley, E. (1999). Immigration to the United States. *Population Bulletin, 54* (2), pp. 1–44. Washington, D.C.: Population Reference Bureau.

Nasir, N. S. (2007). Identity, goals, and learning: The case of basketball mathematics. In N. S. Nasir & P. Cobb (Eds.), *Improving access to mathematics: Diversity and equity in the classroom* (pp. 132–145). New York: Teachers College Press.

National Center for Education Statistics (2008). *The condition of education 2008*. Washington, DC: U.S. Department of Education. Retrieved August 26, 2009 from http://nces.ed.gov/pubsearch/pubsinfo.asp?pubid=2008031

Pollock, M. (2004). *Colormute: Race talk dilemmas in an American school*. Princeton, NJ: Princeton University Press.

Progressive Policy Institute (2008). *50 million Americans speak languages other than English at home*. Retrieved September 2, 2008 from http://www.ppionline.org/ppi_ci.cfm?knlgAreaID=108&subsecID=900003&contentID=254619

Ramírez, M. & Castañeda, A. (1974). *Cultural democracy, bicognitive development, and education.* New York: Academic Press.

Roberts, S. (2008, August 14). A generation away, minorities may become the majority in U.S. *The New York Times,* vol. CLVII [175] (no. 54,402), pp. A1 & A18.

Rogoff, B. (2003). *The cultural nature of human development.* New York: Oxford University Press.

Ryan, W. (1971). *Blaming the victim.* New York: Pantheon.

Sizemore, B. A. (1987). The effective African American elementary school. In W. W. Noblit & W. T. Pink (Eds.), *Schooling in social context: Qualitative studies* (pp. 175–202). Nowrwood, NJ: Ablex.

Steele, C. (2004). A threat in the air: How stereotypes shape intellectual identity and performance. In J. A. Banks & C. A. M. Banks (Eds.), Handbook of research in multicultural education (2nd ed., pp. 682–698). San Francisco: Jossey-Bass.

Suárez-Orozco, C., Suárez-Orozco, M. M., & Todorova, I. (2008). *Learning a new land: Immigrant students in American society.* Cambridge: Harvard University Press.

U.S. Census Bureau (2003, October). Language use and English-speaking ability: 2000. Retrieved September 2, 2008 from http://www.census.gov/prod/2003pubs/c2kbr-29.pdf

U.S. Census Bureau (2008, August 14). *Statistical abstract of the United States.* Retrieved August 20, 2008 from http://www.census.gov/prod/2006pubs/07statab/pop.pdf

United States Department of Homeland Security (2007). *Yearbook of immigration statistics, 2006.* Washington, DC: Office of Immigration Statistics, Author. Retrieved August 11, 2009 from http://www.dhs.gov/files/statistics/publications/yearbook.shtm

Wang, M. C. & Gordon, E. W. (Eds.). (1994). *Educational resilience in inner-city America: Challenges and prospects.* Hillside, NJ: Erlbaum.

Foreword

Achievement gaps in the quality of experiences and outcomes at all levels of U.S. public education are relentless and extensive. The victims are obvious, the causes are complex and debatable, and efforts toward remediation are still producing uneven results. Few if any educators would disagree that poor students of color, especially African, Latino, Native, Pacific Islander, and some Southeastern Asian Americans, are the most negatively affected by disparities and inequities in educational opportunities and outcomes. But this is where the consensus ends; reasons for these disparities and strategies for overcoming them are highly divergent and often contentious. A critical issue too often absent from these debates is a thorough analysis of race, racism, and culture as causes and potential solutions. At first glance it would appear that these are obvious factors in closing the achievement gaps, given that students of color experience higher levels of underachievement than their majority racial group peers. Sometimes the obvious is difficult for educators to see and concede, especially when it involves sensitive issues such as race and racism. Many U.S. citizens, educators, and policy makers are not even willing to acknowledge the existence of racism in education, not to mention subjecting it to careful scrutiny and targeting it for explicit intervention as a means for improving the performance of underachieving students.

Why Race and Culture Matter in Schools is a welcome addition to efforts to counter habits of avoiding and giving only superficial treatment to race and racism in analyzing educational inequities, by focusing first on what actually is before attending to what should be in devising better instructional programs and strategies for ethnically and culturally diverse students. Although the argument is made more forcefully for how race and racism affect the educational opportunities and outcomes of African and Latino Americans, the broad issues raised and the insights provided are applicable to other ethnic, racial, and cultural groups of color as well. The author combines theory, research, and practice to make a compelling argument for educators to give race, racism, and culture the attention they deserve in unveiling

xvii

the deeply ingrained causes of disparities in the educational experiences majority and minority students receive.

This book will be challenging for some readers and affirming for others. It is at times disheartening and other times inspiring, sometimes anguishing but always enlightening. The author presents some sobering statistics about the school achievement of students of color. They are not necessarily new, in that other scholars and analysts have pointed them out previously, but they are graphic reminders of just how dismal current realities and future prospects are for students of color if U.S. education policies and programs continue on their existing courses of action. They make a compelling case for the magnitude of the plight of students of color, and the urgency for immediate and wide-scale transformative interventions. These harsh realities are not pervaded by a sense of fatalism and doom; instead, there is an air of hopefulness and a strong conviction that it is possible to achieve high-quality education for all ethnically, racially, and culturally diverse students. This hopefulness is grounded in thoughtful, informed analysis and practical possibilities, not fanciful dreams.

One message that comes across clearly and persistently in this book is that race, racism, and cultural diversity are real, prolific, and profound factors in teaching and learning. Therefore, dealing realistically with them is imperative if the achievement gaps are to ever close. Tyrone Howard makes a persuasive appeal for educators to confront these realities directly, understand their depth and complexity, and work through the challenges they present to create more viable techniques for teaching students of color and poverty more effectively. A combination of insights gleaned from his academic, personal, and professional experiences makes his explanations more poignant and palatable. He speaks from a position of one who is where he wants other educators to go in improving the quality of learning opportunities and outcomes for racially diverse students. He does not suggest what others should do from a distance, but includes himself in the proposed mandates. Interjecting himself personally into the academic discourse gives credence to his credibility; the readers get the feeling that the author will be as much a part of the process of reform as he expects them to be. The resulting sense of collegiality and camaraderie entices readers to be more receptive and more responsive to proposed actions, since they will be exploring new pedagogical terrains with an empathetic fellow traveler who has already been there. The author's declared experience is a trustworthy guide for other educators in considering alternative techniques for teaching students of color.

Howard speaks candidly to prospective and practicing teachers and teacher educators about dealing with race, culture, and racism in improving the equity of achievement outcomes. He does not placate them or lead them into a false sense of security by suggesting that these tasks will be easily and quickly accomplished. Instead, he repeatedly reminds them that understanding racial and cultural diversity as a basis for closing achievement gaps is a difficult but necessary undertaking. For example, Howard provides explanations of some common errors associated with diversity issues, as well as perspectives and experiences of different ethnic groups with race, culture, and racism and techniques for engaging in constructive race-based conversations and instruction with colleagues and students. Some of the myths discussed are the Eugenics notion that European Americans are naturally more biologically advanced and intelligent than various groups of color; that colorblindness is a feasible ideology for guiding instructional practices for racially diverse student populations; and that good intentions without related culturally relevant knowledge and pedagogical skills are sufficient to accomplish educational equity.

The complexity of these issues is another theme that rings loudly and clearly throughout *Why Race and Culture Matter in Schools*. Some readers may be inclined to interpret Howard's repeated caution about this complexity as a reason to avoid race, racism, and culture in teaching. Most assuredly that is not his intention, because he also tells us over and over again that these are profound realities in U.S. society, in the lives of students and teachers, and in educational programs, policies, and practices. Calling attention to the complexities of race, racism, and culture is Howard's way of underscoring their significance and pervasiveness, and hence the need for teachers to be comprehensive in analyzing them, and to caution against in looking for panaceas that are generalizable to everyone. Antiracist education and culturally responsive engagements with ethnically diverse students are long-term endeavors that require much unlearning, relearning, struggle, vigilance, self-critique, and self-monitoring, as well as changes to the infrastructures of educational systems. They demand personal knowledge, courage, conviction, will, and skill; institutional transformation; and the redistribution of power and privilege. It is refreshing to read analyses of achievement disparities that focus largely on instructional quality, that neither blame victimized students and their families nor romanticize them, and that recognize that necessary changes cannot be accomplished if expedience is given priority over significance. The tone and substance of this book remind educators that achieving academic equality, justice, empowerment, and maximum success for racially diverse minority students who have been marginalized for far too long requires diligence and struggle. The achievement problems that need solving are urgent, deeply entrenched, and a long time in the making, and their solutions will not come quickly or easily. Pointing out this complexity is not intended to intimidate or dissuade teachers from aggressively pursuing educational equity for racially and culturally diverse students, but rather to prepare them realistically for the challenges involved.

Another critical dimension of the complexities of race, racism, and culture in education that comes across loudly in this book is their incredible internal diversity. There is no one version of these issues that is equally applicable to all members within a particular group, and certainly not across groups. Many historical, social, personal, experiential, and ecological variables cause them to vary widely among groups and individuals in different times, places, and circumstances. Thus, African American culture is not identical for all African Americans, nor is it expressed in the same way or manifested identically across individuals, events, and interactions. Similarly, racism is not experienced in the same way by all African Americans, or by all ethnic groups. This variance, however, does not nullify the existence of race, racism, and culture as issues that must be addressed.

Teachers often want the one answer or the one best practice that is good for all students. While this may be understandable on a human level, it is nonetheless a dubious pedagogical pursuit in teaching with and for ethnic and racial diversity (or teaching in general). Students are constantly evolving, complex beings with complex heritages, experiences, needs, and possibilities. These complexities should not incapacitate teachers. As Howard amply demonstrates, the answer is not to bypass cultural and racial complexities and try to deal with students as decontextualized individuals, as some educators are inclined to do. Instead, learning about and responding instructionally to race, racism, and culture must be continuous processes of inquiry, discovery, problem solving, deconstruction, and transformation. These investigations and responses should parallel the inherent complexities of the issues themselves. Howard is astute enough to realize that the demands of the instructional complexities of racial and cultural diversity are likely to intimidate some educators, so he responds by providing actual examples of how classroom teachers and teacher educators have dealt effectively with them, rather than merely telling readers what they should do. This is a wise strategy because of the power of parallel modeling in the professional development of teachers—that is, novices seeing illuminating actions of how they are expected to perform displayed by their more experienced professional colleagues.

Why Race and Culture Matter in Schools is simultaneously sobering and inspiring. The magnitude and pervasiveness of educational inequities it presents are so gripping that readers cannot escape from them, or deny that education for too many children of color is in a state of crisis. If it continues as it currently is without radical reforms the results will be catastrophic, not just for African, Latino, Asian, and Native American students and communities, but for everyone. These gaps in learning opportunities and achievement are not limited to academics in schools or to schools themselves. In the long run all segments of society suffer when the human capital and intellectual potential of groups of color are neglected or squandered. Certainly, settling the educational debt owed to underachieving and marginalized students of color through radical improvements in the quality of their educational experiences and outcomes is a moral imperative. It is the right and just thing to do. But it is more than that. It is a matter of survival, especially when survival is viewed as encompassing not just biological existence, but the maximization of all aspects of human be-ing and be-coming. Howard tells us in so many penetrating ways that we must act now, and at a depth and magnitude that will, in effect, be revolutionary.

At the same time it exposes the horror of inequities, this book is also encouraging and uplifting. It demonstrates that genuine educational equity and excellence can be accomplished for racially and culturally diverse students. The author uses information from both his own and others' theoretical, conceptual, and research scholarship, along with programs in practice, to demonstrate that cultural competence and culturally responsive pedagogy are productive in closing the achievement gaps. The case studies of actual teachers and real schools making a positive difference in performance for poor students of color, which most educators claim as their vision and mission, are a source of inspiration for them to follow suit.

Another important inspirational aspect of this book is its usefulness to different segments of the education profession. Its analytical explanations and practical suggestions are relevant to teachers, teacher educators, policy makers, researchers, and theorists. They are crafted in ways that enable educators from a wide spectrum of participation in the professional community to feel personally included, and to realize that closing the achievement gaps is as much their mandate as anyone else's. This inclusivity should be a source of encouragement for both reluctant and eager advocates of the kind of instructional beliefs and behaviors proposed for closing the achievement gaps. Reading *Why Race and Culture Matter in Schools* is somewhat like joining a community of practice or a collaborative team of change agents devoted to a common cause.

The author tells it like it is by dealing explicitly with the harsh realities of disparities in educational opportunities for poor African, Asian,

Latino, and Native American students, and by being candid about the complexities involved in understanding how race, racism, and culture affect educational opportunities and outcomes. His candor should be a model and motivation for other educators to emulate. However challenging they may be, genuine reality-based educational analyses, decision making, and instructional actions are much better than wishes and dreams for making significant changes that will prevail over time. The educational futures of children of color are too important, and too precarious, for anything less. Our best efforts must be informed by a thorough understanding of how race, racism, and culture have influenced educational practices in the past, and must seek to transform this influence in more constructive ways in the future. High praise is due to Tyrone Howard for repositioning candid analyses of race and culture at the center of efforts to improve the school performance of underachieving African, Asian, Latino, and Native American students. Therefore, this book is a must read for anyone who is genuinely committed to promoting educational equity and excellence for children from diverse ethnic, racial, cultural, and social backgrounds.

—Geneva Gay

Acknowledgments

A project such as this does not happen without a tremendous amount of support, encouragement, constructive criticism, and input from countless people over an extended period of time. I view the completion of this book as a collective endeavor that was influenced by my observations, conversations, and insights from countless individuals to whom I am most grateful.

I would like to thank my friend and mentor Jim Banks for his encouragement on this book project. Jim has been a mentor for close to 15 years. He has been instrumental in my development as a researcher and scholar. I cannot say enough about how much his tough love and constructive editing have helped me to become a better writer and thinker on issues pertaining to disenfranchised populations. Every scholar needs a Jim Banks in his or her corner. Thank you Jim. I am also indebted to Geneva Gay, who also has been a tremendous example of a humane, caring, and compassionate scholar. Geneva has been a vital part of my life personally and professionally, and in many ways has been like another mother. I want to thank her for always caring about me, my family, and my work.

I want to acknowledge a number of my colleagues in the Graduate School of Education & Information Studies at UCLA. My dean, Aimee Dorr, has always been supportive of my endeavors. My current chair, Megan Franke, and past chairs Sandra Graham, Danny Solorzano, and Pat McDonough have all been instrumental in my career as a scholar. I also want to thank Kris Gutierrez, Mike Rose, and Walter Allen for their support and encouragement over the years. I also want to acknowledge Jody Priselac, Gary Orfield, Fred Erickson, John Rogers, Ernest Morrell, and Robert Cooper for their contributions to the work we do at UCLA, and for the conversations that we have shared about creating educational equity. I would also like to acknowledge all of the hard-working and committed faculty and staff in Center X.

I am grateful also to the most intellectually gifted students that I have been fortunate to work with at UCLA for the past decade. My doctoral students have inspired me in more ways than they know. I have learned more from them than I could have ever taught them, and this project is enriched by having their wisdom influence my work. Kerri Ullucci, Glenda Aleman, Ifeoma Amah, Natalia Jaramillo, Jevon Hunter, Rema Reynolds, Cynthia Pineda-Scott, Benji Chang, Nick Henning, LaMont Terry, Danny Cho, Terry Flennaugh, and Patrick Camangian are all bright, young minds that I know will change the face of educational research and practice. Keep up the great work that you do.

There are other colleagues that have influenced my development as a scholar over the years. Rich Milner has been not only a good friend, but more like a brother. Thanks for all you do. Cynthia Tyson and Jennifer Obidah have been invaluable mentors and big sisters to me. Andre Branch, Stephen Hancock, Gloria Ladson-Billings, Carol Lee, Jeff Duncan-Andrade, Garrett Duncan, Donna Ford, Larry Fields, Beverly Gordon, Shaun Harper, Uma Jayakumar, Ron Rochon, Tim Eatman, Adrienne Dixson, Eric Johnson, Keith Harrison, Jeannine Dingus-Eason, Jackie Irvine, Patricia Halagao, Thomas Parham, Pedro Noguera, and Ed Taylor have all helped to shape my views of educational research, scholarship, and commitment to community, equity, and school transformation.

I also want to acknowledge Karen Jarsky, Rema Reynolds, and Kris Gutierrez for reading and editing previous drafts of this work, and Brian Ellerbeck and Lori Tate from Teachers College Press for the development of this book.

I am eternally grateful to the students that I was fortunate enough to teach at Longfellow Elementary School in Compton, California. The students will always be in my heart, because they helped me to learn how to teach, inspired me to think critically about educational equity, and remain a central reason why I do the work that I do. I also want to acknowledge my students from the VIP Scholars Program at UCLA. They are some of the most intellectually gifted high school students that I have ever encountered, and they give me hope for what lies in our future.

While I have been fortunate to have a number of mentors in my professional career, there are people who were instrumental in my life before academia, and to them I am most grateful. My first teachers were my parents, and I am eternally grateful for their unconditional love. My father, Caldwell Howard, has always modeled manhood, work ethic, and integrity. If I can live to be half the father and man that he is, I will be more than happy. My mother, Beverly Sisnett, has always believed in me. She has been a loving and caring mom, and has shown unconditional support for me and my endeavors from the moment of my birth. Love you, mom! Johonna Howard and Leatruce Hill have been my "other mothers." Thank you both for all of your care and concern over the years. Your love, support, and wisdom do not go unnoticed. My brother, Gregory Howard, has been by my side dating back to the Spring Street days, and growing up in Compton. Love you, baby brother! Keith Howard has been the big brother I have never had, and I will always be grateful for his being the role model he has always been in my life. I also must recognize the Cross, Hogan, Hill, and Pendergrass families for their care and support of me, my work, and my family over the years.

I have saved the best for last. The primary reason that I do what I do is to create a better tomorrow for my four children, Jabari, Jameelah, Jaleel, and Jahlani. Each of them is my hero, and they inspire me in more ways than they will ever know. Their intellect, curiosity, humor, dedication, and compassion all fuel my desire to be a better father, man, scholar, and teacher. I love you guys. Thanks for your persistent questions about when the book will be done. Now it's here. Thanks for pushing me. Last but not least, I will always be grateful to my lifetime partner and loving wife Maisah. She has always been in my corner, a constructive critic who keeps me grounded, and a fierce defender and caretaker of our family. She holds it together when I am out trying to save the world. She also has been my best friend, and an excellent example of womanhood. Thank you for being there for the past two decades. I love you.

Finally, I want to thank all the educators and students who have allowed me to spend time in their schools and classrooms, and provided me the opportunity to understand their realities and how we can best improve them.

Introduction

This book addresses perhaps the single most pressing and perplexing issue in education thus far in the 21st century—the achievement gap. This moniker is used often to refer to the discrepancy in educational outcomes and access between various student groups in the United States, in particular African American, Native American, certain Asian American, and Latino students on the low end of the performance scale, and their White and certain Asian American counterparts at the higher end of the academic performance scale. This gap similarly is witnessed between students—regardless of color—who come from low-income backgrounds and their peers who come from middle-class and affluent homes. The purpose of this book is to document the gap in certain academic areas, to shed light on some of the factors contributing to the discrepancies, and ultimately to critically examine what researchers and practitioners have posited as critical interventions that may be useful in ameliorating the disparities in educational outcomes across different groups.

The perennial underachievement of culturally diverse and low-income students is an ongoing concern for educators at all levels. A myriad of factors contribute to the widespread disparities in achievement between these groups of students and their counterparts. However, there are certain areas that remain largely undertheorized and frequently overlooked in analyses of students' school performance—namely, the importance of race and culture in the schooling experiences of today's youth.

This book explicitly examines the roles that culture and race play in the teaching and learning process in multicultural schools. Moreover, this book contends that an improved and more comprehensive understanding of race and culture can play an important role in helping to close the achievement gap. With that in mind, the goals of this book are to: (1) help educators recognize the complexities in the swiftly changing demographics in the nation's schools; (2) describe the ways in which culture and race are two of the primary variables of teaching, learning, and achievement in multicultural school settings; and (3)

1

use a multifaceted understanding of race and culture to inform theory and practices that may ameliorate the academic achievement gap.

The key components of this book are both conceptual and empirical, and build on the work of a number of other scholars who have been concerned with creating equitable schooling conditions for all students, regardless of their racial, ethnic, cultural, gender, linguistic, or social class background (Anyon, 2005; Banks, 2004; Carter, 2005; Darling-Hammond, 2007; Gay, 2000; T. C. Howard, 2001a, Irvine, 2003; Ladson-Billings, 1995, 2006; C. D. Lee, 2002; Milner, 2003; Moll & Gonzales, 2004; Noguera, 2003; Sleeter, 1996; Tate, 1997; R. R. Valencia, 1997; Valenzuela, 1999) . This book attempts to explicitly translate frequently cited theoretical principles into classroom practice based on empirical evidence. Included in the work are data from four different studies conducted over the past 3 years that document classroom practices, teacher–student interactions, programmatic interventions, student and parent viewpoints of schools, and teachers' perspectives on teaching in multicultural school settings. These findings are situated in both a multicultural theory and practice framework, offering important considerations for practitioners and researchers who seek a more fluid synthesis of how race and culture influence the teaching and learning process for students from diverse groups. This book also incorporates tenets of critical race and sociocultural theory, two theoretical frameworks that offer a number of important ramifications for works concerned with race and culture. Finally, this book documents schools where the achievement gap has been closed. Drawing from research at four different school sites, the most promising practices, programs, and principles that were salient in creating high-performing schools are identified and analyzed.

SOCIOECONOMIC STATUS AND SCHOOL PERFORMANCE

Causal explanations of the achievement gap must take into account a multitude of factors. One of the primary foci of this book is that a thorough analysis must be mindful of the myriad of social, cultural, economic, and historical factors that have affected different groups in the United States. To that end, race and culture are the primary units of analysis in this work. At the same time, however, one of the most critical factors behind schooling disparities is socioeconomic status. While it is not the focus of this book, I would be remiss to not acknowledge the powerful role that socioeconomic status plays in the educational opportunities afforded to students in U.S. schools. Some contend that economics, perhaps more than any other factor, explains why academic performance disparities exist across groups (Anyon, 2005; Rothstein, 2004; W. J. Wilson, 2009). Undoubtedly, poverty has deep-seated influences on the manner in which students experience schools: Students from impoverished backgrounds are less likely to have access to medical care and attention, which can allow vision, dental, hearing, asthmatic, and other ailments to go undertreated, or in some cases not treated at all, undoubtedly influencing school performance.

A growing body of research has documented that children living in older, dilapidated homes are more likely to be exposed to lead-based paint, and the direct correlation that this exposure has to delayed cognitive development and behavioral problems (Brooks-Gunn & Duncan, 1997).

Moreover, children from impoverished backgrounds are more likely to have parents with low-wage jobs or no employment at all, increasing the likelihood of moving from place to place, and influencing the quality of continuous schooling they receive. Furthermore, an increasing number of students who attend U.S. schools are homeless, with the number reaching over 1 million during the 2006–07 academic year (National Center for Homeless Education, 2007). Needless to say, the disproportionate occurrences of violence, crime, drugs, and death that young people in impoverished communities are exposed to on a regular basis have an influence on the social, psychological, and emotional well-being that they bring to school, and these effects often go untreated. Thus, it is essential not to ignore these realities but rather to acknowledge and give credence to the deleterious effects that they have on millions of students in this country each and every day. In this current economy W. J. Wilson (2009) reminds us that it is more than just race that explains disparate life experiences and opportunities, and that understanding social structures and culture are salient variables in eradicating poverty.

Unfortunately, despite the economic, social, and emotional challenges that students face as a result of poverty, practitioners are in dire need of the knowledge and skills that can assist them in their classrooms on a daily basis. Many teachers may feel overwhelmed by the large-scale social and economic factors that create hardships for students and their families every day, and may feel powerless in influencing policy and structural change that is desperately needed in the name of school reform. Therefore, providing practitioners with a knowledge base, as well as practical references and skills, from which to better educate students from diverse backgrounds, can be a valuable response to the macrocultural and structural poverty issues that are beyond the scope of individual teachers. The confluence of race, class, and culture plays out in classrooms every day in this country, yet many practitioners and researchers who are well meaning, and committed to helping all students learn, are not well informed on how these differences play out, and are ill equipped to structure teaching and learning arrangements in their classrooms to build on students' cultural knowledge and strengths.

In a similar vein, researchers are frequently in pursuit of theoretical frameworks, literature bases, and conceptual understandings about how to investigate the challenges faced by culturally diverse students in the nation's schools. A legion of scholars have helped to produce important knowledge on many of the challenges faced by nonmainstream students. Despite these noble efforts and rigorous works, there remains a need for additional research to provide insights into plausible models, meaningful explanations, and methodological approaches that may yield new knowledge that can improve schooling experiences for all students, and particularly for those whose learning outcomes are far from ideal.

OUTLINE OF THE BOOK

This book is divided into seven chapters. Chapter 1 examines how current school performance data demonstrate the ongoing achievement disparity between students from culturally diverse and low-income backgrounds and their counterparts from mainstream and more affluent backgrounds. Student outcomes in the area of reading and math proficiency, drop-out rates, SAT scores, and suspension and expulsion rates, among other areas, are examined. This chapter goes beyond mere reporting of achievement data; it also examines historical, social, and economic factors that have contributed to these gaps.

Chapter 2 examines the swiftly changing racial, ethnic, cultural, linguistic, and social class dynamics in the nation and its schools. The unprecedented change in demographics has tremendous local, national, and global consequences for the 21st century. The increase in numbers of students of Latino and Asian descent is indicative of a significant shift in the demographics of students entering the nation's schools compared with previous decades. The challenge educators face is how to effectively educate an increasingly diverse student population, when students of color are no longer a small portion of the national student population.

Chapter 3 provides a comprehensive description of the complicated notion of culture. Borrowing from sociocultural theory, the goal of this chapter is to clarify the manner in which culture is understood. The discussion moves away from static notions of culture that are frequently superficial and thereby have the potential to essentialize various ethnic groups while creating academic and social harm to students. In this book, culture is understood as a multifaceted concept situated within historical contexts, as opposed to intrinsic "traits" that are shaped by one's membership in an ethnic group.

Following the discussion of culture, Chapter 4 offers explicit theoretical arguments concerning how cultural knowledge and skills can be linked with pedagogical practices in ways that can be termed "culturally responsive." This chapter examines theory and research on culturally responsive teaching, and then describes how practitioners can structure learning situations, concepts, and skills in culturally recognizable formats that may contribute to higher levels of engagement, retention, and overall comprehension of course content by students from diverse groups.

Chapter 5 focuses on race. Race is examined as a concept that is different from culture, yet is equipped with a historical legacy that continues to have an influence on the manner in which racially diverse students experience school. Using critical race theory as a framework, this chapter provides an analysis of how race continues to be relevant to education in the 21st century. This chapter also includes data from high school students and how they believe race influences their school experiences. The goal of Chapter 5 is to give readers a better understanding of how racial ideas, beliefs, and attitudes continue to influence educational practice.

Chapter 6 examines the importance of helping novice and experienced teachers acquire, maintain, and build cultural competence and racial awareness that are essential for teaching in today's diverse classrooms. The coincidence of increasing cultural, ethnic, and racial heterogeneity of today's student population with the largely homogeneous teaching population merits important cross-cultural competence and racial awareness. This chapter examines the implications of the demographic divide between students and teachers that are becoming increasingly commonplace in classrooms.

Chapter 7 addresses one of the most important aspects of closing the achievement gap. It describes and examines schools that have been successful in closing these stubborn outcome disparities. By documenting four different schools that were studied over the course of 3 years, this chapter identifies five key themes that were most visible in schools that served predominantly students of color and students from low-income backgrounds. Part of the focus this chapter is to highlight the fact that school leaders, teachers, parents, and students are having success in surmounting odds that suggest that their success is not possible. Moreover, researchers must be willing to engage in research that investigates the primary factors that contribute to these schools' success.

MOVING AWAY FROM THE BLACK–WHITE DICHOTOMY

This book makes a deliberate shift away from the *Black–White* dichotomous terminology in its analysis of the achievement gap, for several reasons. First, the comparison of any particular group to White students, consciously and subconsciously creates the notion of White performance and achievement as being the desired norm or standard against which all other groups are measured. It also seeks to challenge ideas of White supremacy when it comes to school performance. This book makes an explicit shift away from such racial hierarchical arrangements, and suggests that a standard of excellence should be established based on an informed criterion with particular attention to the knowledge, skills, and cultural codes that students are expected to master, regardless of their racial identification.

Second, the usage of *Black–White* terminology creates a binary that is problematic on several levels. Oppression, discrimination, and the quest for equity in the United States cannot be fully understood in only Black and White terms. This approach omits the ongoing struggle, experiences, and contributions of Latinos, Asians, and Asian Pacific Islanders, and Indigenous populations. Moreover, the Black–White binary in school performance excludes the achievement level, educational history experiences, and challenges of non-White students. The racial and ethnic complexity of the U.S. population is such that any analysis of school achievement should be comprehensive and inclusive of large segments of the population that are neither Black nor White. Moreover, a perusal of demographic trends in U.S. schools illustrate the importance of investigating the performance of all students and seeking interventions with gaps no matter where they exist.

Finally, using the Black–White dichotomy as the standard to which Black, Latino, or any other groups of students should seek to achieve, offers its own limitations. Undoubtedly, White students as a group in U.S. schools are performing at higher levels than many of their culturally diverse counterparts. However, absent from the Black–White discourse are the countless numbers of White students across the country who still perform consistently below acceptable academic standards. This became increasingly apparent to me when I spent time as an educator in the Midwest and for the first time was able to see and interact with large segments of White students in Appalachia, and see the challenges that educators face in large and small rural communities. These realities disrupt the idea that all White students are performing at a level that should be the norm toward which all other groups strive. Realities such as those in Appalachia, West Virginia, Kentucky, Iowa, Missouri, and other parts of the country, in rural, suburban, and urban areas, reveal the real difficulties that some White students face in U.S. schools. Thus, while an examination of performance discrepancies is needed, this work is dedicated to helping all students, but especially those on the lower end of the academic performance paradigm, to reach national and international standards of excellence, that will put them in a position to compete in a global society.

This book is driven by a deep-seated desire to help the United States, and its schools, continue to reach toward its lofty principles of democracy, fairness, and justice for all of its citizens in the pursuit of educational equity in a pluralistic society. Historically, this country has promoted education as a tool for social and economic mobility. Unfortunately, too many have not reaped the educational rewards that U.S. schools are purported to offer. Most troubling is that as the educational outcomes become increasingly disparate, it is blatantly clear that many of these discrepancies fall along racial, ethnic, and social class lines. Thirty years ago the persistent school failures of African American, Latino, Native American, and certain Asian American populations would have had little impact on the national landscape because combined these groups made up a less than a quarter of the nation's student population. Current demographic estimates indicate that by the year 2050, these same groups will make up the majority of the nation's population (El Nasser, 2004). Hence, there is a moral imperative, an economic incentive, and a national necessity for the country to do all that is possible to effectively educate what soon will be the majority of the nation's citizenry.

This book is motivated by the belief that educating all students is possible and the belief that when concerned, committed, hardworking, and caring educators, researchers, scholars, parents, and community members work toward a common goal of truly leaving no child behind, school success for all students can happen. It is the intent of this work to navigate through some of the murky terrain that frequently has served as a deterrent to identifying plausible means of transforming the educational opportunities of all students—regardless of race and culture. Moreover, it is my hope that this book will show what is possible when we embrace the richness and complexities that are present in the differences that each of us presents, yet at the same time realize that amidst the differences there are major similarities that we all share that can, should, and ultimately will be our unifying source for recognizing the shared humanity that resides in us all.

CHAPTER 1

Achievement Gap: Contextualizing the Problem

Access to education has been frequently hailed as one of the most valued commodities in a free and egalitarian society. Its importance often is tied to the belief that education offers its recipients better prospects for economic and social mobility, and an improved quality of life. The mantra of education as the proverbial "equalizer" is promoted more in the United States than perhaps in any other nation in the world; it is seen as the commodity that helps to transform life chances, improve economic prospects, change dire outlooks to promising possibilities, and reduce the gap between the haves and the have-nots. As a result, countless people from all over the world have undertaken arduous, at times life-risking, journeys to the United States with the hope of providing themselves, their children, and future generations access to what is purported to be one of this country's most cherished assets—free, high-quality education, with all of the hopes and aspirations that are associated with it.

What is frequently absent from the discourse about individuals who arrive in the United States in pursuit of new opportunities, are the educational circumstances of citizens already in U.S. schools, those who are believed to be benefactors of the institution. A thorough discourse on educational opportunities in the United States would include an examination of the history of education in this nation and would reveal a pattern of highly excluded and racially segregated groups who historically were denied equal equal access to schooling for centuries (R. A. Gutierrez, 2004; Lomawaima & McCarthy, 1999; Min, 2004; Myrdal, 1944; Tyack, 2004). Numerous scholars have produced revealing portrayals and penetrating analyses of the manner in which Indigenous populations, enslaved Africans, people of Latin and Asian descent, women, and poor Whites have been denied educational access (Axtell, 1985; Bullock, 1970; Butchart, 1980; Cremin, 1970a, 1980; Fraser, 2001; Kaestle, 1983; Spring, 2006; Tyack, 1974; Urban & Wagoner, 2000) and thus have experienced a different America. Therefore,

9

as groups from beyond the shores of the United States fight to gain access to what is perceived as a treasured commodity—free education—many citizens of this country continue to question the availability of high-quality education for all students already in this country, regardless of their race, ethnicity, and socioeconomic status.

This chapter examines perhaps the single most pressing and perplexing issue in education today—the achievement gap. The achievement gap is the discrepancy in educational outcomes between various student groups, namely, African American, Native American, certain Asian American, and Latino students on the low end of the performance scale, and primarily White and various Asian American students at the higher end of the academic performance scale. (The term *certain Asian American groups* is used throughout this text for deliberate purposes. Issues pertaining to the schooling experiences and academic outcomes of Asian American and Asian Pacific Islander are best understood when groups are disaggregated by ethnicity. A disaggregated analysis reveals that the performance of Japanese American, Korean American, and Chinese American students, generally speaking, is significantly better than the performance of Filipino, Vietnamese, Cambodian, Laotian, Hmong, Samoan, Thai, and other Southeast Asian students (Lee, 2005; Pang, Kiang, & Pak, 2004). An analysis of the achievement outcomes and educational experiences of Southeast Asian groups in U.S. schools reveals a striking similarity to the performance levels of African American, Latino, and Native American students.)

While the gap between groups of different socioeconomic statuses can be relatively easily tied to factors like parental education, home and community resources, high-quality schools, experienced teachers, and preschool readiness (all of which are more likely to be present for children from more affluent economic backgrounds), racial disparities are more puzzling. Research has shown that even when social class is held constant, sizable gaps are still present between different racial groups (Jencks & Phillips, 1998). In other words, African American and Latino students in affluent school settings still lag behind their White and Asian counterparts; even more disturbing, some research has suggested that Black and Latino students from affluent homes perform *worse* than poor White students on some academic measures (College Board, 1999). This suggests that race still matters. The racial gap in educational performance and attainment sheds an ominous cloud over the idea that education is an equalizer in the United States. What has become abundantly clear over the past several centuries is that high-quality education for all is often a "dream deferred," if not a dream denied, as hopes frequently are shattered for countless students. An analysis of the history of education in the United States provides an important glimpse into the ongoing challenges, victories, struggles, and setbacks of many groups over the past 4 centuries. Spring (2006) documents the manner in which Indigenous populations systematically were removed from tribal lands; forced to abandon their political, spiritual, cultural, and educational arrangements; and subsequently indoctrinated to Christian ideology and beliefs at the hands of European colonists during the 17th, 18th, 19th, and 20th centuries. Moreover, Spring's work examines the role that missionary schools played in the "deculturalization" process of countless Native American and Latino populations over the past several centuries.

The works of Anderson (1988), Siddle Walker (1996), and others capture the experiences of enslaved Africans and subsequently African Americans who were legally excluded from public education in the United States and then—through ongoing struggle, sheer persistence, and unrelenting determination—gained access to public education, but only in segregated and underfunded school settings, where they faced the harsh and discriminatory conditions that were part of the Jim Crow era in the United States.

The work of the aforementioned scholars builds on the intellectual contributions of other noted scholars who lamented the history of disparate societal and educational opportunities available to African Americans in the United States (DuBois, 1903; Woodson, 1919/1968). Similarly, a plethora of scholarship also have documented the manner in which people of Latin and Asian descent have experienced similar types of blatant racism and institutional exclusion from educational opportunities, thus making their efforts to become part of the American mainstream incredibly difficult (Chan, 1993; Donato, 1997; G. Gonzales, 1990; S. Lee, 1996; Low, 1982; Pak, 2002; Takaki, 1993; Weinberg, 1997). The educational exclusion that affected generations of people of color has been endured by women as well (J. B. Cole & Guy-Sheftall, 2003; Eisenmann, 2001; Thompson, 1998) and by various European descendants (Bennett, 1988; Higham, 1972; Roediger, 1994, 2005). This scholarship is essential because it offers inclusive and analytical accounts of the educational experiences of various ethnic and gender groups—whose stories frequently are not told or are told in an incomplete and noncritical manner.

What is imperative about the groups who have been excluded from educational opportunities over the past several centuries is that by and large they are the very groups who continue to be at or near the bottom of the achievement hierarchy today. Therefore, any dialogue concerned with a thorough investigation into how to reduce or eliminate achievement gaps between certain student groups must be informed by both an historical understanding of the experiences of those groups in the United States, and an examination of the correlation between their systemic exclusion from educational opportunities and the current state of their educational performance. It is also important to note that despite the legal exclusion of certain groups from formal education, countless efforts to challenge such oppressive conditions have been waged through the creation of independent schools, freedom schools, and other grassroots movements toward educational freedom in the face of racism, sexism, and exclusion, all of which may offer important examples of potential intervention to address today's challenges.

DOCUMENTING THE ACHIEVEMENT GAP

The term *achievement gap* has become one of the most commonly used catch phrases in school reform over the past 20 years. Although the gap has existed for the better part of the past 2 centuries, it is in recent decades that educational practitioners, researchers, policymakers, and legislators have begun to reference the achievement gap as one of the most pressing and difficult educational and social challenges of the 21st century. As noted earlier, the term usually refers to the disparity in academic outcomes between African American, Native American, and Latino students, and their White and certain Asian American peers. The gap is reflected most clearly in grades, standardized test scores, high school graduation rates, placement in special education and advanced placement courses, and suspension and expulsion rates (Darling-Hammond, 2007; Jencks & Phillips, 1998; Thernstrom & Thernstrom, 2003).

Some of the more typically used areas of achievement in U.S. schools (e.g., reading, math, graduation rates), are examined in this chapter but it should be noted that the idea of "achievement" is called into question by some scholars because traditional measures often fall short in offering a complete picture of the performance and potential of students in general, and culturally diverse students in particular. Some scholars have claimed that the traditional measures of achievement are problematic because they fail to take into account all aspects of school, such as contributing factors to school inequality; place an overreliance on testing outcomes; and define intelligence based on limited constructs (Gardner, 1993, 1995; Hill & Roza, 2004; Kozol, 2005; Perry, 2003; Popham, 2001). By no means do I subscribe to the idea that current school measures accurately reflect the intellectual prowess that resides within all children. I believe that in addition to some of the more common approaches to evaluating what students know, educators need to be steadfast in developing other means of assessing student knowledge and skills.

One of the problems with traditional means of measuring student performance in schools is that such approaches often fail to recognize how students exhibit leadership skills, creative and artistic ability, initiative in analyzing tasks, risk taking, persuasive speaking, consensus building, resiliency, and emotional maturity. Even more problematic is that the intersection of race, intelligence, and testing, upon which racial hierarchies were clearly established and reinforced, has a sordid history in the United States, and most of these measures were tied not necessarily to individual aptitude, but to previous exposure to information and certain types of experiences, and tended to lean toward middle-class cultural knowledge (Cremin, 1988; Gardner, 1995; Kornhaber, 2004; Mercer, 1989; Sternberg, 1985). Finally, this book also operates from the idea that countless numbers of students who are classified as "low achievers" by traditional standards are often some of the most talented, intellectually gifted, creative, and critical thinkers on school campuses across this country. Unfortunately, the manner in which schools are structured frequently inhibits the students' ability to express these skills and show their intellectual prowess. A major challenge before the entire educational community is to identify ways of creating schools and school practices that recognize the gifts and talents of all students, in particular those young people who come from historically marginalized backgrounds.

DOCUMENTING THE DISCREPANCIES

A plethora of scholars have lamented the increasingly disparate levels of achievement, quality of education, and overall school experiences that have been and are being provided to non-White and poor students (Banks, 2004; Darling-Hammond, 2007; T. C. Howard, 2003b; Kozol, 1991, 2004; Ladson-Billings, 1995; C. D. Lee, 2007; Oakes, 2005). Thus, many educational scholars recognize that the distinct differences in academic performance between various subgroups are not a new occurrence, but part of an ongoing struggle for democracy, fairness, and greater educational equity and access for all students.

The primary source used to examine current achievement outcomes across multiple spectra of student performance in U.S. public schools is data from the National Assessment for Educational Progress (NAEP), also referred to as "the nation's report card" (NCES, 2007b).

NAEP is the only ongoing, nationally representative assessment of what students in the United States know and can do in various subject areas. Assessments are conducted periodically in mathematics, reading, science, writing, the arts, civics, economics, geography, and U.S. history. According to NAEP data, persistent gaps have existed in the educational outcomes of White and certain Asian American students in comparison to their African American, Latino, and Native American counterparts across several important indicators of school success for close to 20 years.

Causes of the Gap: Different Perspectives

Some researchers have asserted that the academic gaps that are most prevalent in pre-K–12 public schools are merely a by-product of gaps that exist in society at large and are only magnified in schools (Rothstein, 2004), and that any attempt to place schools at the center of closing the achievement gap is grossly misguided, given that schools did not create it in the first place. Anyon (2005), for instance, cogently reiterates this contention by claiming that:

> We have been attempting educational reform in U.S. cities for over three decades. . . . As a nation we have been counting on education to solve the problems of unemployment, joblessness, and poverty for many years. But education did not cause these problems, and education cannot solve them. (p. 3)

While there is significant merit to accounts such as Anyon's, education and educators have played and will continue to play a vital role in helping to address the disparate types of educational opportunities afforded to different groups of students. To that end, it is worth noting that there are fundamental gaps in readiness levels before many students enter pre-K–12 schools, which may explain disparities in subsequent grade levels. An area where this is best exemplified is in access to preschool, which can provide students with essential knowledge and skills that can help them with future academic success. Researchers have found that access to high-quality, pre-K schooling experiences can have substantial influences on the cognitive, social, and emotional development of children who come from low-income backgrounds (Neuman, 2009). However, an analysis of children attending pre-K programs shows that students who come from low-income backgrounds are less likely to attend such programs, and those who do attend them, do so at later ages compared with their more affluent counterparts, and their schools are usually poorer in overall academic quality. This same research shows that more affluent families tend to send their children earlier and to higher quality pre-K schooling situations (which usually have smaller class sizes, credentialed teachers, more support staff, better facilities, and more user-friendly technology), where they are more likely to gain critical preliteracy experiences and oral language skills essential for classroom learning and overall school success (National Center for Education Statistics, 2001).

The racial and ethnic analysis of children who attend preschools is mystifying because African American children have the highest preschool participation rates. Non-Hispanic White children and those who fall into the "other" category (including Asians and Native Americans) have participation rates in preschool that are somewhat below those of African American children (Barnett & Yarosz, 2004). Given the reported benefits that preschool offers for child development and overall school readiness, it would seem plausible that African American students would fare considerably better in schools. Yet, an analysis of pre-K–12 school performance data across a number of indices shows that African American students perform lower on achievement measures across the board than any other ethnic group (NCES, 2006, 2007a).

Reading and Academic Success

Once students have begun school, reading is arguably the most important subject area for academic success. A litany of research has documented the manner in which overall student achievement is enhanced when students have strong literacy and reading backgrounds (Cunningham, 2005; Snow, Burns, & Griffin, 1998; S. W. Valencia & Buly, 2004; Yopp, 1992). A 2007 study by the National Endowment for the Arts titled *To Read or Not to Read* gathered data from more than 40 comprehensive studies on reading and reading achievement. The findings, which highlight the startling declines in reading as well as the civic, social, and economic consequences of continued reading deficiencies of U.S. students, call for greater attention to reading and reading proficiency, or otherwise warn of the fallout of a growing illiterate population. Thus, examining current reading achievement rates provides an important glimpse into the growing discrepancies that exist across racial and ethnic groups—discrepancies that have even greater ramifications in light of the increasing population numbers of these groups, as will be discussed further in Chapter 2.

To illustrate the concern regarding reading proficiency, the 2006 NAEP reading assessment shows that higher percentages of Asian/Pacific Islander and White 4th, 8th, and 12th graders scored at or above proficient levels than did Native American, African American, and Latino students at the same grade levels. These data, as shown in Figure 1.1, reveal that among fourth graders, 58% of African American, 54% of Latino, and 52% of American Indian students are reading below a basic level, compared with only 24% of White and 27% of Asian American students. To underscore this point, Figure 1.1 also shows that only 13% of African American, 16% of Latino, and 18% of American Indian fourth-grade students are at proficient and advanced levels of reading. Conversely, over 40% of Whites and Asian American students are at these same levels in Grade 4. The following list provides descriptors of how NAEP classifies the four levels of student performance in the area of reading:

NAEP Descriptors for Reading Levels

- Students who are at *below basic* are able to follow brief written directions and carry out simple, discrete reading tasks.
- Students who are at *basic* are able to understand, combine ideas, and make inferences based on short uncomplicated passages about specific or sequentially related information.
- Students who are *proficient* are able to search for specific information, interrelate ideas, and make generalizations about literature, science, and social studies materials.
- Students who are *advanced* are able to find, understand, summarize, and explain relatively complicated literature and informational material.

It is essential that students develop strong reading skills early on because by Grade 3, many schools cease the explicit teaching of core reading skills such as phonemic awareness, decoding skills, phonics, vocabulary building, and comprehension skills. These same core skills are also essential for other academic areas such as history, science, social studies, and mathematical word problems. As a result, students who struggle as readers in Grade 3 fall behind even further as they progress to higher grades, and the likelihood that these students will ever read at their current grade level becomes less. This reality is best exemplified by Figure 1.2, which shows that the percentages of students who are below basic, and at basic, proficient, and advanced levels by Grade 8 remain largely unchanged. These trends hold true at Grade 12 as well.

While reading plays an important role in overall academic success, mathematics often has been viewed as the gatekeeping subject area for postsecondary educational access (Oakes et al., 2006), and this, unfortunately, is yet another area where the academic performance chasm is

Figure 1.1. Percentage distribution of fourth-grade students across NAEP reading achievement levels, by race/ethnicity: 2005

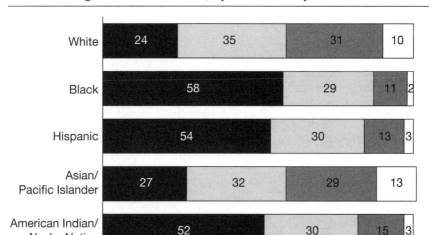

Source: Department of Education, National Center for Education Statistics (NCES, 2006).

clearly pronounced (see Figure 1.3). Students who fail to develop proficient mathematical reasoning are less likely to take important higher level mathematics classes, such as geometry, algebra II, and calculus, which are important for college preparatory courses, college entrance exams, and college acceptance. A growing number of researchers have examined equity and mathematics (Nasir & Cobb, 2002, 2006; Tate, 1997), and have offered plausible interventions that may be viable for reducing the discrepancies in achievement. Many of these recommendations will be detailed in Chapters 3 and 4.

NAEP Descriptors for Mathematics Levels

- Students who score *below basic* have demonstrated basic addition and subtraction facts, and most students at this level can add two-digit numbers without regrouping. They recognize simple situations in which addition and subtraction apply.
- Students who score at *basic* have demonstrated a considerable understanding of two–digit numbers and knowledge of some basic multiplication and division facts.

Figure 1.2. Percentage distribution of eighth-grade students across NAEP reading achievement levels, by race/ethnicity: 2005

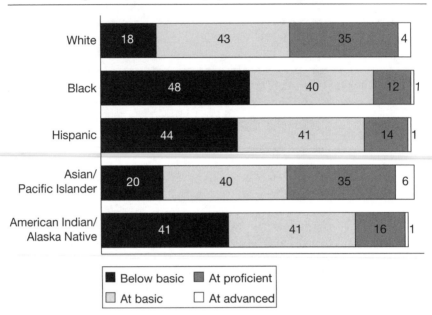

Source: Department of Education, National Center for Education Statistics (NCES, 2006).

- Students who score at *proficient* have demonstrated an initial understanding of the four basic operations (addition, subtraction, multiplication, and division). Students at this level also can compare information from graphs and charts and are developing an ability to analyze simple logical relations.
- Students who score at *advanced* have demonstrated an ability to compute decimals, simple fractions, and percents. Students at this level can identify geometric figures, measure lengths and angles, and calculate areas of rectangles. They are developing the skills to operate with signed numbers, exponents, and square roots.

Figure 1.3 reveals math achievement across racial and ethnic groups in Grade 4 and shows the discrepancies in performance. According to the U.S. Department of Education data, approximately 40% of African American students, 32% of Latino students, and 32% of American Indian students are below basic in mathematics proficiency, compared with 10% of White and Asian American students. The progression of

Figure 1.3. Percentage distribution of fourth-grade students across NAEP mathematics achievement levels, by race/ethnicity: 2005

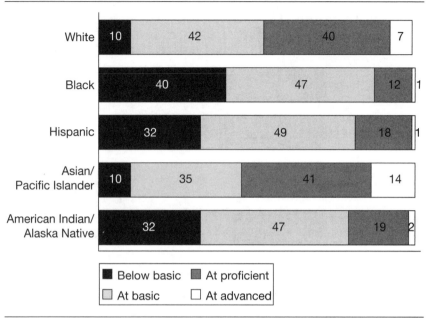

Source: Department of Education, National Center for Education Statistics (NCES, 2006).

mathematics proficiency, as shown in Figure 1.4, reveals that by Grade 8, an even larger number of students of color have fallen behind grade level in mathematics: 58% of African American, 48% of Latino, and 47% of American Indian students are below basic. The fact that only 1% of African American and Latino students are at advanced levels of mathematics underscores one of the more important explanations for the dismally low numbers of African American, Latino, and American Indian students on college campuses.

The focus on reading and mathematics does not negate the fact that other subject areas are in need of attention and examination as well. Indeed, the NAEP data reveal similar types of discrepancies in the areas of science, writing, and citizenship, and appropriate interventions are necessary for these areas. However, because reading and math are foundational to other academic areas, the gaps that exist in these subject areas hold considerable implications for overall school success, and improving student performance in these areas may help to improve students' performance in other academic areas.

Figure 1.4. Percentage distribution of eighth-grade students across NAEP mathematics achievement levels, by race/ ethnicity: 2005

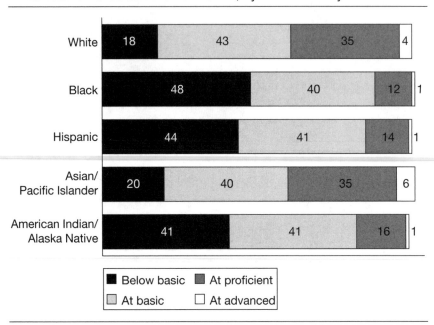

Source: Department of Education, National Center for Education Statistics (NCES, 2006).

RETENTION, SUSPENSIONS, AND EXPULSIONS

Academic performance represents only one of the areas in the achievement gap facing African American, Latino, and Native American students, and their Asian American and White counterparts. For obvious reasons, when students struggle academically with core subjects such as reading and math, their likelihood of not being prepared to move to subsequent grade levels is increased. As a result, in schools where there is a high degree of underachievement, grade retention—the frequency of students repeating grade levels—becomes a prevalent issue. In 2003, approximately 10% of public school students were retained (NCES, 2007b), but an analysis of the ethnic and racial makeup of these students reveals additional discrepancies: A disproportionate number of students who repeated coursework in this time frame were African American and Latino males, continuing a trend that has lasted for close to 2 decades (see Figure 1.5). And, as retention rates escalate, researchers have documented the high correlation between retention and student suspensions and expulsions, as well as subsequent student drop-out rates (Reynolds, 1992; Shepard & Smith, 1990). More precisely, these data reveal that the same groups of students who struggle with reading and math proficiency are the students most likely to be suspended, retained, and subsequently expelled from school (Alexander, Entwisle, & Dauber, 1994).

One of the most daunting dilemmas for educators is how to address the issue of retention as opposed to social promotion, which is the passing of students from one grade to the next, despite students not meeting grade level proficiency (Roderick, 1994). While social promotion creates a host of problems, most of which are concerned with promoting students who are ill prepared for the academic requirements that await them at the next grade level, there are an equal number of legitimate concerns raised around the usefulness of retention, most notably that retention does not to improve student learning and actually increases the likelihood that a student will drop out (Alexander, Entwisle, & Dauber, 1994; Goldschmidt & Wang, 1999; Grisson & Shepard, 1989; Jimerson, 1999; Shepard & Smith, 1989, 1990). Thus, offering interventions intended to improve the prospects of students at the low end of the achievement spectrum can have important ramifications for the retention issue.

Because of the association between retention and school suspension, the rate at which students are retained in schools also indicates which students are most likely to be suspended and expelled from schools. Figure 1.5 shows NAEP data on the rates of suspension by race and ethnicity, and reveals that African American and Latino males are more likely than any other group to fall into this category.

Many studies have examined the relationship between race, class, and special education placement (Artiles, 1998; Artiles & Trent, 1994; Harry & Anderson, 1999; Harry & Klingner, 2006; O'Connor & Deluca-Fernandez, 2006; Orfield & Losen, 2002) and raised a number of important considerations for education practitioners and researchers, particularly with respect to the serious overrepresentation of certain ethnic groups in special education and special services, perhaps in part because students who struggle academically also may be more likely to exhibit problematic behavior in the classroom. Indeed, Harry and Klingner (2006) report that the rates of referral for African American, Latino, and Native American students are significantly higher in what they term "judgment categories," or disciplinary areas that are determined less on clinical judgment and more on individuals' subjective interpretations. Therefore, areas such as mental retardation, specific learning disabilities, and emotional disturbances tend to be disproportionately higher for non-White groups. These findings are supported by data from the Office of Civil Rights, the federal agency that docu-

Figure 1.5. Percentage of public school students in kindergarten through 12th grade who had ever been suspended, by race/ethnicity and sex: 2003

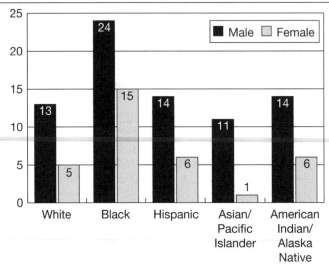

Source: Department of Education, National Center for Education Statistics (NCES, 2006).

ments special education placements, which show that African American, and Native American students make up a larger portion of all students in these categories (see Table 1.1).

These data raise alarming questions about why such disproportionate numbers of African Americans, Latinos, and Native Americans make up special education populations. The contention is that while there are definitely students across all racial and ethnic groups who possess various cognitive, social, and emotional challenges, the overrepresentation of certain groups among those identified as such raises questions about how practitioners make judgments, and what role, if any, cultural misunderstandings and racial beliefs and attitudes may play in the decision-making process. There are a number of considerations to be examined, and these are discussed further in Chapters 4 and 5, where issues of race and culture are discussed.

SCHOOL DROP-OUT AND GRADUATION RATES

A topic that has been the focus of much discussion and analysis in the school reform debate is drop-out rates—particularly for African American

Table 1.1. Minority overrepresentation in special education

The 2006 racial and ethnic makeup of the U.S. population of students ages 6 to 21		The 2006 racial makeup of the special education population in certain disability categories		
		Emotional Disturbance	Learning Disabilities	Mental Retardation
White	61.41%	White	57.44 %	54.82%	58.43%
Hispanic	18.51	Hispanic	11.09	21.22	17.27
Black	14.91	Black	28.79	20.52	20.60
Asian Pacific Islander	4.2	Asian/Pacific Islander	1.12	1.70	2.19
American Indian	0.97	American Indian	1.56	1.74	1.53

Source: U.S. Department of Education, National Center for Education Statistics (NCES, 2006).

and Latino students. Orfield (2004) laments that, in light of the increasing number of students who have been dropping out of the nation's schools over the past 2 decades, we are "losing our future." Among the most disturbing findings in Orfield's analysis of drop-outs is the plethora of social, economic, and political consequences that follow when young people drop out of school. For example, a number of reports have stated that high school drop-outs are more likely to be incarcerated at some point in their lives, to live in poverty, and to send their children to low-performing schools. Moreover, they will earn significantly lower wages over their lifetime compared with their high school graduate counterparts (Orfield, 2004; Orfield, Losen, Wald, & Swanson, 2004).

A closer look at the racial component of high school drop-out research offers an even more dismal look at school underperformance and the ways in which schools have fallen short in helping various ethnic groups successfully matriculate through pre-K–12 schools. During the 2003–04 academic year, for instance, approximately 52% of African American students and 56% of Latino students graduated from high school. These numbers are miserably low, and even more problematic when considering that approximately 77% of Asian American and 76% of White students graduated in the same academic year (Orfield, Losen, Wald, & Swanson, 2004). The situation is even more dire for some specific groups within the Latino and African American community. For example, a 2006 report issued by the Schott Foundation of Education, "Public Education and Black Male Students," reveals that during the 2003–04 school year, only 45% of African American males received diplomas with their classmates 4 years after beginning high school (Holzman, 2006). A number of states had drop-out rates higher than the national average. For example, Florida and Nevada failed to graduate a third of their Black male students. Seven states—Delaware, Georgia, Illinois, Michigan, New York, South Carolina, and

Wisconsin—failed to graduate more than the national average of 45% for Black males. Furthermore, the authors of the report stated that Black males in certain cities, such as New York, Detroit, and Chicago, were in particular danger, as these urban areas failed to graduate between two thirds and three quarters of their African American males. The report's authors state that they studied African American males because "as a group, the cumulative consequences of school failure are most severe for this group of students . . . and this enormity of school failure has created a rip tide of negative results for Black male students and society as a whole" (p. 2). In a follow up to its 2006 report, the 2008 report *Given Half a Chance: The Schott 50 State Report on Public Education and Black Males,* further documents continued educational disenfranchisement of Black males in U.S. schools. States and most districts with large Black enrollments educate their White, non-Hispanic children, the 2008 report says, but do not similarly educate the majority of their Black male students. In the report, a number of disturbing findings are cited:

- More than half of Black males did not receive diplomas with their cohorts in 2005/2006.
- The state of New York has three of the ten districts with the lowest graduation for Black males in the country.
- The one million Black male students enrolled in New York, Florida, and Georgia public schools are twice as likely not to graduate with their class as those who do so.
- Illinois and Wisconsin have nearly 40-point gaps between how effectively they educate their Black and White non-Hispanic male students.

The accuracy of official drop-out statistics has come under increasing scrutiny over the past several years. Warren and Halpern-Manners (2007) maintain that drop-out rates differ dramatically depending on whether drop-outs are measured using data from the Current Populations Survey (CPS) or the Common Core of Data (CCD). CPS data indicate that the national high school completion rate is close to 90%, while CCD data on graduates when disaggregated by race, ethnicity, and socioeconomic status indicate a significantly lower rate of completion (65%–75%). CCD rates examine total numbers of students remaining in school 4 years after they started high school. High schools frequently question the reliability of these drop-out rates because students who transfer to new schools may be considered as drop-outs. Thus, analyzing drop-out rates across race and ethnic groups provides the clearest understanding because it reveals a more comprehensive story of decreasing high school completion rates.

ACCESS TO GIFTED AND AP COURSES

As researchers have continued to investigate the reasons certain ethnic groups are underrepresented in colleges and universities across the country, a number of the previously discussed factors, such as reading and math proficiency and placement in special education, have been identified as contributing variables. However, what is also apparent is that the types of courses that students take in high school are critical to their gaining access to postsecondary education, because certain courses are prerequisites to completing a college application. As the NAEP data reveal, there is a stark difference between the types of courses taken by students from different racial and ethnic groups: Higher numbers of Asian American and White students take advanced placement (AP) courses in English, history, and science, as well as higher level math courses such as algebra II, trigonometry, precalculus, and calculus. The U.S. Department of Education reports that during the 2005–06 school year, 64% of White students took algebra II, compared with 55% of African American and 48% of Latino students. Moreover, 7.5% of White students took AP calculus compared with 3.4% of African American and 3.7% of Latino students (NCES, 2007a). The mathematics proficiency rates highlighted earlier play an important role in explaining and perpetuating much of this difference.

SAT SCORES

The SAT Reasoning Test (formerly the Scholastic Aptitude Test or Scholastic Assessment Test) is another important higher education gatekeeper. Many colleges and universities require applicants to submit SAT scores with their application materials, and the scores become an important component of the admission criteria. Consistent with achievement data presented earlier, it is not surprising that an analysis of student performance across race and ethnicity on the SAT provides disturbing data for large numbers of students of color. The challenge still remains for those students who historically have been on the margins. The data for students' performance on the SAT reveal that Asian Americans/Pacific Islanders and Whites outperform their counterparts from other racial and ethnic backgrounds. Figure 1.6 reveals the performance of the groups in 2006.

EXPLAINING THE GAPS

It is important to put this discussion of educational outcomes into an historical context and to note that widespread gains were made by African American and Latino students from the 1960s until the mid- to-late 1980s. Darling-Hammond (2007) explains how, during the 1960s and into the 1970s, the Great Society's War on Poverty program made noteworthy financial investments in underfunded rural and urban schools, and the result was significant gains in educational input and output. According to Darling-Hammond, an analysis of post-*Brown* educational outcome data reveals that, compared with 1954 data, the number of African American, Asian American, Native American, and Latino students and low-income Whites who graduated from high school increased significantly, to the point where for a brief time during the mid-1970s, the college attendance rates for Whites, African Americans, and Latinos were equivalent. Unfortunately, as investments and resources for urban and rural education were substantially reduced in the 1980s, the gaps in student outcomes began to increase again.

Despite a plethora of policy and school reform initiatives that have sought to reduce the achievement gap between African American, Native American, and Latino, students and their peers from other ethnic backgrounds, the underachievement of the former groups persists and shows little sign of dissipating. Some scholars and researchers have asserted that the issue is not ethnicity at all, but rather low socioeconomic status, which afflicts individuals from all ethnic groups (Anyon, 2005; Bowles & Gintis, 1976; Knapp & Wolverton, 2004; MacLeod, 1995). Students who attend schools and come from homes in more affluent areas perform significantly better than low-income students. At first glance this suggests that socioeconomic status might explain performance differences, particularly in a capitalistic society. However, a careful analysis of school achievement data reveals that even when social class is held constant, African American, Latino, and Native American students still underperform (Jencks & Phillips, 1998; Ogbu, 2003). Data on SAT performance from the College Board (1999) reveal that middle-class African American students perform on a par with Whites from low-income backgrounds. The College Board data also show that the gap between the scores of middle-class African American and White students is wider than the gap between low-income

Figure 1.6. SAT scores by race and ethnicity, 2008

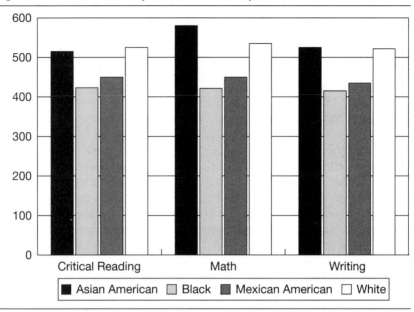

Source: Jashchik, 2008.

African Americans and Whites. Taken together, these research findings suggest that race is a significant factor in explaining achievement outcomes among groups.

The achievement disparities across racial and socioeconomic backgrounds raise several questions that serve as the focus of this book: Why do African American, Latino, and certain Asian American students underachieve compared with other students? What role, if any, do race and racism play in creating and perpetuating academic disparities? Are socioeconomic variables more powerful explanations than race and culture? What does the gender analysis of school performance data reveal? Perhaps more important: What steps can educators take to ameliorate the persistent achievement disparities? When race, socioeconomic status, and gender intersect, what does it mean for school opportunities? How can researchers and practitioners help educators to better understand the discrepancies in academic achievement and offer plausible ways of rethinking schooling in order to create more equitable outcomes for all students?

In order to effectively examine the achievement gap between African American, Latino, and Native American students, and their White and certain Asian American counterparts, it is important to give attention to several explanations—both historical and contemporary—that provide insight into how the existing gaps formed and why they persist today. Although there are many theories in the literature, this discussion is limited to five explanations about the ways in which race and ethnicity are factors in education, in the hope that they may be valuable starting points for intervention into this monumental challenge.

Eugenics Movement

Some would suggest that achievement and opportunity disparities are a contemporary manifestation of age-old racist beliefs about certain racial groups. Thus, in order to develop a more complete understanding of the achievement gap facing students today, it is essential to understand the social construction of race in the United States. While this topic will be discussed further in Chapter 4, it is worth introducing it now as a potential contributing variable to persistent underachievement of racially and culturally diverse students.

The eugenics movement posited that there is a biological basis for the superiority of Whites. These flawed efforts to highlight the racial inferiority of African, Native, and Mexican Americans became part of the fabric of mainstream literature, university research, and popular thinking in the 1920s and 1930s, and reinforced prejudice and racist thinking that was prevalent in the 18th and 19th centuries in the United States (Selden, 1999). Early scholarship on the Eugenics movement highlights the flaws of biological determinism, while also documenting 19th- and 20th-century scholarship and research that established racist paradigms upon which popular thinking about African Americans, Latinos, and Native Americans was based (Gould, 1981; Horsman, 1981; Montagu, 1942).

More recently, Selden's (1999) analysis of the eugenics movement offers an insightful explanation of how the idea of racial superiority was constructed in the name of "science," and the fact that it emerged at a time in the United States when different groups were fighting for greater inclusion into the American mainstream, the establishment of civil rights, economic and social opportunities, and access to greater educational opportunities. The ideas of the eugenics movement generated (and justified) further resistance on the part of many Whites to allowing non-White groups access to mainstream U.S. society.

A close look at educational opportunities during the 1920s and 1930s reveals that African American and Latino students attended underfunded, segregated schools, and in fact were denied access to better funded institutions for no other reason than their racial and ethnic classification. Even as efforts were made to integrate schools, much of the resistance was centered on the belief that non-White students were cognitively inferior, less human, and unworthy of being educated in the same schools as White students (Anderson, 1988; Siddle Walker, 1996).

It is not difficult to draw a connection between these early ideas about racial inferiority and today's educational outcomes. In fact, some scholars argue that remnants of the eugenics movement persist in today's educational practices, policies, and teacher expectations, and that they offer a clear rationale for why students of color continue to underperform (Barry & Lechner, 1995; Smith, Mollem, & Sherrill, 1997). The primary difference, is that these beliefs and behaviors now manifest themselves in more subtle and covert ways, appearing instead in the forms of low expectations, exclusion from enriched academic programs, and inequitable funding for schools attended by students of color (Irvine & Irvine, 1983; Kozol, 2005).

Deficit-Based Thinking

The remnants of the eugenics movement have manifested themselves on multiple levels, not the least of which is the pervasiveness of deficit-based thinking about certain populations. R. R. Valencia (1997) describes deficit-based thinking as a "person-centered explanation of school failure among individuals as linked to group membership. . . . The deficit thinking framework holds that poor schooling performance is rooted in students' alleged cognitive and motivational deficits" (p. 9). Consistent with the thinking of eugenics proponents, individuals subscribing to deficit thinking frequently contend that low-income students and students of color are not "fit" for academic success and social uplift (J. E. King, 1991; Pine & Hilliard, 1990). Earlier examinations of the academic performance of students of color and of students from low-income backgrounds based many of their recommendations on deficit-based frameworks and suggested that these groups suffered because they came from a culture of poverty, lacked motivation for high achievement, did not value education, possessed a poor command of Standard English, were intellectually deficient, or were lacking in their language development, so that their overall academic proficiency lagged (Bernstein, 1961; Glazer & Moynihan, 1963; Hall & Moats, 1999; Riessman, 1962).

There are some of disturbing implications of a deficit-based construction of educational underachievement, most notably the belief that mainstream or European culture and ways of being, thinking, and communicating are considered "normal." Consequently, deviations from mainstream forms of verbal and cognitive processing are viewed as dysfunctional, pathological, or inferior. As a result, students who struggle academically are frequently viewed as cognitively, culturally, or linguistically deficient. Teachers who subscribe to deficit-based paradigms typically seek to "rid" students of their cultural knowledge and means of communicating, and to replace—rather than supplement—their ways of knowing with more standard forms of English and mainstream cultural norms (R. R. Valenzuela, 1999). Deficit thinking speaks to the heart of what many teachers believe about the academic potential of students of color and students from low-income backgrounds (R. R. Valencia, 1997). A plethora of research has uncovered the damaging effects that low expectations can have on students' academic performance (Avery & Walker, 1993; Irvine & York, 1993; Tettagah, 1996)

Cultural Mismatch Theory

Cultural deficit theory as a rationale for underachievement has been challenged by a number of scholars. Scholars have acknowledged that culturally diverse and low-income students are not deficient, but are different in their cultural and cognitive abilities (Boykin, 1994; Hale-Benson, 1986; Kochman, 1981; Lee, 1995, 2007). Because the cultural characteristics that students of color possess may be diametrically at odds with the cultural features of a largely White, middle-class teaching population and institutional ethos of schools, some scholars suggest that a "cultural mismatch" is a primary factor in the underachievement of students of color. Gay (1995), for example, writes, "These incompatibilities are evident in value orientation, behavioral norms, expectations, and styles, social interactions, self presentation, communication and cognitive processing" (p. 159).

Cultural difference proponents argue that people socialized in different environments will vary in numerous areas, including cognitive processes and communication methods. A number of studies have suggested that the language of African American children consists of a highly structured system of oral communication complete with unique grammatical organization, syntax, semantics, morphology, and phonology (Alim & Baugh, 2007; Labov, 1970; Smitherman, 1994). Thus, teaching efforts should be situated in a culturally recognizable format to assist students in developing literacy and numeracy skills. Erickson and Mohatt (1982) discovered that the cultural organization and participation structures of Indian children were different from those of their non-Indian teachers. These findings are consistent with the results produced by other scholars who have examined conflicts between home and school practices (Cazden, 2000; Heath, 1983). Cultural mismatch proponents argue that students of color experience cultural discontinuity in their classroom settings, and for teachers to use culturally responsive teaching strategies. These ideas are discussed in greater detail in Chapter 5.

Opportunity Gap and the Availability of Resources

Some researchers have asserted that the primary culprit in perpetuating the achievement gap is contemporary and historical rates of access to important resources that have a significant influence on school quality. These scholars contend that patterns of structural resource allocation and the social and political context of education and schooling in the United States shed vital light on both the reasons widespread inequities exist and how they are tied tightly to social, political, and economic factors that have a profound impact on schools (Anyon, 2005; Bowles & Gintis, 1976; Kozol, 1991; Oakes, 2005; Orfield, 2004). Darling-Hammond (2007) argues that there is a "legacy of inequality in U.S. education" that explains the different levels of outcomes across racial and social class groups. She maintains that "educational outcomes for students of color are much more a function of their unequal access to key educational resources, including skilled teachers and quality curriculum, than they are a function of race" (p. 320).

Ladson-Billings (2006) agrees with Darling-Hammond's assessment and contends that the achievement gap goes beyond how well students perform in school and requires a more complex analysis to understand and subsequently address it. She calls for a move from the "achievement gap to the education debt" paradigm, wherein the United States must be prepared to take a close look at the mitigating circumstances and historical factors that have contributed to educational inequalities. They include: (1) the economic debt, or the funding disparities that have existed historically and contemporarily between non-White and White schools; (2) the historical debt, which includes social and educational inequities formed around race, class, and gender; (3) the sociopolitical debt, which describes the exclusion of people of color from the civic process; and (4) the moral debt, or the disparity between what we know is right and what we actually do when it comes to the just and fair treatment of all U.S. citizens. Ladson-Billings suggests that addressing the education debt is necessary because it is the "equitable and just thing to do" (p. 9), and that our failure to do so leaves us short in upholding important pillars of democracy such as fairness, equity, and justice.

Stereotype Threat

The ramifications of the racial stigma continue to have an influence on students today, not only in regard to opportunities provided, but also in terms of psychological well-being and academic performance. One of the more important critiques of racial stigma that has important implications for understanding the achievement gap was provided by Claude Steele (1992, 1997). He investigated the salience of race on academic performance. In their research that resulted in the concept of stereotype threat, C. M. Steele and Aronson (1995) conducted research with high-achieving Black and Latino college students and discovered that their test performance faltered when told that they were taking a test that measured verbal ability. They performed higher on the same tasks when they were not told the task measured ability. Most problematic was that when students were asked to identify their racial identity on ability tests, or were told that individuals from their racial or ethnic group had not performed well on given tasks, their performance also faltered. Steele and Aronson posit that students' performance on the assessment was lower because they were concerned about reinforcing widely held stereotypes about members in their racial group. Similar results were found for African American and Latina women college students.

While most of the subsequent work on stereotype threat has been conducted with college students, an emerging body of research has begun to examine whether the effect is present for K–12 students (Kellow & Jones, 2005). If research shows that similar effects exist for elementary or secondary students, it would provide useful insight into the ways in which the salience of race and racism continues to be a significant factor in student performance, and could prove to be an important variable in understanding why academic discrepancies continue to exist across racial and ethnic lines.

FUTURE CONSIDERATIONS

The five variables discussed above do not represent an exhaustive list of the factors that contribute to the achievement gap in schools. Historically, the United States provided one kind of education for the wealthy and elite, and another for the economically disenfranchised and, most often, racially different. As a result of the racial separation that has influenced schooling conditions for students over the past several centuries, some scholars suggest that race is not the most distinguishing factor in educational opportunity; that socioeconomic status is most germane to understanding the problem (W. J. Wilson, 2009). Nevertheless, where achievement gaps persist, there is a greater likelihood of seeing schools that are attended predominantly by students of color and students from low-income backgrounds, as well as students who are English language learners. In addition, these populations usually have high teacher turnover rates, larger numbers of underqualified teachers, inconsistent school leadership and administration, and overall lack of consistency and rigor in school curriculum and instruction (Barton, 2004).

Amidst a host of reform efforts that have sought to eradicate achievement disparities, one of the areas that frequently is overlooked is the importance of high-quality instruction. Darling-Hammond (1997) posits that "in the context of today's higher standards and the growing diversity of students in schools, the lack of adequate teacher preparation for so many teachers in urban and poor schools is troubling" (p. 616). In fact, some scholars assert that perhaps the single most important act that can be done to reverse disparities of educational opportunities and outcomes is to ensure that all students have highly qualified teachers in their classrooms, particularly in those schools where underachievement has remained prevalent (Irvine, 2003; Marzano, 2003; Nieto, 2003).

Some scholars have gone so far as to state that teachers are the most valuable influence on student performance in the classroom. Wright, Horn, and Sanders (1997) conducted research across five subject areas, three grade levels, and 60,000 students, examining factors that contributed to improved student performance. They found that "the most important factor affecting student learning is the teacher. . . . Effective teachers appear to be more effective with students of all achievement levels regardless of the levels of heterogeneity in their classes" (p. 63). Yet, despite these findings, culturally and racially diverse students and those from low-income backgrounds are more likely than students from more affluent areas to have underqualified, noncredentialed, and out-of-subject-area teachers (Dreeben, 1987; R. E. Ferguson, 1991). Research indicates that students are more likely to receive poorer instruction and overall educational quality when they are taught by underqualified teachers (Oakes et al., 2006). In an era of increasing standardization and accountability, it is essential for legislators and policymakers to recognize the importance of supporting the development of programs that produce competent, skilled, and highly trained teachers. More specifically, making a significant financial investment in training high-quality teachers, with incentives for teaching in high-poverty areas, can have a sizable impact on reversing persistent underperformance of various groups (Berry, 1995; Darling-Hammond & Sykes, 2003).

It is essential that political and educational leaders have a sincere commitment to educating all students. Chronic overcrowding in urban schools, inadequate funding, and an overall acceptance of widespread failure in urban and rural schools raise serious questions about the commitment that the United States has to educating all of its students. Although a number of scholars frequently have attributed the achievement gap to cultural deficiencies (Moynihan, 1965), cultural poverty (Riessman, 1962), and oppositional attitudes of poor students and students of color (Ogbu, 1987). They fail to give appropriate recognition to historical, economic, and structural factors that play a fundamental role in students' educational opportunities.

Because an increasing number of factors influence the experiences of all students in schools, it is critical to highlight examples where educators are defying the odds, being successful with students, and making inroads to closing the achievement gap. The goals of this book are to highlight the salience of race and culture in U.S. schools and to provide a useful analysis of the ways in which educators must be equipped to understand the complexities of the changing demographics in U.S. schools. Chapter 2 discusses in more detail the rapid pace at which U.S. schools continue to change, and why the demographic shifts have implications for all educators, particularly those who are most concerned with remedying performance disparities among students from diverse racial, social class, language, and cultural groups.

Changing Demographics

> Change always brings difficult challenges. Change is something that presses us out of our comfort zone. It is destiny-filtered, heart grown, faith built. Change is inequitable; not a respecter of persons. Change is for the better or for the worst, depending on where you view it. Change has a ripping effect on those who won't let go. Flex is the key. Change is won by victors not victims; and that choice is ours. . . . Change is measured by its impact on all who are connected to it. Change happens in the heart before it is proclaimed by our works. Change is like driving in a fog—you can't see very far, but you can make the whole trip that way. . . . Change is here to stay.
>
> —IIE, *What is Change?*

Change is always challenging because it poses new realities, forces individuals to rethink age-old traditions, and places people in different situations where they must consider new outlooks on their realities. Change has been part of the American fabric for the past 4 centuries and in all likelihood will be for the foreseeable future. This change has been far from smooth, and has been detrimental for some people, challenging for many, beneficial for others, and nonending for most. While change in a general sense is always a challenge, change regarding the beliefs, habits, and interactions of people we live near, especially in an ethnically and culturally pluralistic society, is perhaps the most challenging type of change.

This chapter focuses on the changing demographics in the nation and their meaningful influence on public schools. An examination of these changes is necessary because the rapid rate of change along racial, cultural, ethnic, and linguistic lines, combined with individual and group resistance to change, poses a multitude of challenges for each and every citizen in the United States. Demographic changes present unique challenges for educators. Current academic disparities across racial lines hold serious consequences for the future of the United States, which will continue to see major shifts in the ethnic texture of its citizens. If current achievement gaps continue over the next several decades, an increasing proportion of the nation's citizens will be severely undereducated and ill prepared to compete in a global economy. This potential reality would cause grave political, economic, and social consequences for the United States. Our willingness to embrace change—particularly demographic change—is central to the potential success (or failure) of many of the policies, practices and programs that are currently in the nation's schools. This chapter presents a comprehensive account of how fast the United States is changing, and an analysis of the groups who are an essential part of this change. An understanding of the rapid and constant demographic changes in the United States is an essential first component of any effort to advance the strong imperative for why and how citizens must embrace change if we are to truly help all students learn.

A CHANGING NATION

The changing demographics in the United States are exemplified in a number of ways. An analysis of U.S. Census data over the past century shows the rapid change in the ethnic and racial landscape of the United States. According to the 1900 Census, one out of every eight U.S. citizens was non-White, while little more than a century later in 2006, that number had dramatically increased to one in three (U.S. Census Bureau, 2007). Figure 2.1 shows a breakdown of the nation's racial and ethnic demographics in 2006. While the actual number of Whites in this country has increased substantially over the past century—from 66.8 million in 1900 to a little less than 200 million in 2006—their percentage of the total population actually has declined, from 88% in 1900 to 65% in 2006. This shift has resulted primarily from the increased rates of people of Latin and Asian descent, which have been due to birthrate increases in the United States and to immigration, as well as from the steady growth of the African American population.

The United States frequently has been touted as a country of immigrants, and over the past century, ethnic and racial diversity has been one of the primary hallmarks of the nation. The term *e pluribus unum* (out of many one) captures one of the defining and unique characteristics of the United States. While increasing ethnic and racial diversity has been constant since the country's inception, even more noteworthy is the rapid ethnic and racial transformation that has occurred during the past 3 decades. For example, an examination of the Latino population in the United States shows that it more than tripled between 1980 to 2006, growing from approximately 14.6 mil-

Figure 2.1. Racial and ethnic breakdown in the United States in 2006.

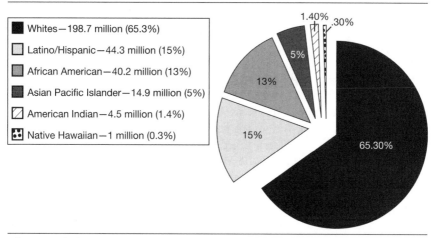

- Whites—198.7 million (65.3%)
- Latino/Hispanic—44.3 million (15%)
- African American—40.2 million (13%)
- Asian Pacific Islander—14.9 million (5%)
- American Indian—4.5 million (1.4%)
- Native Hawaiian—1 million (0.3%)

Source: U.S. Census Bureau, 2007.

lion to more than 44 million, making Latinos the largest non-White population in the United States (Hobbs & Stoops, 2002). The Latino population increased from 6.5% of the country's population in 1980, to 15% in 2006. Furthermore, according to the Pew Research Center's (PRC) projections, the Latino population will triple in size over the next several decades and will account for most of the nation's population growth between 2005 and 2050. PRC states that Latinos will make up approximately 29% of the U.S. population in 2050, compared with 14% in 2005 (Passel & Cohn, 2008).

To further underscore the unprecedented diversity that the United States will experience, PRC states that by 2050, nearly one in five Americans (19%) will be an immigrant, compared with one in eight (12%) in 2005. Moreover, by 2025, the immigrant or foreign-born share of the population will surpass the peak during the last great wave of immigration a century ago. Although the numbers of Latinos in the United States represent an important shift in the non-White populations in the United States, they were the second fastest growing group in the country over the past 2 decades according to the U.S. Census Bureau (2006). An analysis of growth rates by race and ethnicity shows that Asian Americans and Pacific Islanders grew faster in size than any other ethnic group between 1980 and 2005. From 1980 to 2005, the resident population of Asians/Pacific Islanders grew 260%, from 3.6 million to 12.8 million. The Latino population grew 192%, from 14.6 million to 42.7 million. During the same time period, American Indians/Alaska Natives increased by 68%, from 1.3 million to 2.2 million, while Blacks had the slowest growth of the minority groups (39%), from 26.1 million to 36.3 million. In comparison, the White population grew only 10% between 1980 and 2005 (Passel & Cohn, 2008).

DEMOGRAPHIC SHIFTS BY GEOGRAPHIC REGION AND AGE

While the entire United States has witnessed immense growth of various ethnic and racial groups over the past 4 to 5 decades, the West Coast has witnessed the most significant growth. More than 40% of the nation's Latino population lived on the West Coast in 2006, and a majority of the Asian and Pacific Islander populations remained heavily concentrated in California, Oregon, and Washington. Los Angeles County, for example, had the highest non-White population in the United States in 2006 and is home to 1 in 14 of the nation's non-White citizens (DeNavas-Walt, Proctor, & Smith, 2007). Los Angeles County has the largest population of Latinos, Asian Americans, Native Americans, and Alaskan Natives in the United States. It also possesses the second highest number of African Americans (second to Cook Country, Illinois) and Native Hawaiians (U.S. Census Bureau, 2007). In addition to California's increasing diversity, it should be noted that the two fastest growing states in the nation, Arizona and Nevada, also have increasing numbers of Latino and Asian American populations. Population estimates by the Census Bureau indicate that states such as Arizona, Texas, and Nevada will see the most notable increases over the next decade, and that these increases will comprise largely non-White population groups.

Although the changing racial and ethnic demographics in the United States over the past quarter-century may be most visible in certain regions, they are certainly not limited to these regions. In 2006, the number of non-Whites topped the 100 million mark for the first time in U.S. history (U.S. Census Bureau, 2006). The number of non-Whites in the United States today exceeds the total number of all U.S. residents in 1910, and the number is greater than in all but 11 countries in the world. Four states and the District of Columbia are now "majority-minority" states, in which the majority of the population is non-White. Hawaii (75%), the District of Columbia (68%), New Mexico (57%), California (57%), and Texas (52%) each have witnessed unprecedented increases in Latino and Asian populations that have dramatically changed these states and pushed their percentages of non-Whites over the 50% mark.

The U.S. Census Bureau (2007) indicated that in May 2007 there were over 300 counties—more than one in every 10—in the United

States with more non-White than White residents. Some of the counties that are majority-minority are Blaine County, Montana, Shannon and Todd Counties, South Dakota, Rolette County, North Dakota, San Juan County, Utah, and Ford County, Kansas. Each of these counties is located in a state that is not usually known for its racial and ethnic diversity. Their current population trends would suggest that the rapid demographic shifts eventually will touch all facets of the country's landscape.

What is also notable about these demographic changes is the two groups that have experienced the most growth over the past 2 decades are also the youngest groups in the United States. Because age is so closely tied to fertility and birthrates, these numbers further point to their rapid growth over the next several decades. According to the U.S. Census data for 2006, Whites have the lowest reproduction rates of the four major ethnic groups, and have a median age of 40.3 years. This number is significantly higher than the median age for Latinos (27.3 years), which is the youngest of the four major ethnic groups. In fact, approximately one third of the Latino population is under the age of 18, the highest proportion for any group in the United States. In 2006, Asian Americans had a median age of 33.2 years and African Americans had a median age of 30.2. Both groups also had higher percentages of populations under the age of 18 than Whites. These numbers suggest further increases in the numbers of non-Whites in the United States, while the numbers of Whites will continue to decline. Some demographers project that by the year 2050 people of color will make up almost 50% of the nation's population, placing the United States close to becoming a nation comprising mostly non-Whites (El Nasser, 2004).

U.S. SCHOOLS AND CHANGING DEMOGRAPHICS

To provide additional clarity on some of the specifics of the demographic changes occurring within the United States, one only needs to look at the racial and ethnic makeup of the nation's schools. According to the U.S. Department of Education's National Center for Education Statistics (2006), there were approximately 49 million students enrolled in U.S. public schools in 2007. That number is projected to be close to 58 million by 2015. The racial and ethnic breakdown of the nation's student population in 2007 is shown in Table 2.1.

As the United States continues to experience its largest influx of immigrants, along with the increasing numbers of African Americans, Latinos, and Asian Americans, the nation must be prepared to make the necessary adjustments to deal effectively with the changing ethnic texture of its citizens (Banks, 2004). The dramatic shift in ethnic demographics has important implications for schools and, more specifically, classroom teachers, as the changing ethnic and racial makeup of schools undoubtedly will influence the dynamics of teachers and students in classrooms across the entire nation. A pressing question in light of these demographic changes is: "Are educators prepared to teach in diverse schools?" This question has been at the heart of much discussion since the 1970s (Gay & Howard, 2000; Nieto, 2000) and continues to remain a pressing question that defies clear-cut answers.

In 1970, students of color made up approximately 20% of the U.S. student population (NCES, 2003). An analysis of U.S. Department of Education data reveals that in 2007, students of color were 42% of the U.S. student population (NCES, 2007) and demographers project that by 2035 students of color will constitute a majority of the student population (Hodgkinson, 2001). In a number of metropolitan cities across the country, the numbers of non-White students already exceed the numbers of White students. For example, the National Center for Education Statistics reported in 2006 that in 63 of the 100 largest public school districts in the United States, students of color outnumbered their White counterparts; and in a third of these schools, students of color made up at least 75% of the student population (B. Dalton, Sable, & Hoffman, 2006). In a number of cities, such as New York, Los Angeles, Chicago, Philadelphia, Houston, Detroit, Boston, Columbus, Fort Lauderdale, and Washington DC, students of color make up an overwhelming majority of the student population (Hodgkinson, 2001). Furthermore, and certainly related, the number of students whose primary language is not English has increased dramatically over the past 20 years, rising from 1.5 million in 1985 to 5.5 million in 2005 (Genesse, Leary, Sounder, & Christian, 2005; Villegas & Lucas, 2002).

One of the major challenges that educators will encounter amidst these changing student demographics is what Gay and Howard (2000) refer to as the *demographic divide*, wherein teachers face the reality that they are most likely to come into contact with students from cultural, ethnic, linguistic, racial, and social class backgrounds different from their own. In short, U.S. schools will continue to become learning spaces where an increasingly homogeneous teaching population (mostly White, female, monolingual, and middle class) will interact with a mostly heterogeneous student population (increasingly students of color, who come from culturally and linguistically diverse and low-income backgrounds). In 2000, approximately 75% of the U.S. public school teachers were female, 84% were White, and they were almost exclusively middle class (NCES, 2003). Conversely, only

Table 2.1. Demographic breakdown of U.S. student population

White	55.0%
Hispanic	21.1%
Black	16.6%
Asian/Pacific Islander	4.6%
American Indian/Alaska Native	1.2%

Source: Planty et al., 2009.

7.8% of teachers were African American, 5.7% Latino, 1.6% Asian American, and .8% Native American.

To further underscore the dearth of non-White teachers in U.S. schools, the National Collaborative on Diversity in the Teaching Force (2004) reported that more than 40% of U.S. schools do not employ a single teacher of color. The scarcity of teachers of color has remained largely consistent over the past 4 decades: In 1971, 88% of public school teachers were White (Synder, 1998). In all likelihood, the racial make up of the teaching population will continue to be largely White, as evidenced by research done by Zumwalt and Craig (2005), whose meta-analysis of a plethora of studies assessing the racial and ethnic makeup of teacher education students reveals that slightly more than 80% of them are White. Equally serious is the fact that most aspiring teachers are native English speakers and have had little to no contact with non-English speakers as part of their socialization.

ARE TEACHERS
BEING PREPARED TO TEACH IN DIVERSE SETTINGS?

One of the more pressing issues that requires further analysis is the degree to which teachers who are largely White, middle class, monolingual, and female are effectively prepared to teach in diverse settings. A number of studies have indicated that teacher candidates from the above-mentioned categories have had limited interactions with students from diverse groups (Easter, Shultz, Neyhart, & Reck, 1999; Green & Weaver, 1992; Hadaway & Florez, 1987–1988; Terrel & Marck, 2000), and some of these researchers have found that many candidates have negative beliefs about individuals who are different from them, despite their willingness to teach in diverse school settings (Hollins & Guzman, 2005). Consequently, one of the primary challenges for educators is directly tied to the growing schism between teachers and students. When one considers the increasing homogeneity of classroom teachers, many of whom may believe that students of color and students from low-income backgrounds are less capable of being academically successful, one has to question the quality of the instruction, concern, and care that diverse students receive in classrooms (Irvine & Irvine, 1983; Valenzuela, 1999). The lack of knowledge and awareness that many teachers have about diverse groups raises important questions for educational equity, and for our hopes of eradicating the achievement gap. Thus, there is a need to more carefully examine the educational questions such as

1. What types of attitudes and beliefs do teachers have about teaching students from diverse groups?
2. How can negative attitudes and dispositions held by teachers about diverse students be eliminated?
3. What are the important types of knowledge and skills that teachers need to teach students from diverse groups?
4. Are teacher education programs adequately suited to prepare teachers for working in diverse schools?

As future educational inquiry continues to address the implications of the achievement gap, it is essential for both scholars and practitioners to critically analyze what the growing levels of diversity mean for today's teachers. Deficit-based notions of students, low expectations, and less than ideal instructional quality are all possibilities when teachers question the intellectual capability of any student, but these issues are most harmful when students' abilities are questioned based solely on factors such as their socioeconomic status, race, ethnicity, culture, language, or gender.

The demographic divide between White teachers and students of color does not suggest that monolingual, White teachers from middle-class backgrounds are unable to effectively educate students who are from different ethnic and racial groups. Quite to the contrary, as researchers have documented teachers with cross-racial and ethnic teacher competence (Ladson-Billings, 1995; E. C. Parsons, 2005). In my work with teachers, I have witnessed and worked with many White teachers who have been highly successful in working with students of color. Their effectiveness has been tied to their willingness to disrupt colorblind ideologies, to recognize the potential of students' ability to learn, and to structure rigorous learning spaces centered on students' strengths.

Cross-racial teaching and learning arrangements have the potential for varying degrees of misunderstandings between students and their teachers, especially where teachers lack the training and competence necessary to effectively teach students from diverse groups. Both the traditional means of preparing teachers—which frequently utilize superficial ways of addressing diversity—and discussions incorporating issues such as race and culture in the classroom must be significantly improved if teachers are to be more effective with today's diverse student population. Many educators face significant challenges in educating students who are different from themselves. However, too often attention is focused exclusively on the racial disconnect between teachers and students, while not enough attention is paid to cultural differences. The cultural nuances that contribute to this serious schism, as well as how to effectively address them, are discussed in Chapters 3 and 5.

The rapid rates of transformation along ethnic and racial lines in U.S. schools have important ramifications for the ways we think about diversity. Historically, the United States has struggled with its efforts to deal with people who are different from what Audre Lorde (1984) refers to as the "mythical norm" (p. 116). A close look at the experience of Native Americans during the 18th and 19th centuries, the enslavement of Africans for over 4 centuries, the Japanese Internment during World War II, and the economic exploitation of Chinese immigrants in the late 1800s reveals the United States's inability to deal with difference. The conquest of Mexico in the 19th century, the rampant nativism that afflicted millions of Southern and Eastern Europeans at the beginning of the 20th century, and the denial of basic human rights for women over the past several centuries all speak to the challenges that the United States continues to face in its attempt to recognize equality for all of its citizens. The changing face of the United States is another opportunity for it to truly live up to its principles of democracy, fairness, and justice. The ways in which the United States addresses the quality of education it provides to all of its citizens in the coming years will speak volumes about the economic, political, social, and moral prospects of the United States for decades.

MULTICULTURAL EDUCATION FOR SCHOOL REFORM

A number of scholars have worked diligently to help the nation reach its ideological goals of democracy and unity through the education of its citizens (Banks, 2004). The changing demographics in the United States are not a recent phenomenon, but rather have been decades in the making. In response to the changing national demographics,

scholars have articulated the need for a different approach to education, one that recognizes and embraces the values and complexities
of racial, ethnic, cultural, linguistic, and historical differences, while
seeking to achieve academic success for all students (Banks, 2004; Gay,
2000; Nieto, 2000; Sleeter & Grant, 2009).

Multicultural education as a conceptual framework emerged in the
1970s in an attempt to provide teachers with the necessary knowledge
and skills to teach diverse learners. Banks and Banks (2004) summarize
the concept.

> Multicultural education is a field of study and an emerging discipline
> whose major aim is to create equal educational opportunities for stu-
> dents from diverse racial, ethnic, social-class, and cultural groups. One
> of its important goals is to help all students acquire the knowledge, at-
> titudes, and skills needed to function effectively in a pluralistic demo-
> cratic society and to interact, negotiate, and communicate with people
> from diverse groups to create a civic and moral community that works
> for the common good. (p. xi)

Multicultural education emerged out of the struggle to uphold
the nation's democratic ideals of freedom, justice, and equality for all
people. It seeks to hold the country to its promises of equity as noted
by Myrdal (1944) in *An American Dilemma*. Myrdal pondered how the
United States could be viewed as a global model for democracy, fairness, and unity, when so many of its citizens were denied basic human
and civil rights. An outgrowth of the civil rights movement, multicultural education traces its roots back to African American scholars from
the late 19th and early 20th centuries such as Carter G. Woodson,
Charles H. Wesley, and W. E. B Dubois, all of whom worked for greater
societal equity and educational opportunities for African Americans
(Banks, 2004). Since then, multicultural education has grown into
many different forms from its early focus on Black studies, intergroup
education, multiethnic education, finally to multicultural education,
which has come to encompass a myriad of issues related to oppression
based on race, social class, gender, language, disability, and sexuality.
Banks (2006) states that one of the goals of multicultural education is
"to improve race relations and to help all students acquire the knowledge, attitudes, and skills needed to participate in cross-cultural interactions and in personal, social, and civic action" (p. xii).

An important goal of multicultural education is to disrupt the cycle
of hegemony, inequality, and oppression that results in low academic
achievement among students of diverse backgrounds (Banks, 2002).
Multicultural education also was conceptualized as a way of life, and a

school reform movement that should be infused throughout curricula, pedagogical practices, policy, and school culture. It is an approach that embraces the homes and communities of all children to create an equitable educational system, so that all children may become knowledgeable, caring, reflective, and active citizens in a global and multicultural society (Banks, 2004; Grant & Sleeter, 2007).

Multicultural education begins with the assumption that we do not live in an equal and fair society. Scholars in the field assert that we live in a racist, sexist, and classist society where certain aspects of schools and society favor the "haves" over the "have-nots" (Nieto, 2000). As a result of our unequal society, school curricula and practices are frequently Eurocentric, biased, and one-sided, thereby negatively affecting students of color, girls, and low-income students. Dismantling these hegemonic systems is one of the major goals of multicultural education (Sleeter & Grant, 2003), in the hope that interrupting the cycle of inequality and oppression also can counteract the lack of achievement among students of diverse backgrounds.

Multicultural educators posit that any attempt to construct a knowledge base for classroom teachers should recognize the important roles that race, culture, language, gender, and class currently play in U.S. society. Moreover, multicultural educators argue that teachers must teach with what Irvine (2003) refers to as "a cultural eye," wherein teachers view their world and the work that they do through a cultural lens that allows them to be change agents in the academic performance of culturally diverse students.

Banks (2004) introduces five dimensions of multicultural education in an attempt to move the field from a focus on content infusion to a more comprehensive and complex area of study. Each of Banks's dimensions—content integration, knowledge construction, equity pedagogy, prejudice reduction, and empowering school culture—is viewed as a starting point for looking at the breadth and depth of multicultural education theory and practice, particularly in teacher education, and can be a core feature of a teacher's ability to work with diverse learners. Some critique Banks's model as not being critical or reconstructive enough. Most of these critiques center on the idea that the discipline is concerned with "individual mobility within an economic hierarchy more than collective advancement and structural equality, and for reducing problems in the larger society to school solutions" (Sleeter, 1996, p. 89). However, these critiques typically are from scholars outside of the discipline, and tend to group multicultural research and theory in essentializing ways that do not distinguish various approaches to the field. Moreover, multicultural education has served as the foundation upon which more radical or critical approaches to multicultural education have emerged, which are built on many of the same goals. The works of Giroux (1992), McCarthy (1988), and McLaren (1988) are often touted as *critical multicultural education*, which places additional emphasis on structural inequities and calls for radical social and economic reconstruction. These perspectives are equally vital in the quest for school and societal reform, and do not undermine or take away from the fundamental goals and aims of multicultural education.

Cochran-Smith (2003) offered a "conceptual structure interrogating the multiple meanings of multicultural teacher education" (p. 8). She recommends a more comprehensive and complex understanding of multicultural teacher education to inform teacher practice and recognize the value of research and policy in preparing, recruiting, supporting, retaining, and assessing high-quality teachers for multicultural schools. Her framework includes eight penetrating questions that should inform future research on diversity in teacher education, including investigating the complexity of student diversity, examining the purpose of schooling, assessing which knowledge is most useful, evaluating the importance of teacher outcomes, and continuing to document best practices.

The field of multicultural education has grown considerably in its conceptual and theoretical depth, but is nevertheless criticized for being less transparent in its practical implementation (Sleeter & Bernal, 2004). One of the challenges that the field has faced is that it is viewed as a feel-good curriculum, lacking in rigor and depth, and helpful only in improving students' self-esteem. Nieto (2003), for example, notes that one of the frequent questions and criticisms she hears about the field is that "multicultural education is nice, but does it help students do math?" This critique can be refuted by the documentation of additional empirical and practical examples of multicultural practice wherein teachers use the field's concepts, themes, ideas, and paradigms to help students attain academic success.

THE ROLE OF SOCIAL CLASS

One of the primary areas that multicultural education examines is the role of socioeconomic status. Many scholars have posited that U.S. students are becoming increasingly poor, and that school reform efforts need to be mindful of the widespread poverty that afflicts many of the nation's school-aged population. There is undoubtedly a correlation between socioeconomic status and school outcomes, and a litany of data highlights the nexus between race, social class, and school performance, which must be recognized in any analysis of the achievement gap across racial groups (Rothstein, 2004). The U.S. Census Bureau reports that in 2006 there were 36.5 million people living in poverty, and that children under the age of 18 made up approximately 35.2% of that group. Hence, close to 13 million school-aged children, or one in four of all students, come from impoverished economic backgrounds to schools each day. Even more alarming is the racial and ethnic disproportionality of the poor: Approximately 24.3% of African Americans and 20.6% of Latinos lived in poverty in 2006. These numbers were considerably higher than the percentages of Whites (8.2%) and Asian Americans (10.3%) who lived in poverty during the same calendar year (DeNavas-Walt, Proctor, & Smith, 2007).

One of the many challenges in educating students who come from low-income backgrounds is the lack of accessibility to adequate health care. In 2006, approximately 8.7 million students were uninsured and thus lacked access to sufficient medical coverage. At the time, approximately 34% of Latinos in the United States were uninsured (the largest of any ethnic group), followed by African Americans (19%).

Among the more important aspects of understanding poverty is the recognition that while there are complex obstacles involved in teaching students from impoverished backgrounds, students are still capable of being academically successful. To begin the process of reversing underachievement, a number of scholars suggest that it is most important for teachers to internalize the belief that students from low-income backgrounds are capable learners (Gay, 2000; Valenzuela, 1999). They contend that while there is a myriad of reasons for the achievement gap, one of the most important factors in this perennial underachievement is that teachers do not expect all students to succeed, believing instead that poverty makes some students incapable of high academic achievement (Foster, 1997; Ladson-Billings, 1994). Therefore, a critical approach to multicultural education acknowledges the salience of poverty and seeks ways of rethinking schooling practices to be mindful of the intense challenges that poverty presents to students.

One of the concepts that has been instrumental in my own work with teachers is that many who lower expectations for students from low-income backgrounds do so because they feel sorry for the students and their circumstances, and thus become *sympathetic* teachers, who consequently do not challenge students because they have accepted the idea that low-income students are somehow cognitively challenged (Terrel & Marck, 2000). Haberman (1991) refers to this as a *pedagogy of poverty* that is delivered to many low-income students across the country, where teachers water down curricula, lower standards, and develop a vision of students that consists of perceived shortcomings. Conversely, teachers who play a role in transforming the academic plight of low-income students are not sympathetic in their orientation, but are instead *empathetic*, in that they understand the challenges that poverty poses for many students, but they do not become paralyzed by this understanding in their teaching orientation, and instead communicate to their students a firm belief in their ability to be successful. Hence, empathetic teachers listen to, and learn from, their students' experiences and the obstacles that they may be encountering, yet they still hold them accountable for academic rigor. They still expect and demand excellence, and they find creative ways to help students attain success despite circumstances that might suggest that this is not possible. Table 2.2 summarizes additional differences between sympathetic and empathetic teachers.

In addressing some of the challenges that students from impoverished backgrounds face, it is crucial for teachers to develop a realistic, positive vision of where and how they believe students can grow academically and socially. Embedded in an empathetic teaching approach is a deep-seated concern and care for students. Gay (2000) states that caring teachers practice respect, provide choices for students, make information comprehensible, validate students' efforts, and empower them in their quest to be academically successful. Other scholars similarly discuss caring as a concept (Noddings, 2005; Valenzuela, 1999). Multicultural educators contend that any attempt to construct a knowledge base for classroom teachers should recognize the important roles that race, culture, language, gender, and class currently play in the United States (Banks & Banks, 2004; Gay, 2000; T. C. Howard, 2001a; Lee, 2007; Milner, 2003; Nieto, 2003).

Central to empathetic teaching is the eradication of deficit-based thinking that frequently serves as a major obstacle to academic success for countless students, particularly those from culturally diverse and low-income backgrounds. In contrast, a firm belief in students' academic potential can be viewed as a personal and vested interest that teachers take in their students' performance. Ladson-Billings (1994) suggested that one of the central tenets of culturally relevant pedagogy is an authentic belief that students from culturally diverse and low-income backgrounds are capable learners. She maintains that if students are treated as if they are competent, they ultimately will demonstrate high degrees of competence.

Table 2.2. Characteristics of sympathetic and empathetic teachers

Sympathetic Educators	Empathetic Educators
Lower expectations of students due to race, poverty, or language	Hold students accountable despite difficult circumstances
See limitations in students	See promise and possibilities in students
See deficits in students	See assets in students
Paralyzed by problems	Become active problem solvers
Have narrow, limited teaching repertoire due to perceived student capacity	Develop critical and complex teaching practices to engage students
Place little to no value on students' perspectives or voices	Listen and learn from students' experiences to inform teaching
View learning as a teacher-dominated practice, with students having little to offer	View learning as a reciprocal process between teacher and student

In describing the importance and effectiveness of empathetic teachers, I am frequently reminded of my own fifth-grade teacher, Hazel Russell. From Ms. Russell's standpoint, growing up in a difficult inner-city neighborhood in Compton, California, did not excuse students from excelling academically. She was quick to remind us every day that she expected nothing short of excellence in her classroom. Moreover, she refused to allow students to offer excuses about why homework was not returned, or why work was not up to her standard of excellence. She demanded the best of her students in our academic endeavors and frequently would tell our class, "I don't care if you are Black, Brown, or Yellow, you will learn in this classroom. I don't care if you are poor or not, you will learn in this classroom. I don't care if you come from a single-parent household, two-parent household, or ten-parent household, in here [referring to the classroom] you will learn." It was this unyielding belief that she had in us as students that helped most of us find a place on our school honor rolls and in other academic distinctions. In short, even though many students faced a myriad of issues typically associated with poverty (high mobility, hunger, family displacement), we were still given time and attention to develop core academic skills. This was possible because of Ms. Russell's willingness to learn about her students, to be creative in engaging students in learning, and to work tirelessly to make sure that no student would fail on her watch—all of which stemmed from her unwavering high expectations.

The role that social class plays in student learning will continue to be a factor in the 21st century. Some scholars agree that social class is the primary explanation for the discrepancies across racial and ethnic groups in U.S. schools (Coleman et al., 1966; Hilfiker, 2002; Kozol, 2005; Lareau, 2007; Natriello, McDill, & Pallas, 1990). However, as I will highlight in the chapters that follow, the interconnectedness between race, culture, and class is undeniable, and any effort to argue that one of these issues is more important than another is counterproductive. Although a plethora of factors contribute to the structural poverty that has plagued millions of students across the United States, inclusive, critical multicultural education as a school reform movement is a promising path to ensuring educational equity for all students.

CHAPTER 3

Culture

Culture matters because it shapes all aspects of daily living and activities. Unfortunately, the manner in which culture manifests itself for students is frequently not understood in schools and is not used effectively to enhance teaching and learning for all students. This is unsettling because all facets of human conduct are mediated by culture (M. Cole, 1998; Rogoff, 2003). Culture is a complex constellation of values, mores, norms, customs, ways of being, ways of knowing, and traditions that provides a general design for living, is passed from generation to generation, and serves as a pattern for interpreting reality (Damen, 1987; Kroeber & Kluckhohn, 1952; Parham, 2002; Parsons, 1949). Bullivant (1993) describes culture as the way a social group survives and adapts to its environment, and as a defense mechanism in interpreting its reality. Erickson (1986) defines culture as a social science concept that consists of "learned and shared standards for thinking, feeling and acting" (p. 117).

In spite of its centrality to the study of numerous areas—including society, human development, social interaction, and student learning—culture is a misunderstood and misinterpreted construct. Anthropological definitions of culture typically are tied to studying and understanding humans, in particular their behavior and the environments in which it occurs. Anthropological analyses of culture often are done through the use of ethnographic analysis centered on rigorous attempts to examine people's activities, especially individuals' relations with those around them in varied contexts (McDermott, 1977). While the anthropological construct is an important starting point for understanding and examining culture, it often falls short for educators because it fails to make explicit the manner in which culture is manifested in school settings in general, and in the learning processes of individuals from culturally different backgrounds in particular. In light of current academic disparities between students from culturally diverse backgrounds and their peers, there is a need to thoroughly examine culture in new ways—ways that typically have not been part of the dominant education discourse about human behavior, learning, and classroom settings (Erickson, 2002; K. Gutierrez, 2002; C. D. Lee, 2007). Culture in the anthropological context has relevance for human development, but it is the historical and socio-cultural construction of culture that is most relevant for educators as they seek ways to improve outcomes for students who have perenni-ally underperformed (K. Gutierrez & Rogoff, 2003).

Culture is conceptualized in most social science literature as the learned norms, values, beliefs, behaviors, and ways of knowing—more in line with a "mental abstract or code"—that people use in response to their social environments (Trumbull, 2001). All human conduct is culturally mediated and culture is all-pervasive, representing a social system of accumulated beliefs, attitudes, habits, and values that are responses to specific circumstances. Banks and Banks (1989) add com-plexity to the traditional definitions of culture, and assert that

> Most social scientists today view culture as consisting primarily of the symbolic, ideational, and intangible aspects of human societies. The es-sence of a culture is not its artifacts, tools, or other tangible cultural ele-ments but how the members of the group interpret, use, and perceive them. It is the values, symbols, interpretations, and perspectives that distinguish one people from another in modernized societies. (p. 13)

The degree to which we understand how these intangible aspects shape attitudes and behaviors has tremendous consequences for teachers and students in diverse schools. Many practitioners now rely on mainstream learning theories such as behaviorism, information processing, and cognitive constructivism to understand and influence student behavior, and they fail to incorporate theories of learning that take into consideration the influence of culture, historical group expe-riences, and the role of environment on thinking and learning (Artiles, Trent, & Palmer, 2004; K. Gutierrez & Rogoff, 2003). This is in spite of a plethora of research that has examined the ways in which human development, as mediated by culture, influences student cognition, communication, and problem solving (Erickson, 2002; K. D. Gutierrez, 2002; K. Gutierrez, Baquedano-Lopez, & Tejada, 1999; K. Gutierrez & Rogoff, 2003; Lee, 2007; Nasir, 2000).

CULTURE, RACE, AND ETHNICITY

Clear distinctions exist between culture, and race and ethnicity, two other misunderstood concepts that frequently are linked to culture.

While race—which is discussed in greater detail in Chapter 5—tends to be defined as a social construct based primarily on phenotype, ethnicity usually is tied to a group's ancestral homeland or place of origin. Culture, while closely tied to race and ethnicity, is a different concept that shapes learning in unique and meaningful ways.

A number of scholars have stated that the culture–ethnicity–learning link is an effective means for increasing student performance, in particular for students from culturally diverse backgrounds. For example, some theorists have suggested that there are traits or learning styles that are common among working-class students and students of color, and as a result teaching styles that are congruent with these traits should be constructed (Boykin, 1994; Dunn & Dunn, 1992; Hickson, Land, & Aikman, 1994). These scholars try to identify essential cultural components of non-White students to generate a discourse on ethnically based cultural differences. This work has been valuable in the discourse and scholarship on nonmainstream students and learning because it was developed to respond to theories of the late 1960s and early 1970s in which school failure of students of color and working-class students was attributed to cultural deprivation (Bloom, Davis, & Hess, 1965; Riessman, 1962). These deficit-based accounts often described students of color as having no culture, coming from a culture of poverty, or having pathological versions of mainstream culture. Scholars who focused on learning styles sought to disrupt these portrayals and shift the discourse from cultural deficit to cultural difference (Boykin, 1994, Hale-Benson, 1986; Ramírez & Castañeda, 1974; Shade, 1997). While the cultural difference model has enabled a much-needed shift away from harmful cultural deficit models (which still exist), nevertheless many of its approaches lack sufficient depth and rigor as educators seek to understand how cultural nuances play out in schools and other learning spaces.

A more comprehensive, complex account of culture must recognize that culturally diverse groups frequently bring cultural and social capital to the classroom that is not mediated exclusively by ethnicity (C.D. Lee, 2002). Culture is *not* bound exclusively by one's race, ethnicity, or place of origin, but is shaped by a myriad of factors. A narrow view of culture fails to recognize how geography, immigration status, generation, social class, gender, family history, migration patterns, language, and religious affiliations all have major influences on how culture is developed. These cultural factors can differ greatly between members of the same ethnic group, and at times can be quite similar to those of individuals who are from different ethnic groups. Figure 3.1 documents some of the factors that influence student learning.

Figure 3.1. Factors that influence student learning

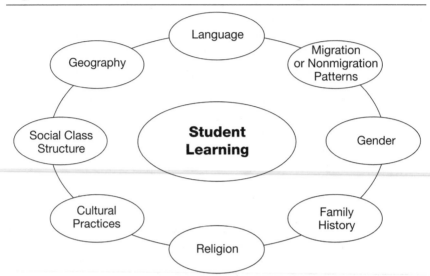

A further complicating factor is that many individuals from dominant groups mistakenly believe that culture is something possessed only by people of color, and thus view it as tied to the ethnic customs, rituals, and celebrations of "minority groups," reducing it to a static concept that is directly tied to one's ethnic or racial group membership. This is the most widely held view of culture in schools today, and it poses many problems. As Ingold (1994) argues, it is essential that we understand that all individuals have culture and, more precisely, how all people live culturally.

THE COMPLEXITY OF CULTURE

To develop a more complex notion of culture needed to ameliorate the achievement gap, it is critical to understand how culture plays out in schools and connects to varying types of knowledge. While schools are widely believed to be institutions that transmit academic knowledge, they also transmit certain types of cultural knowledge that are frequently consistent with mainstream concepts, paradigms, and experiences (Banks, 1996; Carter, 2005). It is the transmission of what Banks (1996) refers to as *mainstream academic knowledge,* taught in both explicit and implicit ways, that is problematic for culturally diverse students in their attempt to exhibit academic proficiency, as it conflicts with what Banks (1996) calls students' personal and cultural knowledge—or the "concepts, explanations, and interpretations that students derive from personal experiences in their homes, families, and community cultures" (p. 11). Where these conflicts occur, outcomes for students' experiences in schools may be compromised because of the cultural disconnect or discontinuity that students may encounter in the different cultural contexts that they participate at home and in school (Heath, 1983).

Some scholars assert that this cultural discontinuity from home to school is one explanation for lower educational outcomes for students from culturally diverse groups. Fordham and Ogbu (1986) contended that for low-income African American students, academic struggles are often attributable to the disconnect between their personal and cultural knowledge and the type of knowledge that is highly valued in schools. Some students in their research stated they had to "act White" in order to achieve academic success. Subsequent works by Fordham (1991, 1998) and Ford (1996) supported these findings. They indicate that African American students believe they must suppress their racial identity or surrender their own cultural knowledge in order to achieve high academic success in school. Similarly, Delpit (1995) found that many students from culturally diverse groups feel they must learn the codes of power or intentionally underachieve in order to maintain cultural integrity. Existing research confirms that personal and cultural knowledge is an important attribute of students' identity and behavior, underscoring the importance of developing a more comprehensive knowledge base of how students live, think, and act culturally.

One of the ways that cultural manifestations play out in the larger social realm is discussed by Bourdieu (1986). Bourdieu's theory of cultural capital emerges from a Marxist standpoint and examines culture through a sociological lens. He defines cultural capital as the knowledge, skills, education, experiences, and/or connections one has had through the course of his or her life that do or do not enable success. Bourdieu uses the term *habitus* as part of the social capital paradigm and defines it as the dispositions that are inculcated in the family but manifest themselves in different ways in each person. Although social class is formed not only by the habitus, or activities of the family, Bourdieu ties these tendencies to the social class to which an individual belongs, claiming they are essential for social mobility. Young people who come from social class backgrounds that afford them the opportunity to travel regularly, visit museums, study arts and music, and learn about other cultures, possess cultural capital that is consistent with the type of knowledge (capital) that is valued of the dominant society.

Bourdieu's (1986) analysis has been useful as a starting point for understanding and examining cultural capital, but some have challenged its usefulness for communities of color and for working-class individuals. Yosso (2005) states that Bourdieu's cultural capital framework makes "the assumption that People of Color 'lack' the social and cultural capital required for social mobility" (p. 70). She contends that the idea of a particular type of capital that is required for social mobility, operates from the standpoint that "some communities are culturally wealthy while others are culturally poor" (p. 76). Yosso provides a compelling and inclusive framework that builds on Bourdieu's work by recognizing the cultural complexities, richness, and uniqueness of culture that non-White communities possess. She refers to it as Communities of Color cultural wealth. It is composed of six forms of capital: (1) *aspirational capital*, which refers to the resiliency and ability to nurture hopes and dreams for upward mobility despite constant obstacles; (2) *linguistic capital*, which is the intellectual and communicative skills and experiences used in multiple languages; (3) *familial capital*, which refers to the capital produced and maintained by family members; (4) *social capital*, which is the people and community resources used for educational or professional opportunity and advancement; (5) *navigational capital*, or the skills and ability to maneuver through institutions that are frequently hostile or oppositional to people of color; and (6) *resistant capital,* which is the knowledge and skills used to challenge inequality and oppression.

Yosso's (2006) framework is valuable because the cultural capital that is most desirable in U.S. schools tends to be Eurocentric, male-oriented, English speaking, heterosexist, and middle class. Conversely, the norms, knowledge, values, forms of expression, and ways of being that many students from culturally diverse groups bring from home conflict with those valued most by schools—arguably one of the most important explanations for current and historical educational performance disparities (Gay, 2000; T. C. Howard, 2001).

SOCIOCULTURAL THEORY

Sociocultural theory has gained increased prominence in the psychological literature and serves as a fundamental lens for understanding how culture contributes to learning and human behavior. This body of literature draws heavily on the works of Vygotsky (1978) and assumes that children's development cannot be understood by studying the individual exclusively but must be understood within the context of participation in activities that require cognitive and communicative functions. This type of situated learning draws attention to cognitive processing that occurs in authentic situations, such as how students interpret their surroundings, make meaning of new information, process existing knowledge, communicate likes and dislikes, express a sense of what they comprehend, and convey that sense of understanding (Brown, Collines, & Duguid, 1989; Lave, 1988). Sociocultural theory seeks to move culture away from simply an individual construct that resides in a person's mind, to one that is also influenced by the external or outer factors that shape human cognition (M. Cole, 1996). Sociocultural theorists recommend examining culture as a construct that influences not only cognition, but also motivation, modes of interaction, everyday practices, and ways of viewing the world and navigating one's place within it (Cole, 1996; K. Gutierrez & Rogoff, 2003; C. D. Lee, 2004; Nasir & Cobb, 2002).

An important aspect of the sociocultural paradigm, cultural historical activity theory asserts that the process of learning requires the use of signs, symbols, and other cultural tools and artifacts (e.g., language, skills, knowledge, and beliefs) that individuals use to embody their collective experiences in external forms (such material objects as words, pictures, letters, numbers, and books), which is the essence of learning. Cole (2001) cites Wartofsky's (1973) three-level hierarchy, which delineates different artifacts that are part of the human experience. Wartofsky states that *primary artifacts* are used directly in production—namely, words, writing instruments, communication networks, and the like—while *secondary artifacts* tend to be representations or modes of action to utilize these primary artifacts, such as beliefs, norms, and other modes of transmission. Finally, *tertiary artifacts* serve as an interpretive lens through which individuals make meaning of the first and second levels. This third level thus becomes important, especially for teachers, because it serves as the impetus for understanding various practices. Teachers who have an understanding of the different accounts of artifacts, and are able to connect them to student learning and cognition, are much better equipped to structure pedagogical practices that are more accessible for students who come from culturally and linguistically diverse backgrounds.

CULTURAL MODELING

While more complex and comprehensive accounts of culture are important and can provide educators with insights into the ways that cultural norms play out in learning and social settings, many practitioners are searching for what these manifestations look like in learning settings. Many teachers want to know how to use students' cultural knowledge in meaningful ways in classroom settings in order to contribute to increased academic performance. A cogent example of how cultural practices are incorporated into classroom learning situations is C. D. Lee's (2007) cultural modeling. Lee describes cultural modeling as a framework that "address[es] the demands of complex problem solving in the various subject matters" (p. 8). The framework is built on an anti-deficit model that recognizes the wide range of cultural repertoires of practice that all students bring from their homes and community experiences to the classroom.

The premise in C. D. Lee's (2007) framework is that everyday, practice-based knowledge can and should be used to help students develop problem-solving skills with academic content. The essential idea is that out-of-school knowledge can and should be used as a conduit to acquire in-school knowledge. Similar to Moll's (1992) funds of knowledge approach, cultural modeling centers on three basic tenets: (1) positioning students as sources of authority to use their firsthand knowledge to solve academic problems; (2) the selection of texts or learning materials that deal with problems and issues that students face in their day-to-day environments; and (3) privileging students' knowledge as intellectually rich and valuable in the learning process, thus reversing the manner in which many schools tend to devalue it.

C.D. Lee (2007) describes examples of how students' cultural knowledge can be used to analyze and interpret literature such as *Beloved* (Morrison, 1987), *Damballah* (Wideman, 1998), and other notable works. Following more traditional curricula, students are asked to identify symbolism, irony, satire, plot configurations, and character types, but they are not given narrow or predetermined rubrics in which to develop their interpretations. In Lee's cultural modeling approach, students are encouraged to use their own cultural data sets to "provide them with a language to talk about their problem-solving processes, and to help them make connections between what they already do and what they are expected to do with canonical, school based problems" (p. 61).

C.D. Lee's (2007) work with cultural modeling complements nicely the work of other scholars who have examined the culture knowledge–subject matter connection. For example, Nasir (2002) examined cultural knowledge, identity, and schooling in mathematics proficiency for African American adolescents. Building on the students' knowledge of dominoes, Nasir's qualitative and quantitative findings indicate that when mathematical concepts became a normalized and mandatory part of a particular familiar activity like dominoes, mathematical goals naturally arise. Nasir (2000) found similar types of connections between cultural knowledge and learning when she explored how the practice of basketball afforded different levels of engagement with statistical thinking and mathematical reasoning for African American males. Nasir's findings suggest that when students' cultural experiences are used as their own data sets to help them analyze new information, cultural experience can be valuable parts of the learning process.

Au and Jordan's (1981) research is another example of how students' cultural knowledge or data sets can inform instructional practice. They conducted a case study of the Kamehameha Early Education Program (KEEP), a language arts development project, to examine how a team of teachers, psychologists, anthropologists, and linguists devised culturally relevant methods to teach Native Hawaiian children how to read. They concluded that KEEP's method of reading instruction was successful because greater emphasis was placed on comprehension than on sound–symbol relationships and instruction was individualized through the organization of a system of learning centers. They also attributed the majority of KEEP's success to the similarities between how the reading lessons were conducted and the linguistic patterns, such as "talk-story," that are found in Native Hawaiian cultural communication styles.

An additional study that examined the culture–cognition connection is T. C. Howard's (2001a) study of urban elementary school students. He uses the phrase *culturally consistent communicative competencies* to describe a form of culturally situated instruction that teachers use to develop literacy proficiency for African American students. According to Howard, this principle includes teachers organizing their interactions and using vocabulary in ways that are consistent with many of the culturally formed communication modes that students bring from home. Teacher pedagogy is arranged in a way that enables students to use cultural forms of expression, interpretation, and analysis in ways that do not have negative influences on their teachers' perceptions of their intelligence or academic potential.

A second-grade teacher from T. C. Howard's (2001a) study stressed the importance of recognizing the verbal propensities her African

American students brought to the classroom. She noted that one of the factors that hinder the literacy development of many African American students is typical classroom reliance on written tasks to assess reading comprehension. She discovered that many of her African American students performed better with oral than written forms of expression. Consequently, verbal opportunities as a form of student assessment became an integral part of her teaching. Considerable improvement occurred in student performance as she made these modifications.

CULTURAL REPERTOIRES OF PRACTICE

One of the most insightful and useful paradigms of culture and human development is Rogoff's (2003) work on cultural repertoires of practice. Rogoff states that human development is a cultural process and people develop as participants in cultural communities. Moreover, the processes of human development in cultural communities are guided by what Rogoff calls "orienting concepts" that influence cultural activities. These concepts are: (1) culture is not what other people do, but culture processes occur through everyday activities; (2) understanding one's own cultural heritage requires taking the perspective of people of contrasting backgrounds—everyday subtleties that may seem insignificant in one cultural context may be viewed with the utmost significance elsewhere; (3) cultural processes are multifaceted relations among numerous aspects of community functioning; (4) culture changes, because culture and the communities that shape it are in a state of continual transformation; and (5) there is not likely to be one best way to engage in human behavior, and cultural practices do not entail having to identify "the right way" to do things.

A number of theorists have discussed how culture shapes student thinking, learning, situated cognition, and the social context of cognition (M. Cole, 1996, 2000; K. D. Gutierrez, 2002; K. Gutierrez & Rogoff, 2003; C. D. Lee, 2002, 2004; Rogoff & Angelillo, 2002; Tharp & Gallimore, 1991). These approaches to culture are important for all educators to understand and incorporate into their knowledge bases. They attempt to move teachers beyond traditional methods of conceptualizing learning, and beyond superficial, essentialized notions of student and group culture, both of which have important implications for learning in today's classrooms. Many of the simplistic approaches to culture are centered on what Rogoff and Angelillo (2002) describe as the "box problem," wherein individuals from various ethnic groups are viewed by the mainstream as homogeneous. Many of these constructions of individuals are based primarily on race or ethnicity, with little consideration of student individuality or group variability.

The box problem that Rogoff and Angelillo (2002) discuss, plays out in various ways in the classroom. Based on widespread stereotypes, for example, teachers may assume that all African American students are purported to learn best when they are taught with rhythm and work in groups; Asian American and White students are viewed as highly individualistic, and thus should be taught in a particular way; Latino students all come from large family backgrounds, so teachers should include family-oriented activities in their approaches (Ramírez & Castañeda, 1974). These notions of students can be highly problematic and stereotypical, and may reinforce institutionalized racist beliefs if they are not fully comprehended because they give little consideration to the heterogeneity that exists within every group. Ethnically based learning styles can place unfair confines on the manner in which teachers view their students, and as a result teachers may fail to see, for example, why certain strategies that worked with a Korean American student one year would not work with a new Korean American student the next year. Rose (1988) states that ethnically based learning styles are examples of "cognitive reductionism," which seeks to reduce the complexity of individual cognition into nice and neat dualities. These approaches, while seemingly convenient for teachers because they allow broad, yet oversimplified categories in which to place students, can result in highly problematic outcomes for students (K. D. Gutierrez, 2002). Moreover, these notions also border on derogatory stereotypes of students, which can be highly destructive for students' learning prospects (M. Cole, 1998; C. D. Lee, 2007).

K. Gutierrez and Rogoff (2003) describe the value of cultural historical approaches to understanding culture and argue that in educational spaces, learning is not segmented into different times and spaces, but is instead a process of ongoing activity in both within-school and out-of-school contexts. They contend that to comprehend cultural practices, there is a need to understand the historical, social, and political contexts from which groups emerged. They discuss "the importance and benefit of knowing about the histories and valued practices of cultural groups rather than trying to teach prescriptively according to this broad, underexamined generalities about groups" (p. 20).

Cultural historical theorists such as Engestrom (1987, 1990, 1999) and others seek to find ways of identifying people's practices in varied communities over time (Brown & Cole, 1997; M. Cole, 1996, 1997; Cole & Engestrom, 1993, 1995). This cultural variation leads to what

K. Gutierrez and Rogoff (2003) refer to as "cultural regularities," or practices that shape how the individuals live their lives and carry out practices with the individuals with whom they come into contact as they make meaning of their worlds. The cultural historical framework suggests that practitioners and researchers should give more attention to repertoires for participating in practices, which are understood through examinations of the ways that young people participate in different communities, and understand how the histories of these communities influence learners.

An example of a repertoire of practice is the way in which young people communicate in different communities. When my oldest son Jabari was a preschool student, he continually brought home pictures, paintings, and drawings that he had produced throughout the day in his classroom. I became intrigued by the fact that his peers tended to have significantly fewer paintings and drawings, but instead possessed a litany of number and letter books and activities centered on mastering beginning words and preliteracy skills. When I asked Jabari's teacher why he did not have the same materials as his peers, she explained that he was "not ready" for the more academic tasks being done in his preschool classroom. To my chagrin, when I asked his teacher to explain what led her to this conclusion, she stated that on a number of occasions when the class was prepared to do the more academically oriented work, she would *ask* Jabari to join the circle group or *invite* him to participate in the literacy circle, or in some cases *encourage* him to engage in the numbers activity the rest of the class was completing. When he was "asked," "invited," and "encouraged" to join such groups, Jabari would state that he did not want to join the groups, politely declined such requests, and instead stated his preference to paint or draw during class time.

This exchange touches on issues raised in the works of Cazden (2000), Heath (1983), and other scholars who have documented interaction patterns in classrooms to highlight the complex nature of communication across different cultural spaces. When I informed Jabari's teacher that there appeared to be a communication disconnect between the two of them, as opposed to a cognitive deficit or an inability on his part to perform the tasks, she seemed dumbfounded by what I meant. I recommended that instead of asking and inviting Jabari to participate in these activities, she communicate with him in more direct terms, and *tell* him to participate instead of asking or inviting him. In this particular instance, Jabari's interpretation of his teacher's invitations seemed to be that his participation in learning tasks of this type was optional. This particular cultural repertoire was quite different from what he was accustomed to at home, where directives are much more common than invitations to perform particular tasks.

I told Jabari's teacher that he was not *invited* to go to bed or *encouraged* to clean his room, and that a more direct form of communication would yield different results. Through our conversation, she learned that she had been using a form of communication that was not consistent with his cultural norms of interacting; upon modifying her questions to more direct requests, she discovered his mastery of and interest in the skills that days earlier she did not think he was capable of performing. One can only wonder how many other students experience these types of disconnects in the teaching and learning process similar to the one Jabari and his teacher experienced and, without advocates to intervene and clarify cultural or communication gaps, fall short of their academic potential. The cultural historical point of view suggests that educators' awareness of modes of interaction across different spaces is crucial. K. Gutierrez and Rogoff (2003) state:

> Students who have participated in varying cultural traditions would differ in repertoires in terms of familiarity with engaging in discussions with authority figures, answering known-answer questions, analyzing word problems on the bases of counterfactural premises, seeking or avoiding being singled out for praise, spontaneously helping classmates. (p. 22)

Other scholars have addressed similar issues related to communication patterns such as spontaneity in discourse practices (Kochman, 1981; Smitherman, 1977), topic-centered and topic-chaining approaches to speaking (Au, 1993; Gay, 2000), and speech rate (Boggs, 1985). What is central in these facets of culture is understanding communities' practices and the ways in which individuals construct practices within certain parameters. An understanding of culture requires a level of observation, examination, and reflection that rarely is used by practitioners (Milner, 2003). However, for teachers to think critically about ways of improving teaching and learning for students from culturally diverse groups, they must be cognizant of a wide range of students' cognitive processes, and should not be informed only by the surface levels of culture, such as foods, dress, festivals, and dance.

In my experiences in schools, I have talked to classroom teachers about how they relate student culture to learning, and I am continually dismayed by the numerous references to cultural fairs that require students and their families to bring foods or rituals from their home cultures. At the secondary level, this question typically is answered by mentioning lessons or units that deal with some type of foreign empire, namely, the cultures of ancient Egypt, Greece, or Rome. To develop a more complex and comprehensive notion of culture, practitioners should ponder these questions:

Questions for Understanding Student Culture

- What are the expectations and experiences my students have had with school?
- What are the factors that shape students' understandings of school?
- What do I know about my students' home and community life?
- How can I learn more about my students' home and community life?
- Who are the individuals that influence my students most?
- What are the tools, skills, and practices that students use to navigate their homes and communities?
- What are the contexts that seem to motivate my students to learn?
- How do my students express themselves in different settings?
- What are the topics, issues, and themes that generate high levels of student engagement, effort, and interest?
- What are the cultural practices that seem to be most common among my students? How and where were they acquired?
- What, if any, contradictions or tensions seem to exist between the cultural practices and traditions that my students bring to the classroom and the practices and traditions that I operate on?

NORMALIZING CULTURE IN EVERYDAY PRACTICE

One of the critical aspects of understanding culture is a recognition that cultural dispositions and practices held and displayed by one individual are not universal for other people. Any variations from these "normal" behaviors too often are viewed with suspicion or scorn, and they are likely to be seen as problematic and as needing immediate efforts to make them "correct." Rogoff (2003) states that we need to develop a deeper sense of how and why people carry out their practices in their respective ways, separate from value judgments about cultural differences. Therefore, it is essential to understand human behavior within a cultural framework derived from observations of events and behaviors. She writes:

> Interpreting the activity of people without regard for *their* meaning system and goals renders observations meaningless. We need to understand the coherence of what people from different communities *do*, rather than simply determining that some other group of people do *not* do what "we" do, or do not do it as well or in the way that we do it, or jumping to the conclusions that their practices are barbaric (p. 17, emphasis in original).

Rogoff (2003) calls for individuals to move beyond the typical initial assumptions we create when coming into contact with cultural activities and displays that are different from our own. To do so, we also must examine our own cultural frameworks and recognize that our own ways of being are not necessarily shared and embraced by others: "Even without being immersed in another cultural system, comparisons of cultural ways may create discomfort among people who have never before considered the assumptions of their own cultural practices" (p. 14). Germane to culture, as has been stated previously, is context. Cultural displays typically are developed in response to the settings in which individuals are seeking to thrive and survive, and many of their practices may look abnormal, irregular, or out of context. The dissonance that frequently is experienced with respect to different cultural displays typically is tied to individuals' cultural comfort zones. These zones are centered on a person's belief that his or her own ways of being are correct and proper, and social and cultural disequilibrium may result when one steps outside of these zones. An example that demonstrates this cultural context is provided by the Native American Tribe of Five Nations in responding to an invitation from Benjamin Franklin in 1784 to send some of their young men for training at William and Mary College.

> We are convinced . . . that you mean to do us good by your proposal and we thank you heartily. . . . But you, who are wise, must know that different nations have different conceptions of things; and you will therefore not take it amiss, if our ideas of this kind of education happen not to be the same with yours. We have had some experience of it: several of our young people were formerly brought up at the colleges of the northern provinces; they were instructed in all of your sciences; but when they came back to us they were ignorant of every means of living in the woods unable to bear either cold or hunger, knew neither

how to build a cabin, take a deer, nor kill an enemy, spoke our language imperfectly, were therefore neither fit for hunters, warriors, or counselors; they were totally good for nothing. We are however, not the less obliged by your kind offer . . . and to show our grateful sense of it, if the gentlemen of Virginia will send a dozen of their sons, we will take great care of their education, instruct them in all we know, and make men of them. (cited in Reimer, 1971, p. 60)

Culture is a messy, complex, ever-changing, and at times contradictory concept. K.D. Gutierrez' (2002) describes the contradictions that exist within culture and states that while some beliefs, values, and practices remain constant within particular groups over time, other cultural practices and knowledge are not necessarily universal and remain in a state of flux. Trying to identify and interpret these contradictions within culture is a difficult and ongoing endeavor. The multifaceted and intricate features of culture contribute to it being widely misunderstood and misused when we examine student learning. The literature on culture continues to expand and inform our understanding. It is important for educators at all levels to move away from static and contracted cultural categories that lend themselves easily to scholarly discourse about how ethnicity dictates learning preferences, despite transparent evidence that offers contrasting views of simplistic categories and offers more nuanced understandings of culture. Culture is too important to understanding the human condition for us not to examine it, analyze its meaning, and find out how cultural practices are used by people every day in their attempts to navigate the world around them. Attempts to view culture in a simple, neat, cohesive, and seamless fashion fail to recognize its complicated and dynamic nature. In Chapter 4 I will locate culture within pedagogical practices that offer critical implications for future research and practice for educators concerned with the disparate achievement outcomes for diverse cultural groups.

CHAPTER 4

Culturally Responsive Pedagogy

This chapter will examine culturally responsive pedagogy, which has gained increased attention over the past decade as a way to rethink instructional practice in an effort to improve the educational performance of African American, Latino, Native American, and various Asian American students (Gay, 2000). The merger of culture and pedagogy is a more complex and intricate set of processes than many practitioners and researchers have suggested. While it may improve student learning, researchers continue to evaluate its effectiveness for helping culturally diverse students improve academically. The marriage of culture and pedagogy is built upon a comprehensive and informed set of knowledge and skills that many practitioners often lack in their attempts to engage diverse students in the teaching and learning process.

Culturally responsive pedagogy is more than just a way of teaching or a simple set of practices embedded in curriculum lessons and units. It seeks to move away from the "methods fetish" (Bartolome, 1994) that has become far too commonplace in teacher education as being the most useful way to teach certain types of student—especially low-income and students of color. Practitioners who seek to reduce culturally responsive teaching to a simple act or who ask, as one preservice teacher once asked me in a class, "Can you just show me how to do it?" fail to recognize the intricacies of the concept. Culturally responsive pedagogy embodies a professional, political, cultural, ethical, and ideological disposition that supersedes mundane teaching acts; it is centered in fundamental beliefs about teaching, learning, students, their families, and their communities, and an unyielding commitment to see student success become less rhetoric and more of a reality. Culturally responsive pedagogy is situated in a framework that recognizes the rich and varied cultural wealth, knowledge, and skills that students from diverse groups bring to schools, and seeks to develop dynamic teaching practices, multicultural content, multiple means of assessment, and a philosophical view of teaching that is dedicated to nurturing student academic, social, emotional, cultural, psychological, and physiological well being.

Culturally responsive teaching is a response to the ongoing achievement disparities between African American and Latino students, and their White and certain Asian American counterparts. A plethora of school reform initiatives, research agendas, and school intervention programs have been designed to eradicate chronic differences in the educational outcomes of students (R. Ferguson, 2000). A host of explanations have been offered to explain the differences in academic performance and outcomes among underachieving groups. One of the more troubling explanations for disparate educational outcomes that culturally responsive teaching attempts to disrupt is deficit-based explanations of low-income students and students of color. These explanations usually are centered on low-income students and students of color lacking or being devoid of culture, coming from a culture of poverty that is not suited for academic success, possessing an oppositional culture, having a disdain for academic achievement, or having parents who lack concern for their children's academic aspirations (McWhorter, 2000; Ogbu, 1987; S. Steele, 1990; R. R. Valencia, 1997). These deficit-based explanations also have derided students' language as being deficient because of its variation from Standard English (Alim & Baugh, 2007). Some scholars have maintained that academic achievement outcomes are caused by innate differences in intelligence between racial groups (Herrnstein & Murray, 1994), a belief that is not as prevalent as it was half a century ago, but still present nonetheless. Ryan (1971) asserted that accounts of deficit thinking are essentially *victim blaming*, or a way of shifting deep-seated structural inequities to individual, family, and community deficits. Deficit theorists have advocated changing student knowledge, language, culture, and behavior to be more consistent with mainstream ways of being (Olson, 1997; Pearl, 1970; Valenzuela, 1999). These efforts typically have been been met with student resistance, disengagement, and ultimately educational disenfranchisement for millions of low-income and culturally diverse students (Kohl, 1995; Solorzano & Delgado Bernal, 2001).

A number of scholars respond to cultural deficit theory by stating that students from diverse backgrounds are not deficient in their ways of being, but are different (Ford, 1996; Irvine, 2003; C. D. Lee, 2007; Moll, 2000). These scholars describe different ways of thinking about students, their families, and communities, and offer different ways of thinking about closing the achievement gap. Table 4.1 briefly describes how deficit and difference theorists view fundamental aspects of diverse students and their families.

Table 4.1. Deficit and difference viewpoints

Cultural Deficit Theory	Cultural Difference Theory
Culture is nonexistent or abnormal	Cultural is rich, unique, and complex
Language is a deficit	Language is an asset
Home environment is pathological	Home environment has capital
Genetics matter	Environment matters
Solution: Transform the Child	**Solution: Transform the School**

In response to the deficit explanations offered for the chronic academic underachievement of culturally diverse and low-income students, some scholars have asserted that the performance discrepancies are a result of cultural discontinuity that exists between culturally diverse students and their teachers. Cultural discontinuity has generated increased attention to culturally responsive pedagogy. A growing number of scholars have posited that teacher beliefs and practices should recognize and respect the intricacies and complexities of culture, and the differences that come with it, and that pedagogical practices and ideological stances should be structured in ways that are culturally recognizable and socially meaningful (Foster, 1989, 1993; T. C. Howard, 2001b, 2003a; C. D. Lee, 2007; Nasir, 2000). A significant increase in professional works concerned with culturally responsive teaching occurred between 1999 and 2009. Culturally responsive pedagogy assumes that if teachers are able to make connections between the cultural knowledge, beliefs, and practices that students bring from home, and the content and pedagogy that they use in their classrooms, the academic performance and overall schooling experiences of learners from culturally diverse groups will improve (Gay, 2000; Hollie, 2001; T. C. Howard, 2001a; Irvine, 1990; Ladson-Billings, 1995; C. D. Lee, 1995, 1998; Lipman, 1995; Lynn, 2006; E. C. Parsons, 2005; E. Pierce, 2005; Sheets, 1995; Tate, 1995; Wortham, 2002).

SEEKING CLARITY IN CULTURE AND PEDAGOGY

A perusal of the works concerned with culturally responsive pedagogy reveals that it continues to grow as both scholars and practitioners recognize the potential of rethinking pedagogy in a way that belies traditional approaches to content, instruction, and assessment. A multitude of terms have been used in the professional literature to describe culturally responsive teaching, including *culturally embedded, cultur-*

ally relevant, culturally congruent, culturally mediated, culturally sensitive, and *culturally synchronized teaching.* Because there are at least 3 decades of theoretical and empirical work on culturally responsive teaching, it is important to determine what we know about the concept and where gaps exist in the knowledge base, and most important, to assess whether there is sufficient evidence to show that it contributes to students' performance in schools. It is also important to examine where we have observed success, because this knowledge will help to inform future research, theory, and practice, as well as areas that may need to be re-examined and reconceptualized. Gay (2000) asserts that culturally responsive teaching is a "very different pedagogical paradigm" (p. 24). An examination of research and theory on culturally responsive pedagogy reveals that it is based on five key principles.

- The eradication of deficits-based ideologies of culturally diverse students.
- The disruption of the idea that Eurocentric or middle-class forms of discourse, knowledge, language, culture, and historical interpretations are normative.
- A critical consciousness and sociopolitical awareness that reflects an ongoing commitment to challenge injustice and disrupt inequities and oppression of any group of people.
- An authentic and culturally informed notion of *care* for students, wherein their academic, social, emotional, psychological, and cultural well-being is adhered to.
- A recognition of the complexity of culture, in which educators allow students to use their personal culture to enhance their quest for educational excellence.

These principles are informed by the growing body of research that examines the utility and complexity of culturally responsive pedagogy and serves as a critical blueprint upon which all students can be educated, particularly in multicultural schools.

Varying questions and objections have been raised about the appropriateness of culturally responsive pedagogy. Some scholars have suggested that cultural instantiations are lacking in depth and rigor, while others have claimed that the emphasis on culture denies students access to core academic skills such as reading, writing, and math, which are purported to be culturally neutral (Hirsch, 1987; Ravitch, 2003). Another commonly cited critique is that culturally responsive pedagogy seems appropriate only for students of color. Irvine and Armento (2001) respond to this critique by stating that culturally responsive teaching is not a novel or transformative approach to teaching. In fact, they maintain that culturally responsive teaching has been a staple in U.S. schools for centuries, but it has been most responsive to only one group of students—U.S.-born middle-class, English-speaking, White students.

Irvine and Armento (2001) assert that curriculum, instruction, and assessment that are responsive primarily to one group (middle-class White students) is one of the fundamental reasons why, historically, middle-class White students have performed better than all other student groups. The epistemological origin of school knowledge is heavily steeped in a Eurocentric worldview and ideology that largely omit the experiences, histories, contributions, and cultures of people of color, the poor, and women. Banks's (1996) typology of the types of knowledge is as an important exemplar of how different types of knowledge inform school content. Juxtaposing Banks's typology within a K–12 school framework cogently highlights the way in which academic and school knowledge most frequently taught in U.S. public schools can conflict with the cultural knowledge that students bring from home and can contribute to cultural confusion, disconnects, and misunderstandings that frequently occur in classrooms across the United States. Culturally responsive pedagogy seeks to offer the same types of educational opportunities, personal enhancements, school structures, and experiences in schools that have been in place for dominant groups since the establishment of U.S. public schools. Gay (2000) reaffirms this contention by suggesting that "the fundamental aim of culturally responsive pedagogy is to empower ethnically diverse students through academic success, cultural affiliation, and personal efficacy" (p. 111).

EMPIRICAL AND CONCEPTUAL
WORK ON CULTURALLY RESPONSIVE PEDAGOGY

Culturally responsive pedagogy is becoming more comprehensive and more concrete—as it shifts from conceptual theory to grounded practice. Gay (2000) suggests that culturally responsive pedagogy recognizes the uniqueness of student culture by using "the cultural knowledge, prior experiences, frames of reference, and performance styles of ethnically diverse students to make learning more relevant to and effective for them. It teaches *to and through* the strengths of these students. It is culturally *validating and affirming*" (p. 29, emphasis in original). Ladson-Billings (1994) describes the concept, which she calls culturally relevant, as one that "empowers students intellectually, socially, emotionally, and politically by using cultural referents to impart knowledge, skills, and attitudes" (p. 18).

Ladson-Billings's (1994) explained how teachers influence students' literacy development through the incorporation of culturally recognizable content. Her work also stresses how teachers' conception of self, ethic of care, and clear and deliberate instructional focus are important components of developing culturally relevant teaching practices. Culturally responsive teaching has been critiqued because there are few studies that examine the concept in mathematics. Over the past decade a number of studies have begun to address this void. For example, Tate (1995) examined culturally relevant teaching in mathematics and discovered teachers who used community issues as a framework for improving math proficiency. Other scholars have examined culturally relevant approaches to mathematics (Gutsetin, Lipman, Hernandez, & de los Reyes, 1997; Nasir & Cobb, 2006; Nelson-Barber & Estrin, 1995). Nasir's (2000) research investigated the construction of identity, culture, and learning. In her work she found the relationship between identity and schooling to be an integral one in the area of mathematics proficiency for African American adolescents. Building on the students' knowledge of dominoes, Nasir's qualitative and quantitative findings revealed that, in dominoes, mathematical goals were reached in the context of activity when math concepts became a normalized and mandatory part of a particular activity.

Civil and Khan (2001) studied teachers who used students' home experiences in planting gardens to develop important math concepts. Ensign (2003) documented how one teacher used students' experiences within their local stores and price comparisons as a conduit to build better comprehension of math concepts. Martin (2000) examined mathematical proficiency of African American students and suggests that the history and context of the African American experiences are crucial for improved mathematical proficiency and reasoning; he recommends that educators develop an awareness of the socioeconomic issues that influence African American students' educational experiences.

E. C. Parsons (2005) studied how teachers disrupt cultural hegemony in school curriculum and discourse. She examined how a teacher used the approach of affirming students' best qualities and challenged dominant discourses that silenced African American students and privileged White students as a form of culturally sensitive teaching. Powell (1997) investigated how White teachers in diverse school settings and discovered that the teachers used biographies to examine their own backgrounds and as a result developed a critical consciousness that helped them to develop a more inclusive and affirming form of pedagogy that increased student engagement. Powell's work builds on one of the key tenets in Ladson-Billings's (1995) framework that identifies teachers' conception of self as an integral element of culturally responsive teaching.

Beauboeuf-Lafontant (1999) investigated teachers' construction of self-concept by studying six African American teachers and discovered that the teachers' "psychological worldviews" had a significant influence on the way in which their culturally relevant teaching approaches were carried out. She also asserted that teachers who used culturally embedded approaches were explicitly aware of the political nature of their work. She suggested that *politically relevant teaching* might be a more appropriate term for this approach to teaching than culturally relevant teaching, because teachers in her study were acutely aware of the political context in which their work was situated. By problematizing the salience of gender in his study, Lynn (2006) looked at culturally relevant teaching by analyzing the role of African American male teachers and discovered that they placed an important premium on students' lived experiences. Lynn also noted that the teachers adopted an activist orientation in their teaching that examined critical issues in the local context, which engaged students.

Each of these studies highlighted the multifaceted way in which culturally responsive teaching is implemented. Much like Ladson-Billings's (1995) seminal work, the studies stressed teachers' conception of self; this means self-examination is instrumental in recognizing the importance of racial and ethnic identity for students. There is an explicit commitment to improving student academic performance. Teachers view their roles as pedagogues who teach in a way that helps students improve in core academic areas such as reading, language arts, mathematics, and writing.

In addition to enhancing academic performance, culturally responsive pedagogy seeks to develop a critical consciousness and commitment to social justice, wherein students understand the social, historical, and political issues within an historical and contemporary context and seek to identify and address inequities that exclude marginalized groups. Another contribution of these studies of culturally responsive pedagogy is the much-needed attention they have placed on key subject areas such as English language arts, mathematics, and social studies. Teachers use the students' cultural knowledge (through family, community, personal, and home experiences) as starting points to engage them in academic content. Several of these studies identify White teachers who use culturally responsive teaching with students of color. One of the frequent comments I hear from White teachers is that these approaches can be used only by teachers of color because "they understand" students' culture in ways that White teachers do not. I am quick to challenge and refute such assertions by stating that one of the essential elements of culturally responsive teaching is getting to know and understand students, their cultures, their families, and their communities. A teacher's ability to know and understand students is not restricted by her or his race; it is tied to a willingness of educators to know and understand the complexities of race and culture, develop a healthy sense of their own racial identity and privilege, develop a skill set of instructional practices that tap into cultural knowledge, reject deficit views of students of color, and have an authentic sense of students' ability to be academically successful.

Another element that these studies reveal that is significant is the importance of care. Gay (2000) elaborates on the importance of care to culturally responsive teaching.

> Caring is one of the major pillars of culturally responsive pedagogy for ethnically diverse students. It is manifested in the form of teacher attitudes, expectations, and behaviors about students' human value, intellectual capability, and performance responsibilities. . . . This is expressed for their psychoemotional well-being and academic success; personal, morality, and social actions, obligations and celebrations; community and individuality; and unique cultural connections and universal human bonds. (pp. 45–46)

These studies acknowledge the political nature of teaching. Reflecting on Freire's (1970) notion of reading the *word* and the *world*, these studies each highlight teachers who view their work as a more than just a job but as a specialized craft, a unique calling, a moral endeavor embedded in a cultural context that seeks to defy conventional thinking about culturally diverse and low-income students. These teachers are informed by a genuine desire to empower students, and they see themselves as transformative agents in that process.

While the knowledge base of culturally responsive teaching has grown, in order for the area to continue to advance in depth and breadth, additional studies are needed that will continue to inform both researchers and practitioners. Culturally responsive teaching can be strengthened if research answers these questions.

1. What means of assessment are best suited to measure the effectiveness of culturally responsive teaching?
2. What are the best methods to prepare teachers to develop culturally responsive teaching approaches?

3. How do practitioners develop culturally appropriate methods of teaching in classroom settings where there are students from various cultures?
4. How can culturally responsive teaching methods disrupt essentializing accounts of students' cultures?
5. How can researchers document the wide variations of culturally mediated teaching when tacit knowledge of student culture is possessed by teachers?

One of the challenges in moving culturally responsive teaching forward is to continue to disrupt the static notions of culture that dominate educational discourse. The challenge of static notions of culture is tied to the idea that practitioners must be able to move beyond cultural fairs, ethnic celebrations, and multicultural feasts in order to diversify their curricula. For further explanations on how to move beyond these superficial accounts of students' culture, see J. A. Banks's (1989) work on the five levels of multicultural content.

THE IMPORTANCE OF PEDAGOGY

After developing a clear and complex understanding of culture, it is vital that teachers develop a conception of what Shulman (1987) refers to as pedagogical content knowledge. Shulman states that pedagogical content knowledge is a form of practical knowledge that is used by teachers to guide their actions in classroom settings. Shulman bases the concept of pedagogical knowledge on three key areas: (1) knowledge of how to structure and represent academic content for direct teaching to students; (2) knowledge of the common conceptions, misconceptions, and difficulties that students encounter in the learning process; and (3) knowledge of specific teaching skills that can be used to address students' learning needs in the learning context. Constructing pedagogy in meaningful ways is important in culturally responsive teaching. An in-depth understanding of each of Shulman's principles is fundamental especially when situated within a culturally specific manner. The mere understanding of culture cannot translate into effective teaching strategies. Far too often I have seen practitioners who possess a solid grasp of students' backgrounds, families, and cultural practices, but still fall short in assisting students to become optimal learners, because of their lack of knowledge about how to teach concepts, and structure instructional practices, and their overall lack of pedagogical knowledge.

Some researchers and theorists have called for effective teaching that recognizes the complexities of teaching and the need for teachers to develop breadth and depth of pedagogy, content, and students' backgrounds in order to enhance learning. Dalton (2008) sets forth five pedagogical standards that she maintains are essential for transformative teaching:

1. Teacher and students producing together through joint activity,
2. Developing language and literacy competence across the curriculum,
3. Connecting school to students' lives by linking teaching and curriculum to students' experiences at home and in their communities,
4. Teaching complex thinking,
5. Teaching through conversation, in particular engaging students in instructional conversation.

It is essential for teachers to have a firm grasp of how students learn and the types of pedagogical knowledge and skills that can be used to tap into students' prior knowledge in ways that will pique their interest in learning, increase their levels of engagement, and encourage them to feel a part of the learning process. Hess (2009) describes effective ways to facilitate discussion, including incorporation of multiple perspectives around a particular topic or issue. Knowledge is not viewed as a static entity that is not open to multiple interpretations. The multiple vantage point perspective is stimulated by instructional approaches that encourage students to think critically about information, analyze various sources of information, contemplate opposing viewpoints, gather additional information, and make informed decisions. Culturally responsive teaching values different viewpoints about topics and encourages students to offer insights and perspectives that may not be majority ones, but are still equally respected by teachers and students. Culturally responsive teaching asks students to question, deconstruct, and then reconstruct knowledge. Culturally responsive teaching is also a mutual exchange of knowledge and information, wherein educators are learning from students, and vice versa. Ladson-Billings (1995) states that for culturally relevant teachers, knowledge is not static but is viewed critically from multiple vantage points. Knowledge should be viewed as a mechanism for developing a critical consciousness in students, wherein they acquire information that allows them to critique social inequities locally, nationally, and globally (Banks, 2009). The development of critical consciousness is a domain where subject areas such as history, sociology, language arts,

English literature, biology, and business can be taught in transformative ways that seek to incorporate culturally responsive teaching approaches that encourage students to go beyond surface-level comprehension of course content. Social studies, and language arts content in particular, allow teachers to use concepts, issues, themes, literature, and events (historical and contemporary) as contexts to help students think democratically and develop decision-making and social action skills (Banks, 1990).

PROGRAMS WITH CULTURALLY RESPONSIVE TEACHING

While considerable attention has been placed on the conceptual understanding of culturally responsive pedagogy, a number of school districts have implemented action plans, mission statements, and teacher training designed to translate theoretical principles of culturally responsive teaching into classroom practice and school culture. One example of this implementation is in the Los Angeles Unified School District. In 2001, concerned about the persistent failure of its African American student population, the district developed a program called the African American Learners Initiative (AALI), a resolution committed to improving the academic performance of African American students. One of the essential components of the AALI is the Academic English Mastery Program (AEMP, 2008). According to its Web site:

> AEMP is a comprehensive, research-based program designed to promote equity in access to the District's core language, literacy, and mathematics curriculums for Standard English Learners (SEL's). AEMP's program's mission is to eliminate disparities in educational outcomes for African American and other underachieving students. Working in alignment with the District's instructional initiatives the Program advances the acquisition of school language, literacy, and learning in SEL through culturally and linguistically responsive pedagogy, and forwards the Superintendents priority to close the achievement gap.

AEMP's framework classifies SELs as students for whom Standard English is not native and whose home language differs in structure and form from standard academic English. These students often are classified as "English only" because their home language generally incorporates English vocabulary but embodies phonology, grammar, and sentence structure rules borrowed from indigenous languages other than

English. The AEMP mission expands upon the idea of distinguishing English language learners (ELLs) from Standard English learners by stating that the former are students for whom English is not native and the latter are students for whom Standard English is not native.

The AEMP assumes that both ELLs and SELs are considered linguistically diverse, but SELs generally can understand Standard English when it is spoken, whereas ELLs may have language comprehension difficulties. Languages spoken by SELs may include African American language (sometimes referred to as African American English), Mexican American language (also referred to as Chicano English), Hawaiian American language (also referred to as Hawaiian Pidgin English), and Native American language (NL) (sometimes referred to as American Indian English or Red English). Both ELLs and SELs need to acquire knowledge of the rules of Standard academic English in its oral and written forms in order to be successful in U.S schools. In their work with schools, AEMP teachers stress that language acquisition is a highly complex, structured, and dynamic process that students engage in varying ways. Even for students whose only language is English, there is a need to recognize the richness in linguistic diversity, yet provide them with assistance to master the acquisition of Standard English without having to sacrifice the unique nuances, structures, and patterns of their use of English, which is a fundamental attribute of culturally relevant teaching. AEMP's work has been most effective when teachers have fully embraced the rich linguistic differences and cultural knowledge students bring from home. Teachers from AEMP classrooms have reported significant improvement in students' reading proficiency, Standard English acquisition, literary interpretations, and vocabulary. Consequently, these teachers reported decreases in behavior problems and student absences, and increases in overall self-efficacy, engagement, and problem-solving skills.

Teaching in Action

Part of the work I have been involved in over the past 2 years has examined teacher practice with students from culturally diverse groups. One of the aims of this work has been to investigate how teachers may use students' cultural knowledge in ways that increase student engagement, improve learning, and enhance students' levels of comprehension of academic content. This work has been done across elementary and secondary schools in Los Angeles County. The makeup of these classrooms was predominantly African American and Latino, and each of the schools was located in a low-income neighborhood and was classified as a Title I school, meaning they had high numbers of low-SES students, high numbers of students qualifying for free and reduced lunch, and a growing number of students who spoke English as their second language. To highlight culturally responsive pedagogy in action, I will discuss different episodes of teaching, learning, people, and programs that exemplify how the idea of culture and instruction can be used to foster student learning, and critical thinking, and therefore improve educational outcomes.

In the city of Inglewood, California, the charter school Culture and Language Academy of Success (CLAS) places an explicit emphasis on African American culture to help students master academic success. CLAS focuses on incorporating African and African American cultural knowledge as part of the professional development of teachers to help them acquire a deeper understanding of how to structure pedagogical practices that can build on African American culture. A wide range of instructional practices defy traditional teacher–student interactions in this K–8 school. Teachers are rarely in their seats as they actively interact with students, providing a wide range of instructional strategies. Students are engaged in hands-on problem solving, and there seems to be a palpable sense of energy and excitement about teaching and learning that rarely is seen or felt in most schools.

In Mrs. Johnston's 5th-grade classroom, the methods that were incorporated were directly tied to the ideas and principles associated with the Gifted and Talented Education Program (GATE). She never referred to her teaching as culturally responsive, but she made several references to the idea of "knowing what my students know, and understanding how they see the world," as the general premise that guided her work. As a former GATE teacher, she stated that classrooms assume that there are two different types of curriculum and instruction in most schools: the type received by students in GATE classes, and the type provided to the rest of the students. She found these distinctions most disturbing because the quality of teaching that students in non-GATE classes received was "downright appalling."

The use of gifted principles is critical in that it offers students important opportunities for learning that frequently are missing from schools where low-income students and students of color are present. VanTassel-Baska (1992) identifies five goals that are essential to gifted education and cognitive development, and that all teachers should help students develop: (1) increasing high-level proficiency in all core subject areas; (2) becoming independent investigators; (3) appreciating the world of ideas; (4) enhancing higher level thinking skills; and (5) encouraging the spirit of inquiry.

The belief that all students are capable learners is essential to culturally responsive teaching, and was clearly evident in Mrs. Johnston's classroom. One of the approaches that Mrs. Johnston used in her fifth-grade classroom from day 1 was to have students write often. The students wrote in their daily journals about their experiences on a multitude of topics, such as their likes, dislikes, fears, hopes, dreams, and aspirations. Mrs. Johnston stated that the purpose of these writing activities was to find out about students' lives outside of schools, to tap into their thinking, and to try to assess how they think. She also mentioned that she used this approach to engage the students in a process that allowed her to look into students' lives outside of school and "take a walk into their brains" so that she could make connections to what they knew and understood. Writing has been cited by a number of scholars as a way to engage underperforming urban youth in the learning process (Morrell & Duncan-Andrade, 2005). Culturally responsive instructional practices are implemented when teachers are able to take the personal and cultural knowledge that students bring from home and use it as a conduit to course content. Mrs. Johnston frequently would teach the writing process, introduce parts of speech, and teach key grammar and punctuation concepts using students' daily journal writing. She informed me that she was always careful not to compromise the integrity of the students' thoughts by having them change their topics or alter the essence of their content. However, she stated that she pushed her students to think about how they expressed their thoughts in writing and how they would capture a reader's attention, and she sought to make sure that they developed a command of how to use Standard English in conveying their ideas.

Mrs. Johnston's approach to developing a rigorous writing program in her class offers a direct response to critics of culturally responsive teaching who have asserted that such approaches are lacking in rigor, are devoid of depth, and essentially do not assist students to become proficient learners (D'Souza, 1995; Ravitch, 2003). Mrs. Johnston's emphasis on writing represented the ideal nexus of using cultural knowledge to promote higher order thinking in order to engage students in rigorous reading and writing. Her approach was exemplified in her assigning students to develop persuasive speeches. The cultural relevance in this particular assignment was evident when she allowed students to identify topics that they would write their speeches about. She stated that the topics should be areas that students were passionate about and really had strong conviction toward and would "fight for the right to believe." The following were topics or guided questions for persuasive speeches:

- Why gang members should be given harsher penalties
- Why city leaders should listen to students' ideas about improving the city
- The top three reasons kids join gangs and how we can stop it
- Why the neighborhood Boys and Girls Club should not have been closed
- Why drug dealers should not be given long prison sentences
- Why teachers should not give homework
- Why the government does not care about poor people

The majority of the topics that students selected had connections to issues they faced in their own experiences with their families, communities, or schools. Many of the topics dealt with what they believed to be inequities in laws and circumstances, such as one young man's topic that was centered on why new school funding formulas should be established, or a young woman's topic that addressed the negative impact rap music has on young girls' self-esteem and educational performance. The way students were required to identify topics and conduct independent research on them using five different sources (newspaper, Internet, magazines, books, and personal conversation) really challenged them to think deeply about their topics. Students also were required to identify consenting arguments to their speeches and to identify rebuttals. They had to be prepared to give a 3- to 4-minute speech on the topic, which also had to be accompanied by a three-page written paper. Extra credit was offered to students for developing a plan of implementation that would consist of the student taking steps to address the topic on which he or she had become an "expert."

Mrs. Johnston's assignment was in many ways similar to tasks that countless teachers across the country give to their students. However, the fundamental difference was the students' ability to select the topics of their choice to which they felt an emotional connection and to take what otherwise could be a mundane task and transform it into a more socially meaningful and culturally responsive task. One of the shortcomings of many traditional classroom activities is that students are expected to access only limited types of knowledge, usually dictated by teachers' experiences and preferences that are often at odds with students' backgrounds and interests. Or in some cases, the examples, concepts, and themes that students are required to use are directly from textbooks or school-sanctioned mainstream knowledge. Consequently, one of the key components that teachers must remain mindful of is students' ability to learn core academic proficiencies by tapping into different knowledge sources—particularly their own culturally and individually mediated knowledge. Equally important to culturally responsive teaching is a teacher's willingness to educate herself about students' cultures, communities, and experiences.

A teacher's ability to connect with student knowledge is a concept that researchers have examined. Central to these works and also integral to the concept of culturally relevant teaching is the use of what Moll and Gonzales (2004) refer to as students' *funds of knowledge*. They define the concept as "the knowledge base that underlies the productive and exchange activities of households" (p. 700). The funds of knowledge approach to teaching also entails using anthropological approaches to understand students' lives outside of school, most specifically students' roles within their families and their relationships with assets in their respective communities, and developing a more profound and holistic sense of how students interpret their world. Moll and Gonzales (2004) state:

> A major limitation of most classroom innovations is that they do not require (or motivate) teachers or students to go beyond the classroom walls to make instruction work. Consequently, sooner or later the classroom comes under the control of a restrictive status quo. Capitalizing on cultural resources for teaching allows both teachers and students to continuously challenge the status quo. (p. 711)

Challenging the status quo is a critical element of the way in which students can critique inequities by using their own worldviews. To highlight this point, one of the core ideas embedded in critical thinking, as laid out by researchers of gifted education, is that students are able to synthesize and evaluate information in one context and apply the same knowledge and skills in different contexts; this ability demonstrates higher levels of cognitive processing (Ford, 1996; VanTassel-Baska, 1992). Building on Moll & Gonzales' (2004) idea of challenging the status quo, a critical analysis of traditional or mainstream ways of knowing can be an important element of the way in which students can critique inequities by using their own worldviews. For many students of color, and from low-income backgrounds, challenging the status quo can entail evaluating harsh realities in their schools, neighborhoods, and communities and comparing these occurrences with the experiences and communities of more affluent students and questioning the dominant script about why such inequities exist. One of the core ideas embedded in critical thinking as laid out by researchers on gifted education, is that students are able to synthesize and evaluate information in one context and apply the same knowledge and skills in different contexts.

More Culturally Responsive Teaching in Action

In another classroom that I observed at a Los Angeles school, Mrs. Givens, a seventh-grade math teacher, used community assets that students viewed or frequented in their respective communities to teach the concept of ratios and proportions structured within a culturally responsive framework. She asked students to pay particular attention to various businesses, buildings, parks, homes, and other structures that they observed on their daily treks to and from school. The students made note of the fact that there were a disproportionately high number of churches, liquor stores, abandoned buildings, and billboards in their communities. To further develop the concept of ratios and proportions, Mrs. Givens asked the students to identify various buildings and billboards per square block and develop an inventory. One student in Mrs. Givens's class documented seven different stores that sold liquor on her three-block walk home. Another student described the 20 billboards that he noticed on his seven-block walk home, and identified a 3:1 ratio of billboards to blocks. Most important in his assessment of billboards was what was advertised on each of them. To his dismay, he tabulated that six of the twenty billboards advertised some form of liquor, while five advertised cigarettes, and four encouraged the purchase of lottery tickets. Mrs. Givens encouraged the student to make inferences about what these occurrences mean in a low-income community, to point out the extensive promotion of alcohol, tobacco, and gambling. This math concept contributed to the type of critical questioning that is an essential part of culturally relevant teaching.

The importance of teaching core academic concepts, while also helping students to develop a critical consciousness about issues, events, and occurrences in their own communities, is germane to culturally responsive teaching. The way in which Mrs. Givens was able to use assets or occurrences from a community standpoint was quite creative and appeared to engage students. They analyzed the number of homicides in Los Angeles from the current year to the previous year to determine the percentage increase. They tabulated demographic shifts among different ethnic groups to understand percentage, decimal, and fraction values. Much of what Mrs. Givens created in her classroom was exemplary models of rigorous, standards-based instruction, with explicit ties to community wealth, knowledge, and assets with which most of her students were familiar.

UCLA *Sunnyside* GEAR UP

To illustrate how the concept of culturally responsive teaching is a complex commitment and idea that can aid in improving the achievement of students at the high school level, and how it can help to reduce the achievement gap between African American and Latino students, and their White and Asian counterparts, I will describe my work the UCLA Sunnyside GEAR UP (Gaining Early Awareness and Readiness for Undergraduate Program). For 2 years, I was fortunate enough to serve as the principal investigator of the GEAR UP program, a multiyear project at Sunnyside High School, located in southern California. Working in conjunction with the UCLA Graduate School of Education and Information Studies, the program provided intensive academic support (e.g., in-class and after-school tutoring, study skills preparation, California High School Exit Exam preparation, and CAT 6 test preparation) for any student interested in support services for preparing for college entry. UCLA Sunnyside GEAR UP also coordinated school activities that informed parents, teachers, and students about college requirements, the college admissions process, and financial aid.

During the 2006–07 school year Sunnyside High School was made up of approximately 2,100 students, of whom 50% were Latino, 48% African-American, and 2% White, Pacific Islander, Filipino, and Asian. Sunnyside High School is a Title I school with a 24.6% English language learner population. Approximately 450 students participated regularly in GEAR UP activities (3–4 times a week), over a 3-year period. Approximately 85% of the students were African American. The program sought to challenge the idea that students from low-income, urban areas, where resources and access to information for academic success are frequently limited, can be high achievers if they are given access to adequate resources, academic support, and committed and qualified personnel working toward the same goal.

The manner in which culturally responsive teaching was manifested at Sunnyside High School was not through specific teaching acts or the incorporation of culturally sensitive or inclusive learning materials. It was embedded in authentic and genuine care and concern for the students, coupled with an ongoing commitment to rigorous, high-quality, individualized and small-group tutoring and academic support for students. This care was manifested through the program's mission to increase the numbers of African American and Latino students who would be competitively eligible for admission to the country's top universities. Care also was manifested through the hiring of a multiracial staff of more than 40 people who devoted countless hours to counseling, tutoring, and mentoring a plethora of students in a multitude of ways. Finally, culturally responsive tenets were manifested in the staff's refusal to allow historically low expectations, limited funding, and school bureaucracy to limit the types of opportunities that the students deserved, and the type of academic success that was possible as students pursued postsecondary options.

The work that was done by the GEAR UP staff also highlights the way in which one element of the achievement gap was ameliorated—improving the college-going rates of African American and Latino students. Historically, Sunnyside High School was one of the more understaffed and underperforming schools in Los Angeles County. One indicator of this perennial underperformance was the fact that less than 10% of its graduating seniors had gone on to 4-year universities prior to our work at the school. One of GEAR UP's major goals with Sunnyside High School was to implement a program that could begin to identify students during their freshman year who showed academic promise and prepare them for college by the time they graduated.

The GEAR UP office, which was housed in a trailer on the school's campus, became the unofficial source of information for college preparation, academic counseling, and tutoring. Critical to the development of this space was the importance of relationships that were built between the project's director, the program coordinator, the five full-time staff members, and the more than 40 tutors who worked with the students daily. GEAR UP staff conveyed an authentic sense of care by going out of their way to visit students' homes and meeting parents, siblings, and legal guardians; providing financial assistance on occasion for students; and conveying a steadfast message that anyone involved in the program was required to have an unyielding belief in students' academic potential. Care, rigor, and accountability became the hallmarks of the support that GEAR UP provided to Sunnyside High students.

Care was manifested through a deep-seated concern for students' academic, social, and emotional well-being. Rigor was apparent in the intense tutoring sessions that occurred every day between students and tutors in class and after school covering subjects such as AP chemistry, history, calculus, algebra, English, and Spanish. Accountability was prevalent in that students understood that if they were to benefit from the GEAR UP program, being in good academic and behavior standing in all of their courses was a prerequisite. GEAR UP staff engaged in regular dialogue with classroom teachers about students' performance. Specific recommendations frequently were offered by classroom teachers on ways to assist students in tutoring sessions. Students were required to go over test preparation in tutoring sessions, complete enrichment work with tutors, and be accountable to tutors in addition to classroom teachers.

The initial findings from our research with students at Sunnyside High School revealed a significant improvement in academic performance during the 2005–06 academic year, when the initial group of targeted students were in their junior year, as demonstrated by the Annual Performance Index (API) and shown in Figure 4.1. The AP Index score increased from 475 during the 2001–02 school year (the year prior to GEAR UP arrival) to 578 during the 2005–06 school year, an increase of 103 points.

A vital part of the success with the GEAR UP program at Sunnyside was the ongoing support of its administrative staff and the dedicated classroom teachers who played a critical role in our work. Sunnyside High School staff worked with GEAR UP staff in myriad ways to ensure student academic success. Allowing GEAR UP tutors to be in classrooms each day to support teachers was critical to improving student performance; offering space on campus for a continued presence was instrumental; and having a school leader who encouraged GEAR UP's work to help students surpass academic expectations was fundamental to the program's success. This university–school partnership revealed the way that an educational alliance with common goals, shared responsibilities, and ongoing lines of open communication can work toward improving student achievement.

As we examined our findings of the graduating class of 2007 (the group that was targeted as high school freshmen), the data showed that the students who were consistent participants in GEAR UP programs (meaning they attended tutoring and academic support 4–5 times a week) performed significantly better than students who did not participate in programs on a consistent basis. Our analysis identified 59 of the 385 students in the graduating class of 2007 to be consistent participants in GEAR UP programs. This group, identified as "core" students, had a mean GPA of 3.29 compared with their non-GEAR UP counterparts, who had a mean GPA of 2.51. Table 4.2 shows this breakdown across gender lines as well.

An examination of the student GPA by race and ethnicity also revealed marked improvement of students who participated in GEAR UP programs. Table 4.3 shows that the mean GPA for the core African American students at Sunnyside was close to 2.56, while the GEAR UP students' mean GPA was 3.26. Even more noteworthy is an examination of student performance across race and gender. African American

Figure 4.1. Annual performance index scores for Ing School

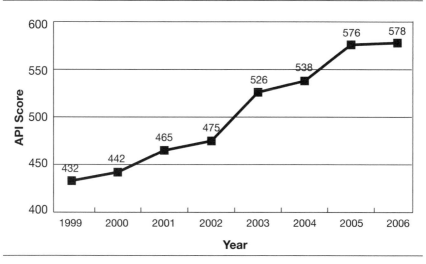

Source: California Department of Education, 2006.

males in particular showed noteworthy gains. This was meaningful given the dismal performance of Black males across the country and in southern California, where in some districts the drop-out rate is reported to be close to 50% (Orfield, 2004).

In addition to the significant gains that were made by African American students in the GEAR UP program, equally impressive gains were made by Latino students, who were frequent participants in the program as well. Table 4.4 shows the disaggregated data for Latino student performance at Sunnyside High School during the 2006–07 school year.

During the 2006–07 school year, the number of students participating in advanced placement (AP) courses increased in algebra I and II, geometry, precalculus, calculus, chemistry, and physics. For example, the percentage of 10th graders taking geometry increased from 23% during the 2004–05 school year to 65% during the 2005–06 school year. In addition, of the juniors at Sunnyside, 35% were enrolled in algebra II and 40% were enrolled in chemistry during the 2005–06 school year. Much of this work also helped students to develop the skill set and knowledge base that would enable them to compete in more academically rigorous courses.

Another major accomplishment of the GEAR UP program was the increased educational expectations participating students developed

Table 4.2. 2006–07 GPA breakdown

Class of 2007 Average GPAs	GEAR UP Class of 2007 Average GPAs	Difference
Graduating Class (n = 385): 2.51	2007 Core Cohort (59 students): 3.29	+ 0.78
Avg. Female GPA: 2.67	Avg. GEAR UP Female GPA (37 students): 3.26	+ 0.59
Avg. Male GPA: 2.31	Avg. GEAR UP Male GPA (22 students): 3.32	+ 1.01

Table 4.3. 2006–07 Semester 2 GPA breakdown by ethnicity and gender: Black students

Class of 2007 Average GPAs	GEAR UP Class of 2007 Average GPAs	Difference
Entire Class: Avg. Black GPA = 2.56	2007 Core Cohort: Avg. GU Black GPA (40 students) = 3.26	+ 0.70
Avg. Black Female GPA = 2.65	Avg. GU Black Female GPA (24 students) = 3.23	+ 0.58
Avg. Black Male GPA = 2.51	Avg. GU Black Male GPA (16 students) = 3.29	+ 0.78

Table 4.4. 2006–07 Semester 1 GPA breakdown by ethnicity and gender: Latino students

Class of 2007 Average GPAs	GEAR UP Class of 2007 Average GPAs	Difference
Entire Class: Avg. Latino GPA = 2.45	2007 Core Cohort: Avg. GU Latino GPA (20 students) = 3.31	+ 0.86
Avg. Latino Female GPA = 2.59	Avg. GU Latino Female GPA (14 students) = 3.19	+ 0.60
Avg. Latino Male GPA = 2.27	Avg. GU Latino Male GPA (6 students) = 3.59	+ 1.32

for themselves. In 2006, the Advanced Readiness in Students' Education (ARISE) program, a 2-week (12-day) academic intensive series, focused on preparing new sophomores and juniors for courses in AP geometry, algebra II, calculus, English language, and literature. The courses were selected based on the University of California's competitive eligibility formula. Along with the program's strong academic focus, the students also were able to participate in a variety of enrichment activities, which included poetry/spoken word, art, drama, nutrition, and fitness, and a computer technology program. During the 2007 academic year, we offered the ARISE program again, and it continued to help students to develop a strong educational foundation and prepare them for success in a college or university. By providing a space where students could thrive with adequate resources at hand, GEAR UP helped students to develop their confidence and mentored them to raise their own academic expectations and performance.

Even with limited funding, GEAR UP continued to provide a high level of service and intensified programs that met the needs of those who were served. As the program drew to a close after the 2006–07 academic year because of limited funding, we celebrated many measures of success over our final year, such as seeing 85% of seniors who participated in the California High School Exit Exam tutoring program pass the exam. In addition, we witnessed the largest graduating class (385) from Sunnyside High School in nearly a decade, which was approximately a 25% increase in the number of graduates from the previous year (291). Furthermore, in a senior survey of 247 of the 385 (65%) graduating seniors, almost 80% reported that they were going to either a 2-year or 4-year college the following year. Moreover, of the graduating class, 80 students were accepted by 4-year colleges, which meant that a little over 20% of the class entered universities the following fall. This number is double the previous year's number. Nine African American students (six of whom were males) were accepted by UCLA, typically one of the more difficult colleges to gain admission to, compared with only four students in 2006, more than doubling the number of students accepted to UCLA from Sunnyside High School.

The knowledge base on culturally responsive teaching continues to emerge. Although this information has been critical to inform the larger educational community, there is a need to ask more questions that will help scholars and practitioners expand the concept, in particular if it is successful in improving the academic performance of underachievers. Despite arguments to the contrary, there is growing evidence that shows that culturally responsive teaching approaches are having an influence on student outcomes, improving student learning, and engaging students who often are disengaged from teaching and learning. Culturally responsive teaching, like much of teaching, is a multifaceted, dynamic, and intellectually intense endeavor. It has to be undergirded by a deep-seated commitment to the holistic development and well-being of students, their families, and their communities.

Culturally responsive teaching also can be enhanced by examining policies and large-scale programs that have been implemented and that have helped underachieving students. While individual accounts of teachers who possess the knowledge, skills, and cultural competence to assist culturally diverse learners are valuable, there are far too many teachers who still lack this viable knowledge that can enable them to implement transformative approaches to teaching and learning. Identifying and replicating effective programs will be fundamental to closing the stubborn achievement gap that continues to result in countless numbers of learners who experience school failure. In addition to identifying these programs, researchers and practitioners must engage in information exchanges about where such interventions are having success and try to replicate them. The premise of replicating effective programs is centered on the belief that many teachers want to use practices that will improve students' performance, but lack the necessary knowledge and skills about the culture–cognition connection.

CHAPTER 5

The Role of Race in Learning

When examining the academic achievement gap that exists in U.S. schools, the topic that frequently lies beneath the surface yet rarely is addressed in an explicit, thoughtful, and critical manner, is the role of race. The obvious, yet often neglected questions that educators at all levels must ask as part of any detailed analysis of achievement disparities are: How does race play out in academic outcomes? What role, if any, does race play in the achievement gaps in U.S. schools? Where are these discrepancies most recognizable? How does race affect the schooling experiences of students of color? What steps can be taken to reduce perennial discrepancies along racial lines? Any detailed analysis of U.S. achievement outcomes usually has some racial implications, but what these implications mean, and more important, how educators address the issue of race, has been a source of consternation, confusion, avoidance, and uncertainty for far too long. The difficulty in examining race—and assessing whether, how, where, and when it is having an impact on the educational outcomes of students—is not a challenge unique to scholars and practitioners (Singleton & Linton, 2006). In fact, the dissonance and discomfort surrounding the topic of race in education are reflective of the larger societal context in which race has been viewed historically and contemporarily in the United States. A more detailed analysis of race, racism, and each of their manifestations is long overdue if viable interventions are to close racial achievement gaps in U.S. schools.

DuBois (1903) prophetically stated at the turn of the 20th century that "the problem of the twentieth century is the problem of the color line, the relations of the darker to the lighter races of men in Asia and Africa, in America and the islands of the sea" (pp. 15–16). Nearly a century later, West (1993) reminded us that even with high levels of education and increased economic mobility and social status, "race matters" (p. 3). In between these two notable works, a plethora of scholars, philosophers, researchers, and practitioners have lamented the way in which we talk (and do not talk) about race, and its manifestations in our everyday lives (Baldwin, 1988; Bonilla-Silva, 2003; Dixson & Rousseau, 2006; Marable, 1992; Solorzano, 1997; Takaki, 1993; Woodson, 1933).

A 21st-century analysis of race would reveal that it remains the elephant in the room, the issue that no one wants to acknowledge. As much as we attempt to ignore it, look around it, over and under it, race remains a constant reality in these United States. Given the complexity of race, the challenges it poses, and our national fixation on it, it has become our ticking time bomb, set to explode on a moment's notice. Race is our historical lightning rod, equipped with centuries-old baggage, uninformed epistemologies, and sordid axioms that, at its mere mention, quickly can divide people who are seemingly united citizens. Edelman (2008) says that throughout America's history, race has been a noose choking our capacity to soar. Race is our eternal taboo, and as much as we try to rid ourselves of its salience in our collective psyches it seems to linger in our minds, hearts, and actions. In many ways, it is like the oxygen in our stratosphere—it is always there. Scholars have asserted that it is time to move beyond race and engage in more cultural, structural, and social class-based analyses of schools and society (Darder & Torres, 2004; W. J. Wilson, 2009). The calls to move beyond race have important merit that must continue to inform the racial dialogue. Yet, when it comes to education, and more specifically disparate racial outcomes in schools, investigators should be mindful of the murky terrain that must be traveled in search of better understandings and greater clarifications about racial outcomes. Only then can we move beyond race.

INTERROGATING RACE

Any authentic investigation of the achievement gap should be mindful of falling prey to the extremes that are in place at both ends of the racial spectrum. The conservative, *race is nonessential* approach contends that race and/or racism has nothing to do with the current academic outcomes of students in U.S. schools, and refutes any inquiry that even raises the racial question or seeks analysis along racial lines (McWhorter, 2000; S. Steele, 1990; Thernstrom & Thernstrom, 2003). Thus, the history of racial segregation in U.S. schools, Jim Crow laws, and destructive racial ideologies quickly are dismissed as nonfactors of the past that skirt the importance of individual merit and personal responsibility. Scholars who support the *race is nonessential* approach maintain that the failures of people of color in the United States are more a result of individual choice and lack of merit, and have little to do with institutional or historical structures or policies.

A second, more liberal approach, *race was essential, but we have overcome the vestiges of racism* approach, operates from the standpoint that there was an ugly racial past in the United States, but collectively the nation has transgressed this period. Bonilla-Silva (2003) refers to believers in this approach as "racial optimists," or individuals who maintain that a profound transformation has occurred in the United States over the past several decades, that the country has become more egalitarian and just, and that racial issues are not important variables in explaining outcome disparities. Frequently lacking from this analysis is an examination of the existing institutional practices and policies that remain situated in past racial ideologies and hierarchies. Moreover, racial optimists tend to believe that any mention of race is unwarranted and only contributes to a regression of the tremendous racial progress that has been made.

Third on the continuum is the *race is the determining variable in all that ails schools and society* approach, which posits that academic differences are a direct result of racist structures, racist educators, and a long history of race baiting and racial exclusion. Frequently absent from this discourse is any real investigation into the important educational progress that has been made over the past century, or the family arrangements, cultural practices, levels of parent engagement, structural conditions, and amount of individual effort and accountability that may play a role in student outcomes. Also missing from this analysis is acknowledgment of the steady progress that has been made in race relations and the overall racial climate for diverse groups in the United States over the past 5 decades, as well as the increases in academic opportunities to non-Whites, which were virtually nonexistent two generations ago.

A fourth approach operates from a more balanced perspective and centers on the *institutional responsibility–individual accountability* approach. This approach assumes that race and racism have always played a significant role in the way life is experienced in the United States and that over the past several decades important progress has been made in race relations and racial justice (Noguera, 2003; Tough, 2008). However, race remains relevant. To that end, institutions must remain vigilant, responsible, and ever-mindful in assessing hiring practices, promotion opportunities, learning environments, admission criteria, counseling tactics, and leadership approaches. They also must remain committed to the establishment and maintenance of a racial climate that is conducive to racial equity. Questions about whether practices or certain incidents are racially insensitive are welcomed, evaluated, and addressed. Coupled with such an approach is the willingness of individuals to take ongoing inventory of and accountability for their own individual efforts, merits, and commitments to success in their respective capacities as teachers, school leaders, students, or researchers. The individual responsibility aspect of this approach does not convey that race is never a determining factor in various occurrences, but it operates from the standpoint that, for particular outcomes, individual choice, efforts, and behaviors are evaluated on an equal status with other factors, including race.

While evaluating race as a variable in academic achievement outcome gaps between racially diverse students and their peers is essential, seeking to identify simplistic solutions or unexamined fixes to this issue is counterproductive. In many ways, our work as practitioners, school leaders, researchers, and scholars can be guided by penetrating questions that are rarely part of the dialogue in education, but must be asked if we are to move toward eliminating racial gaps in school performance, no matter how we define and measure performance. We should ponder questions such as the following:

- What explanatory variables exist for the poor academic outcomes at predominantly African American and Latino schools?
- How do we make meaning of the disproportionate numbers of African American and Latino students who are placed in special education classrooms?
- What are the ramifications of an increasingly homogeneous teaching population educating an increasing racially heterogeneous student population?
- Are there correlations between the preponderance of White female teachers and African American and Latino males' performance in schools?
- What role, if any, do teachers' racial attitudes and beliefs play in student performance?
- How do we best prepare teachers to work in racially diverse schools?
- How do we eradicate the pervasiveness of colorblind approaches to teaching?
- How do school leaders develop a culture of racial awareness, sensitivity, and inclusiveness?
- What coping strategies can students adopt when confronted with racially insensitive teachers and administrators?

RACE AND EDUCATION IN THE UNITED STATES

To best understand race and its complexities in education, it is imperative to examine and understand race and its legacy in the United States. Race, in many ways, has been and remains a powerful dynamic that has shaped U.S. history, its landscape, and way of life (Horsman, 1981; Marable, 1997, 2002; Oliver & Shapiro, 1997). Failure to engage in critical discussions about race will further polarize a nation with increasingly rich racial diversity. As Marable (2002) points out, "Instead of talking abstractly about race, we should be theorizing about the social processes of racialization, of how certain groups in U.S. society have been relegated to an oppressed status, by the weight of law, social policy, and economic exploitation" (p. 10). Marable's claim is a resounding call to scholars and practitioners to incorporate race as an essential ingredient in how we examine life and schooling opportunities in the past, present, and future of the United States.

In a multiracial nation such as the United States, examinations of race are most critical within the domain of democracy. Whether the case is the systemic removal and elimination of the Indigenous peoples of North America (Bowden, 1981; Thornton, 1987), the inhumane enslavement of Africans in the United States and subsequent Jim Crow laws (Anderson, 1988; Franklin, 1988), the cruel and callous treatment of Japanese Americans in Internment camps during World War II (Pak, 2002; Takaki, 1993), the economic exploitation of Chinese immigrants (McClain, 1994; Takaki, 1989), or the geographical and cultural ramifications of the colonization of Mexico (M. G. Gonzales, 1999; R. A. Gutierrez, 2004), race has always played a critical role in the evolution and advancement of democracy in the United States.

We must include the ugly history of race and racial hierarchies in the United States in the dialogue if we are to ever move beyond race. Until there is a recognition of this tragic aspect of life in the United States, as long as there is a failure to explicitly examine how race has influenced life in the United States, there remains the potential for creating a more fractured nation, with a large segment of the populace remaining resentful, bitter, angry, and unable or unwilling to ever develop a climate of racial harmony and cohesion. Baldwin (1988) often referred to the *rage of the disesteemed* caused by the United States's refusal to acknowledge historical injustices. According to Balfour (2001), Baldwin implies that the United States is guilty of "innocence" or

> a willful ignorance, a resistance to facing the horrors of the American past and present and their implications for the future. This unwillingness to confront these horrors accounts for the resistance of racial in-

justices to remedy by formal, legal measures. For innocence sustains a mind-set that can accommodate *both* an earnest commitment to the principles of equal rights and freedom regardless of race *and* a tacit acceptance of racial division and inequality as normal. (p. 27, emphasis in original)

Exploring race-related issues, particularly in relation to school outcomes, is difficult, tedious, and complex work. One of the first questions that needs to be examined is, "What is race?" Most social scientists concur that race is a social construct that has both self-prescribed and externally ascribed meaning. In the United States, race has had more social and political meaning than biological reality (Jacobson, 1999). Since the 1980s scholars have examined the intricacies and contradictions of racial construction (Haney-Lopez, 1996; Omi & Winant, 1994). These works have helped to clarify the ambiguity of racial categories and stratification. Banks (1995) states that "race is a human invention constructed by groups to differentiate themselves from other groups" (p. 22) and to defend the disproportionate distribution of wealth. Singleton and Linton (2006) write:

Scientifically, race is nothing more than the color of our skin, texture of our hair, and shape, color, and dimension of physical features such as eyes and lips. So much social and political meaning has been attached to these physical determinations of race, however, that the simplicity has given way to a complex phenomenon in this country over the past four centuries. (p. 158)

It is the social and political meanings to which Singleton and Linton (2006) refer that remain a significant factor in the way in which many students of color are viewed in U.S. schools.

Another question that merits problematizing is, "What is racism?" Solorzano, Allen, and Carrol (2002) highlight three important characteristics of racism: (1) the belief that one group is superior, (2) the ability of the group believed to be superior to carry out racist acts, and (3) the ability of racist acts to affect multiple racial/ethnic groups. Marable (1992) defines racism as "a system of ignorance, exploitation and power used to oppress African Americans, Latinos, Asians, Pacific Americans, American Indians, and other people on the basis of ethnicity, culture, mannerisms, and color" (p. 5). An integral part of the analysis of race in schools is the question of what meanings educators assign to students who come from racially diverse groups. This question has even-greater significance when educators (teachers in particular) have had limited or no interaction with students who come from racially diverse backgrounds (Hollins & Guzman, 2005).

The relationship between race and intelligence has always been complex, contradictory, and complicated terrain in the United States (Gould, 1981). The construction of race and, more important, intellectual acumen tied to different racial groups has been rooted in at least 2 centuries of racist discourse in the Western hemisphere. In the early 19th century, the science of phrenology, which involved the study of human skulls, their shapes, sizes, and inferences about mental capacity, was popular among various scientists, who used their work to argue the innate superiority of White groups over Native American, Mexican, and Black populations (Chernow & Vallasi, 1993; Gould, 1981; Jacobson, 1999). Charles Caldwell, a prominent physician, published an influential book titled *Thoughts on the Original Unity of the Human Race* (1830), which posited that the Caucasian race was intellectually more endowed than the other races (Horsman, 1981). The works of scholars at the time reinforced and validated beliefs that people of African, Latin, and Indigenous descent lacked the mental strength and intellectual acumen of Whites (Gould, 1981). More important, the dissemination of this information in the name of science was widespread and institutionalized during the 19th century, and had a significant influence on popular thinking at the time (Gould, 1981). The remnants of the racial hierarchy—and subsequent racist ideologies that came with it—were reinforced during the 20th century by the eugenics movement. Selden (1999) documents how American Mendelian eugenists promoted racial and ethnic superiority of Whites over non-White groups by "pursuing policies of immigration restriction, segregation, and eugenic mating . . . they also saw the public schools as one important venue for the popularization and dissemination of eugenics policies" (p. xiii). The eugenics movement played a similar role to that of phrenology in the 1800s—it used a form of scientific reasoning to justify the racial hierarchy. It also used mental testing to reinforce the hierarchy.

A perusal of the works of Lewis Terman, Edward Lee Thorndike, and Robert Yerkes, all noted members of the American Eugenics Society in the mid-1920s, reveals how race, ethnicity, and intelligence became socially constructed, and how schools became places where the mental superiority of certain groups could be "proven" based on students' performance on cognitive tasks or intelligence tests. In particular, Terman's and Yerkes's work on intelligence testing was done using Army Alpha and Beta examinations, which were based more on Army recruits' familiarity with American culture at the time than on innate intelligence (Selden, 1999). Moreover, these tests were widely used to measure intelligence and were given to native-born Americans and immigrants. Not surprisingly, the test outcomes resulted in superior performance of native-born Americans and justified the purported superiority of certain groups, while creating the notion that immigrants were inferior in cognitive ability. Similar steps were taken to create the illusion of the intellectual inferiority of native-born groups of African and Latin descent (Gould, 1981), which also influenced popular thinking at the time about education, who deserved access to it, and who would be denied. While the influence of the eugenics movement has waned significantly over the past 7 decades, the works of Jensen (1969) and Herrnstein and Murray (1994) have continued to argue that a race–intelligence connection is tied to genetic factors. While the premise in this book is that instances of prejudice, racism, and discrimination have decreased over time, it is clear that important work remains to be done, and that critically analyzing how opportunities are afforded in U.S. schools is an important aspect of the ongoing American democracy project.

CRITICAL RACE THEORY:
A FRAMEWORK FOR EXAMINING RACE AND ACHIEVEMENT

As both a theoretical lens to examine race and its complexities as well as a framework to examine the relationship between race and achievement, critical race theory is invaluable in this investigation, primarily because it places race at the center of the discussion of the achievement gap in education. Critical race theory is a movement born out of critical legal studies seeking to address issues of racial inequality and the overlooked role that race and racism have played in the construction of the legal foundation (Bell, 1992, 2002; Crenshaw, 1997; Harris, 1993; Matsuda, 1993). As critical race theory has emerged in the field of education, it has sought to move the dialogue about race and racism from the realm of the experiential to the realm of the ideological (Ladson-Billings, 2000; Lynn, 1999; Parker & Lynn, 2002; Tate, 1997; Taylor, Ladson-Billings, & Gilborn, 2009). Leading critical race theorists have argued that the marginalization of race and consequently racism is interwoven into the historical conscious and ideological framework of the U.S. legal system (Bell, 1992; Delgado, 1995). Consequently, critical race theorists argue that a thorough examination of race within the legal context is desperately needed.

Critical race theory in education seeks to give much-needed attention to the role of race in educational research, scholarship, and practice (Dixson & Rousseau, 2006; Ladson-Billings, 2000; Solorzano, 1998; Solorzano & Yosso, 2001, 2002). The inclusion of a critical race framework in education is essential when one considers the perennial underachievement of African American, Latino, Native American, and certain Asian American students in U.S. schools (NCES, 2001, 2004, 2006, 2007b). Educators can ill afford to subscribe to the notion that mere coincidence explains the perpetual school failure of students of color. At some point, the question must be posed: What's race got to do with it? (Parker & Lynn, 2002).

Critical race theory in education is an evolving methodological, conceptual, and theoretical construct that attempts to dismantle racism in education (Solorzano, 1998). It provides scholars with unique ways to ask the important question of what racism has to do with inequities in education, by centering the discussion on racism and thereby examining racial inequities through a more critical lens than multicultural education or achievement gap theorists do. Thus, the question from a critical race standpoint is not, "Does racism play a role in educational disparities?" Rather, critical race theory presupposes the historical and contemporary role that racism plays and has played in education, and asks a more penetrating question: "How has racism contributed to educational disparities, and how can it be dismantled?"

Critical race theorists anchor their interrogation of racism in education in four primary ways: (1) by theorizing about race along with the intersectionality of racism, classism, sexism, and other forms of oppression in school curriculum; (2) by challenging dominant ideologies that call for objectivity and neutrality in educational research; (3) by offering counterstorytelling as a liberatory and credible methodological tool in examining racial oppression; and (4) by incorporating transdisciplinary knowledge from women's studies and ethnic studies to better understand various manifestations of discrimination (Smith-Maddox & Solorzano, 2002; Solorzano, 1997, 1998).

As explanations become clearer concerning what race and racism have to do with the widespread failure of students of color, we can begin to understand the wide influences of inequality, discrimination, and, most important, race and racism, and how they may influence achievement disparities. As we grapple with race, it is important to note Lewis's (2006) notion that "race (then) is not a real or innate characteristic of bodies but a set of signifiers projected onto these bodies—signifiers we must learn about and negotiate in order to successfully move through the social world" (p. 6). She further states that "race is about who we are, what we do, how we interact. It shapes where we live, whom we interact with, how we understand ourselves and others. But it does so in specific ways based on our social and historical location" (p. 7). It is within this context of race, within our social and historical locations, that we investigate outcome disparities between African American and Latino students and their higher performing counterparts.

More important, it is essential to understand how these students themselves believe these "signifiers" of race influence their realities in schools and in classrooms and shape their prospects for learning. Rarely have students on the lower end of the academic continuum been offered a deliberative space to diagnose, examine, and describe what role, if any, they believe race plays in their educational experiences and ultimately their academic performance. Far too often, students from racially diverse groups have been told that race does not matter, and teachers have espoused their commitment to a colorblind ideology, which purports to render race a non-factor (Schofield, 1999). However, the mere mention of a colorblind approach to educating students poses a set of contradictions, as Crenshaw (1997) notes, because the use of a colorblind approach seeks to conceal the power and ugliness of race, but at the same time highlights the very significance of it by claiming that to acknowledge it would lead to troublesome outcomes.

Gotanda (1991) reiterates the problems with colorblindness, stating that it serves to maintain racial subordination. Hence, to many educators race becomes the pedagogical paradox, the conversation that many least want to engage in, as they are cognizant of the explosive nature that it can have if they do. The solution becomes to avoid it, rendering it unimportant, making it useless within the context of teaching and learning. In the United States, this avoidance takes place in many school settings where millions of racially diverse young people continue to be defined in racial terms—some good, and most negative (Carter, 2005; Conchas, 2006; Noguera, 2008). Educators ignore race or adopt colorblind approaches, while failing to realize that the greater avoidance of the topic denies students an essential part of their being, and only increases the likelihood of race becoming an explosive topic (Lewis, 2006).

EMPIRICAL WORKS EXAMINING RACE

A number of works have addressed the salience of race in schools and have documented the persistence with which colorblind approaches continue to have a deleterious influence on the schooling experiences of students of color—in particular African American, Latino, and certain Asian American student populations (Schofield, 1999). Pollock's (2004) anthropological study at a California high school revealed how "race talk matters" in normal, everyday schooling situations. She uncovered the murky terrain that is race talk, and how it presents paradoxical dilemmas for educators and students alike. Her analysis of students' and teachers' conversations around schooling experiences on a racially diverse campus revealed that as much as both groups asserted that race did not matter in their schools, it was profoundly a part of their ongoing discourse.

Pollock's (2004) work problematizes the manner in which adults at the school were quite at ease in explicitly acknowledging race and race relations when it came to describing students or their interactions with one another, but were extremely uncomfortable in discussing race when it came to adult–student interactions. Hence, the ambiguity and the contradictions in how adults and students deal with race can create harmful environments for some students. Pollock suggests that "although talking in racial terms can make race matter, not talking in racial terms can make race matter too" (p. 16). Her findings revealed that adults effectively "ignored black students in racial terms" (p. 16) and as a result Black students became loathed by many adults at the school. Pollock's work has important implications for rethinking how educators talk about race in school settings, to avoid reinforcing and institutionalizing the same racial stereotypes, patterns, and beliefs that we claim to despise.

Conchas's (2006) study also revealed how race played a significant role in the schooling experiences of and academic opportunities afforded to African American and Latino youth. His work cited three areas that negatively affected students' engagement and performance: racial segregation in schools, division within racial groups, and lack of institutional support based on race. One of the intriguing findings in Conchas's work is that teachers believed that students were stratified along racial but not social class lines. This finding is intriguing because it highlights the complexity of the confluence between race and class, and how they are manifested in school settings. The teachers in Conchas's study were seemingly unable to disaggregate the difficult racial and social class terrain, and as a result engaged in highly racialized discourses that placed Black and Latino students at an academic disadvantage. A number of teachers stated that most of the AP and college prep courses were disproportionately filled with White and Asian students, even though African American students were the largest subgroup in the school. Furthermore, the students echoed the teachers' contention that counselors and teachers were covertly and overtly racist in their treatment of African American and Latino students.

Lewis (2006) described how "racially coded ideas and assumptions were a regular part of the school space, both implicitly and explicitly"

(p. 53) at the elementary school she studied. Moreover, certain students of color adopted negative beliefs about other students of color. For example, Latino third and fourth graders made a number of racially demeaning and offensive comments when describing Black students. These realities offer stinging and painful insights into the way racially constructed categories, which are produced by dominant ideologies, become reified and explicated by and onto the very groups of people they were designed to marginalize. Huber, Johnson, and Kohli (2006) contend that acts of racial hostility displayed by individuals of color against other individuals of color reflect internalized racism, which they define as "the internalization of the beliefs, values, and worldviews inherent in White supremacy that can potentially result in negative self or racial group perceptions" (p. 184). They frame the argument of internalized racism around three key areas in education—teacher attitudes and perception, curriculum bias, and school resources—all of which embrace racial hierarchies that marginalize people of color.

Rousseau and Tate (2003) examined the ways in which high school mathematics teachers addressed race in student data, and discovered that the teachers consistently avoided examining race-related patterns in students' performance; they attributed discrepancies in performance to socioeconomic status, although there were clear racial ramifications in students' performance. T. C. Howard (2008) investigated Black males' accounts of their schooling experiences and found that the participants identified both overt and covert accounts of racial discrimination coming from teachers and school administrators. The findings also revealed that Black males consistently believed that they were scrutinized and excluded more than any other group of students. These findings were consistent for Black males across suburban and urban school settings, and reveal ways that race seems to be the overriding variable in how some students experience schooling.

The accounts provided in these studies reveal how racial discrimination plays out in schools for students of color, or what Webb-Johnson and Larke (2002) refer to as *instructional racism*. Tatum (2007) poses fundamental questions about the importance of race, racism, and their influence on academic achievement by stating that there is a pressing need to talk about race. She maintains that the conversation must be authentic and connected to the schooling experiences of students from racially diverse groups. She asks: "Can we get beyond our fear, our sweaty palms, our anxiety about saying the wrong thing, or using the wrong words, and have an honest conversation about racial issues?" (p. xiii). The ability to talk about racial issues in school practices may be a fundamental variable in helping to reverse the performance patterns of underachieving students. A summary of the works concerned with race reveals that race continues to be omnipresent in schools on multiple levels, both explicitly and implicitly. It is imperative for educators to recognize that race, racism, and their complexities are present in school curriculum, teacher expectations, teacher–student interactions, disciplinary practices, GATE recommendations, AP and Honors course opportunities, college preparatory courses, instructional practices, and special education referrals, and that they influence parental involvement, counseling opportunities, and testing procedures (Oakes et al., 2006).

GRANTING VOICE TO THOSE WHO RARELY ARE HEARD

To underscore the persistent role that race plays in the schooling experiences of students, there is probably no better source than students themselves. An important part of critical race theory is the inclusion of the voices of those who rarely are heard. Delgado and Stefancic (2001) state that "Engaging stories can help us understand what life is like for others, and invite the reader into a new and unfamiliar world" (p. 41).

To learn more about the new and unfamiliar world that Delgado and Stefancic (2001) refer to, I conducted a study with a high school English teacher from the Los Angeles area, where we surveyed 250 African American and Latino male students about what role, if any, they believed their race played in their schooling experiences. Over 90% (n = 241) of the respondents agreed with the statement, "My race plays a role in how teachers perceive me." In addition, more than 80% (n = 232) of these same respondents answered "yes" to the follow-up question, "Do you think your race causes teachers to view you negatively?" Responses such as these shed light on how race shapes the schooling experiences of students of color. More important, one can only begin to wonder about the quality and rigor of classroom instruction, the levels of authentic caring, the overall schooling climate, and ultimately the ways in which academic performance is influenced by the ways that teachers and students view race.

I have been fortunate to be part of a research team for the past several years that has collected data from a group of African American and Latino high school students participating in a summer outreach program, which provides an additional window on their schooling experiences. The primary focus of the project was to explore students' college readiness. However, the research team became intrigued by the repeated references to what the students believed were acts of racial discrimination, racial preferences, and in some cases racial hostility directed toward them by school staff and other students. A series of focus groups and individual interviews with 90 high school sophomores and juniors highlighted the ways in which they believed race was a factor in their experiences. In some cases it was blatant, as when one student informed us that his biology teacher repeatedly referred to the class of Latinos and Blacks as "stupid" and "lazy." In other cases it was more subtle. For instance, Jasmine, a high school junior, stated:

> Race has been a factor in our schools because teachers make it a factor. They look at you like you can't learn. They talk down to you. And you just know they think this about us because we are Black.

Taylor, another high school junior, said:

> Being a Black female, I am always looked at different when I am in my AP and Honors classes. My counselor said that I should not take the class because it might be too hard for me. I asked some of my friends [who are not Black] who I got better grades than, if she told them they should not take it, and they said no, and she said that they would do well in class. How do you think that makes me feel?

Several of the students mentioned teachers being surprised or having doubts about their ability to do well in academically demanding courses, and in many ways the students seemed to not allow such comments to influence their work. Rafael, a high school junior, was one such student.

> The [AP English] teacher looked at us [the two Black students in the class] and said "this class might be hard for you guys" . . . I knew in my mind that it was because we were the only Black students in there. But I also knew that no one could tell me what is too hard for me, and that I could end up being one of the top students in the class.

Some of the students' responses provide insights into the resilience they have acquired as a protective defense against doubts about their intellectual abilities. In many instances, students seem to accept teachers' comments as common. Michael, a high school junior, said:

> You can ask all the students about which teachers are racist, and there are quite a few of them around here. But we [the Black students] are used to it . . . that's why you don't even let them get to you. You just do what you have to do to shut 'em up.

Some of the students felt their perceived language was another way to make them feel racially excluded. Maribel stated:

> They [the teachers] just assumed I was an ESL student without even knowing me. I was born here [in the United States] and lived here my whole life, so why would they think that? I have never seen them [teachers] do that to Asian kids, but the Mexican kids get treated that way all the time.

Another student stated that he was told by his teacher that "this would be a better place if you and your people just went back to where you came from." The students' sentiments around racial mistreatment seemed to center on the perceptions, beliefs, or comments that they recalled teachers, administrators, and school staff repeatedly making. These comments are tantamount to what C. Pierce (1974) refers to as racial microaggressions, which he characterizes as subtle insults (verbal, nonverbal, and/or visual) and insinuations directed toward people of color, often automatically or subconsciously. C. Pierce (1974) states that in isolation racial microaggressions may seem innocuous and nonthreatening, but the damage comes from the cumulative burden of a lifetime of microaggressions, which can have a detrimental influence on students' perception of themselves, their confidence, and ultimately their performance. He states that "one must not look for the gross and obvious. The subtle, cumulative miniassault is the substance of today's racism" (p. 516). When examining achievement disparities across racial groups, one has to contemplate whether students who have been targets of racial microaggressions for years have experienced subpar performance as a result of these subtle assaults on their intelligence because of their race. Indeed, a growing group of scholars have investigated the impact of racial stereotyping on academic performance and found that it can lead to levels of anxiety and doubt that can negatively influence school performance (C. M. Steele, 1995; C. M. Steele & Aronson, 1995, 1998).

Although a number of students stated that teacher insults and putdowns were frequent occurrences, others thought that racial inequities were most apparent in the quality of their schools, and believed that if there were more White students in their schools, they would be different. This was best summed up by Juan:

> If you look at our school, it is 99.9% Mexican. We don't have
> resources like books, pencils, computers, and things that would
> help you learn. But if this school was 99% White, I bet that it
> would look a lot better than it does.

It becomes apparent on some level that for many of the students, racial
discrimination was more structural than individual, and this seemed
to be more of a pressing issue for them because they believed that their
learning prospects were severely compromised as a result. One of the
most poignant quotes came from Miguel, who made vivid compar-
sions of the quality of two different high schools he attended.

> You know when I lived on the east side, Adams High School
> where it's like mostly Latinos, there's metal detectors to get
> in, the bathrooms are all messed up, we had subs [substitute
> teachers] all the time. The campus was all dirty, and it seemed
> like nobody cared. Then we moved to the valley and went to
> McKinley [High School], a school that had a lot of White and
> Asian kids and it was way different; clean schools, clean bath-
> rooms, teachers were never absent. I mean it was so nice, and I
> just kept wondering, you know, like how come you could not
> have a school like this for the Latinos? It just makes you won-
> der if they really care about us.

Comments like these raise a number of important issues when evaluating the achievement gap. Nationwide, schools have become increasingly segregated along racial lines, and some scholars have argued that
issues of racism and discrimination are most evident in areas such
as per-pupil funding, school resources, and teacher quality, and this
is where change is most needed (Darling-Hammond, 2007; Orfield,
Losen, Wald, & Swanson, 2004). A number of scholars have lamented
the fact that it is no accident that school quality is largely shaped by
issues of race and social class (Anyon, 2005; Kozol, 2005; Oakes et al.,
2006).

INTERNALIZED RACISM:
EDUCATORS OF COLOR AND ACTS OF EXCLUSION

One of the missing elements from the discourse on race and racism in
schools has been the way that individuals of color can adopt, maintain, and promote many of the same racial ideologies and racialized

deficit views of students of color that frequently are purported to be held only by Whites (Derman-Sparks, Phillips, & Hilliard, 1997; hooks, 1995). One of the more intriguing findings from our research on students' perceptions of the racial climates at their high schools was that the majority of the students said that racially offensive comments were not made exclusively by White teachers and administrators, but that teachers and administrators of color were equally complicit in delivering racial microaggressions. This fact adds further complexity to the way race seems to be manifested in schools and how it plays out for students of color. Huber and colleagues (2006) amplify this point through their work on internalized racism, which they define as the "conscious and unconscious acceptance of a racial hierarchy in which Whites are consistently ranked above People of Color . . . [and] the internalization of the beliefs, values, and worldviews inherent in White supremacy that can potentially result in negative self or racial group perceptions" (p. 184). Their argument is critical because any authentic attempts to interrogate teacher attitudes and practices that place students of color at a disadvantage must be removed from the belief that acts of discrimination come exclusively from racist White teachers and administrators. While the overwhelming majority of the teaching population in the United States is White, and undoubtedly many of them do engage in acts of racist thinking and behavior that afflict millions of students of color in U.S. schools every day, our discourse also must acknowledge that there are many teachers of color who do just as much damage, if not more, to students of color (Obidah & Teel, 2001).

As a former classroom teacher, I witnessed a number of African American, Asian, and Latino teachers make disparaging comments about African American, Asian, and Latino students. Our research supports my own anecdotal evidence. Thus, the tentacles of racism are not limited to one group of people, but permeate across groups, which makes the need for a probing analysis of race even more necessary. Moreover, while racial politics have always played a role in schooling experiences for students, most of the analysis of the topic has subscribed to the White–Black binary (Jencks & Phillips, 1998; Rothstein, 2004).

RACIAL FRAMES OF REFERENCE

In moving forward, our understanding of the complexities of race reveals that there is tremendous work that needs to be done. This work must be done simultaneously at theoretical, practical, research, and leadership levels because of the ways race plays out in each of these areas of education. Much of the challenge lies in educational communities' willingness to take a probing look at how race remains a part of the everyday realities of young people. Thus, there should be the development of frames of reference that will assist in creating a more racially inclusive way of delivering educational theory, practice, and research. I describe three areas that can be useful in the development of these frames.

Talking Explicitly About Race

The ability to engage in honest, thoughtful, respectful dialogues about race, racial perceptions, and racism is sorely needed in school settings and research spaces. The inability of school leaders, practitioners, and researchers to talk about race and what it means in the work that is done on behalf of students undoubtedly has influenced the way that students experience schools. The changing demographics in U.S. schools make the need to discuss race mandatory when dealing with school research, practice, or policy. The failure to do so places the very future of the nation at grave risk, in particular when we consider the sizable proportion of the U.S. student population that will be non-White in the coming decades. An explicit focus on race does not advocate a fixation on race, but rather a more inclusive, honest, and critical dialogue about how it shapes educational opportunities and outcomes.

Race in Research

One of the increasingly apparent realities in dealing with issues of race is our lack of knowledge about the racial realities that students experience every day within schools. As race-conscious as the United States is, beyond widespread anecdotal accounts about racial realities, race remains severely underresearched and undertheorized. Our knowledge base must improve if we are to transform the schooling experiences of racially diverse students. Thus, one of the more important racial frames of reference is the way race must become a central focus of research efforts across multiple levels. At the academy level, researchers can begin to interrogate the experiences that racially diverse students report in schools. Using race as a variable in experimental designs, survey research, interview inquiry, and case study research is important.

Racial realities are so complex that no one set of experiences can serve as a representative reality for all individuals of a particular racial group. Thus, there is a need for greater diversity and viewpoints of racially diverse students to evaluate how generalizable or representative various experiences are in schools. The experiences of people of color are not monolithic. Yet one criticism of the critical race theory paradigm is that the realities of a few become generalized to become the experiences of all (Darder & Torres, 2004). One of the ways to dismantle potential overgeneralization is to conduct large- and small-scale studies of how students experience race. Moreover, different methodological approaches and theoretical frameworks that contribute to this diversity in how young people experience race can be fundamental in generating new knowledge about race and schooling. These efforts should recognize the importance of young people in naming, describing, and critiquing their own experiences. Student voice is imperative in such efforts. At the school level, further disaggregation along racial lines can inform reform efforts. Despite the criticism that No Child Left Behind has received, one of the laudable features of the legislation is that schools are required to examine the performance of subgroups and they face penalties for failure to show improvement in these groups' academic performance. Not surprisingly, many schools consistently fall short in adequate yearly progress with students of color, primarily African American and Latino students, and these shortcomings have been present in low-income, middle-class, and more-affluent schools.

Postracial Paradigm

Race has always played an integral role in U.S. law, life, and social arrangements. Critical race theorists contend that race and racism are endemic to American life (Delgado & Stefancic, 2001). However, the ultimate goal in examining race and all of its manifestations is to gain greater clarity about how it shapes the realities of millions of U.S. citizens, to recognize the privileges it has afforded various racial groups and how it has denied freedom and justice to millions of citizens, and subsequently to work tirelessly to dismantle the racial hierarchies that have provided economic, social, and political opportunities for some, while denying them for others. Thus, a willingness to examine race and its complexities moves the United States one step closer to a postracial paradigm—a paradigm that recognizes the human connectedness that binds all citizens and calls for the interrogation and interpretation of human behavior to be tied to individual characteristics, as opposed to group classifications. The postracial paradigm allows for a deeper structural, class-based, and gendered analysis to be conducted on group disparities. Issues around capitalism, wealth distribution, widespread poverty, and the overall improvement of the global human condition need immediate attention; however, the way race frequently overshadows our realities undermines our ability to be effective problem solvers. In sum, the postracial paradigm would not render race insignificant, but it certainly would move us to a more transparent space in the analysis of difference, and remove the ambiguity, fear, and dissonance that we currently have around race.

CHAPTER 6

Developing Cultural Competence and Racial Awareness in Classroom Teachers

This book focuses on the important roles of race and culture in the teaching and learning processes for culturally and racially diverse students in U.S. schools. It asserts that race and culture are critical factors in how disparities in academic outcomes have developed over the past 2 decades. It is explicit in its standpoint that while race and culture play cogent roles in the achievement gap, they are by no means the sole or determining variables in disparate school outcomes. (The myriad factors that contribute to academic success and failure have been elaborated on further in Chapters 1 and 2.) I argue that by developing and maintaining a better understanding of race and culture and how they play out in school settings, educators can begin to take important steps toward ameliorating persistent gaps in educational outcomes between African American, Native American, and Latino students, and many of their Asian American and White counterparts on the opposite end. This chapter examines the importance of helping novice and experienced educators and researchers acquire, maintain, and build the cultural competence and racial awareness that are essential for teaching and working in today's diverse classrooms and schools.

The coincidence of the increasing cultural and ethnic heterogeneity of today's student population with the largely homogeneous teaching population requires important cross-cultural and racial awareness, as well as sensitivity to and understanding of diversity in all of its manifestations. This chapter describes how educators across various levels can develop and maintain the cultural competence and racial awareness necessary for optimal and equitable schooling experiences for all students. The primary purpose of this chapter is to describe specific ways for practitioners, school leaders, teacher educators, and researchers to acquire the skills, knowledge, and dispositions needed to become effective teachers and researchers in multicultural classrooms.

CULTURAL COMPETENCE

The concept of *cultural competence* gained prominence in health care and social work in the 1980s but has acquired increased attention and relevance in education during the past several decades. Cultural competence usually is conceptualized as a set of behaviors, attitudes, and policies that come together in a system or agency, or among professionals, to allow for effective work in cross-cultural situations (Cross, Bazron, Dennis, & Isaacs, 1989; Isaacs & Benjamin, 1991). The National Center for Cultural Competence (2008) offers a cultural competence framework that consists of five key concepts: (1) valuing diversity; (2) conducting ongoing self-assessment; (3) the ability to manage the dynamics of difference; (4) the willingness to acquire and institutionalize cultural knowledge; and (5) the ability to adapt to diversity and the cultural contexts of the communities that the individual serves. These five concepts provide a comprehensive account of how individuals must remain reflective about their beliefs, behaviors, and dispositions, while also recognizing how the cultural knowledge of others holds as much value for them as others hold for their own.

Operationally defined, cultural competence entails the integration and transformation of knowledge about individuals and groups of people into specific standards, policies, practices, and attitudes used in appropriate cultural settings in order to increase the quality of services, thereby producing better outcomes (Davis, 1997). Cultural competence conveys the idea of individuals being able to acquire the knowledge, skills, and dispositions that allow them to effectively work in cross-cultural settings (Cross et al., 1989), and rests on the belief that individuals are able to effectively function, communicate, and coexist in settings with individuals who possess cultural knowledge and skills that differ from their own.

The development of cultural competence is an ongoing process and is rooted in the idea that individuals continue to learn from, respect, and appreciate the broad range of cultures in a diverse society. Equally critical to the concept is that different forms of culture are not viewed in a hierarchical manner, which assumes that certain types of culture are superior to others, but rather that cultures exists on a continuum, giving equitable credence to the different variations of culture. Darder (1991) discusses the importance of creating cultural democracies in learning settings, wherein the range of cultures that students possess all maintain an equitable location in the quest for learning. She builds on the work of Ramírez and Castañeda (1974) by stating that cultural democracy asserts that students should be able to be educated in their own language and cultural context, and that they have the right to maintain a bicultural identity. Educating students in their own cultural context can include structuring instruction, content, and assessment in ways that are tied to students' lived experiences, personal background, or cultural ways of knowing and being (see C. D. Lee, 2007).

One of the significant aspects of creating cultural competence begins with developing a more nuanced understanding of culture and its complexities. Much of the important work that is associated with culture, cultural knowledge, and the contradictions and complexities that are part of culture was discussed in Chapter 4. A plethora of research documents how culture influences cognition, motivation, and behavior (M. Cole, 1996, 1998; K. Gutierrez & Rogoff, 2003, C. D. Lee, 2007; Rogoff, 2003). Much of this work has been centered on the idea that culture is not static across groups, but is constantly changing, deeply complex, highly nuanced, and manifested differently across and within groups. W. J. Wilson (2009) describes "cultural repertoires," or habits, styles, and skills, as a comprehensive means to understand culture (p. 15). In his words, these are "the micro-level processes of meaning making and decision-making—that is the way individuals in particular groups, communities, or societies develop an understanding of how the world works and make decisions based on that understanding" (p. 15). One of the first steps that educational practitioners and researchers must take is to gain a comprehensive understanding of how cultural knowledge is acquired, expressed, maintained, and transformed across space and time. Understanding what cultural knowledge is, and how it plays out in teaching and learning situations, is not easy, but it is essential to the creation of more culturally inclusive teaching, learning, and research environments. At the outset, practitioners and researchers must engage in important self-reflection or self-assessment about their own ways of being and knowing, forms of expression, and communication across different time and space, in particular when it comes to learning communities in schools. Self-reflection and assessment are fundamental because culture shapes all aspects of the human condition, and, as noted in Chapter 4, it is a better indicator of who people are than race is.

CRITICAL SELF-REFLECTION ON RACE AND CULTURE

One of the most fundamental elements of cultural competence is the development of ongoing critical self-reflection. Critical self-reflection on race and culture within a diverse cultural context requires education practitioners and researchers to engage in one of the more difficult processes for all individuals: honest self-assessment, critique, and evaluation of one's own thoughts, behaviors, cultural patterns, methods of expression, and cultural knowledge and ways of being (Gay & Kirkland, 2003). Critical reflection and self-assessment draw on one's ability to seek deeper levels of self-knowledge and to acknowledge how one's own worldview shapes one's perspectives and beliefs about oneself as well as one's students, their families and their communities (Schon, 1983). Palmer (1998) states that "we teach who we are" (p. 2) and that for teachers, separating one's own lived experiences from the act of teaching is an arduous, yet necessary task. Palmer writes:

> Teaching, like any truly human activity, emerges from one's inwardness, for better or worse. As I teach, I project the condition of my soul onto my students, my subject, and our way of being together. The entanglements I experience in the classroom are often no more or less than the convolutions of my inner life. Viewed from this angle, teaching holds a mirror to the soul. If I am willing to look in that mirror and not run from what I see, I have a chance to gain self-knowledge—and knowing myself is as crucial to good teaching as knowing my students and my subject. . . . In fact, knowing my students and my subject depends heavily on self-knowledge. When I do not know myself, I cannot know who my students are. I will see them through a glass darkly, in the shadows of my own unexamined life—and when I cannot see them clearly, I cannot teach them well (p. 2).

Palmer (1998) notion of "we teach who we are" has significant implications for teachers of today's learners in diverse schools and offers important implications for developing greater cultural competence. What is important within a critical reflection and self-assessment framework is for educators to ask themselves the important question, Does "who I am" contribute to the underachievement of students who are not like me? Critical reflection and self-assessment and the development of cultural competence can help educators to recognize whether they consciously or subconsciously hold deficit-based notions of culturally diverse students, distorted views of low-income communities, and negative perceptions of students' families.

The formation of a critical reflection paradigm is extremely difficult, if not impossible, without honest and sustained self-reflection (Gay & Kirkland, 2003). Critical reflection can be difficult because it forces individuals to ask challenging questions related to their construction of individuals from diverse racial, ethnic, and cultural backgrounds. While posing these questions can be difficult, answering them is the bigger and more difficult hurdle. Yet, the stakes for educators and the students they teach are too high not to engage in critical reflection. Freire (1973) states:

> Those who authentically commit themselves to the people must re-examine themselves constantly. . . . Only through comradeship with the oppressed can the converts understand their characteristic ways of living and behaving, which in diverse moments reflect the structure of domination. (p. 42)

Critical self-reflection may be more difficult for some White teachers because race is not often spoken about by those from racially privileged or dominant positions. G. R. Howard (2006) talks about the salience of White dominance and how "most White educators want schooling to become more than a mechanism of social control that favors White children" (p. 51), and strongly advocates the importance of self-examination to disrupt racially favorable beliefs toward Whites. Sleeter (2008) found that White teachers generally resist examining long-held beliefs and "bring little awareness or understanding of discrimination, especially racism [and], are dysconscious of how racism works in schools and society" and about "how it is reproduced daily" (p. 560). Moreover, she asserts that these teachers typically "bring virtually no conceptual framework for understanding visible inequalities rather than the dominant deficit framework . . . [are] generally ignorant of communities of color, fear them and fear discussing race and racism," and "lack awareness of themselves as cultural beings" (p. 560).

Given the changing demographics of U.S. schools, reflections on racial and cultural differences are essential, and notions of White dominance must dissipate if cultural democracy and educational equity are to become a reality. The need to create cultural democracy is particularly vital when many students' notions of their own academic potential, social adjustment, and emotional well-being are dependent on how teachers perceive them, the expectations that teachers hold for them, and the spaces teachers create for them to reach their full potential. Whites are not the only individuals that may subscribe to, or act upon, attributes of White dominance. Huber and colleagues (2006) describe how internalized racism can be held by persons of color, wherein they are capable of behaving in ways that convey a belief in White superiority and adopt a deficit or inferior viewpoint of people of color and their cultural ways of knowing and being.

A number of emerging frameworks provide educators with useful steps that can be taken to develop cultural competence and racial awareness. Duncan-Andrade (2008) offers five core pillars of racial and cultural competence for teachers of culturally diverse students: (1) *critically conscious purpose*, where teachers ask, "Why do I teach?" and "Whom do I teach?" and have clear and realistic answers to these questions; (2) *duty*, in which teachers have a commitment to the communities and students that they teach; (3) *preparation,* which entails teachers having solid classroom management skills and giving intense commitment and time to their curricular decision making, lesson planning, and assessment; (4) *Socratic sensibility*, or teachers' ability to find a balance between their confidence as teachers and their ability to engage in frequent self-critique; and (5) *trust*, or the building of authentic relationships between students and teachers in ways that are predicated on mutual levels of trust and respect.

RACE, CULTURE, AND THE ADAPTIVE UNCONSCIOUSNESS

An essential aspect of culturally competent teaching is the willingness of the educator to examine his or her own ways of knowing, sources of information, and value-laden perspectives, and then to be willing to acknowledge the fact that students frequently bring their own unique skill sets and knowledge bases to the classroom. Teachers can work toward the establishment of a relationship that is undergirded by a mutual respect of the positionality of the teacher and the learner in a way that promotes reciprocal teaching and learning of content across different contexts. Essential to this particular stance of cultural competence is the way it can enhance all aspects of the learning environment. Teel and Obidah (2008) contend that cultural competence is "as important as competence in classroom management, curriculum, lesson planning and delivery, and assessment . . . all those competencies become stronger and stronger as a teacher becomes more and more racially and culturally competent" (p. 3). Cross and colleagues (1989) stress the importance of competence because it implies having the capacity to function within the context of culturally integrated patterns of human behavior defined by a group.

Perhaps the biggest challenge in critical reflection, and one rarely examined in education, is what T. D. Wilson (2002) refers to as the *adaptive unconsciousness*—a social psychological concept that refers to as the deeper embedded meanings that we tend to act on unconsciously, those meanings that influence people's judgments, feelings, and behaviors. Wilson states that people can cognitively process in sophisticated ways, yet be thinking—and in some cases behaving—unconsciously about certain concepts, people, and situations. Within the context of educational practice in diverse school settings, race and culture easily can become areas where the adaptive unconscious contributes to the ways which student-teacher interactions are manifested. Consider, for example, a teacher who may have limited interactions or experiences with individuals from diverse or low-income backgrounds, yet undoubtedly has been exposed to many of the distorted and often inaccurate portrayals of various populations that frequently are found in the media and mainstream press. Add to this equation the possibility that the same teacher may have friends, colleagues, or family members who share experiences about their interactions with people from diverse backgrounds that may have been less than ideal. Hence, one can begin to question the manner in which this fair-minded teacher is going to view, judge, teach, and evaluate students who come from the groups that she has heard a plethora of negative information about.

T. D. Wilson (2002) suggests that beliefs may be formed in ways that connect to a person's own psychological well-being and belief systems. He writes:

> The adaptive unconscious is not governed by accuracy and accessibility alone. People's judgments and interpretations are often guided by a quite different concern, namely the desire to view the world in the way that gives them the most pleasure. (p. 38)

T. D. Wilson (2002) argues that "what makes us feel good depends on our culture and our personalities" (p. 39) and that people can go to great lengths to see the world in a particular way, and as a result see the world in a way that is consistent with existing paradigms and comforting epistemological stances. Wilson and Gilbert (2003) refer to this as the *psychological immune system*, or a protective set of ideologies that protect people's psychological well-being. The adaptive unconscious may seek to identify the pleasure or feel-good aspect of the belief system or to connect to the individual's own psychological well-being to accommodate information that is inconsistent with the existing data set about different groups of people. For example, if a teacher accepts the idea of White students being academically superior to non-White students, there may exist a flurry of examples that suggest the contrary, but those examples are dismissed as aberrations. What is especially important about Wilson's work within the context of race, culture, and learning, is that in subtle and subconscious ways teachers continually may deny the fact that students from culturally diverse groups possess the intellectual skills to be academically successful.

In many ways, the adaptive unconscious can provide a glimpse into the authentic or real feelings and beliefs about particular people or circumstances that an individual may not want revealed, yet are demonstrated in ways that we are usually unaware of. While a classroom teacher engages in what he may view as fair practices, equitable teaching, and a positive learning climate, students from the teacher's class may paint a very different picture. Certain students may feel as though they are unfairly criticized, harshly evaluated, or treated in a less than desirable way, and may describe a negative climate. Social psychologists maintain that individuals often project something different from what they believe they are projecting; therefore, in situations like the one just described, a teacher may object to a description of himself as being unfair, discriminatory, or hostile toward particular students (Aronson, Wilson, & Akert, 2002; T. D. Wilson & Dunn, 1986). Given such a situation, a critical step in developing cultural competence would be not to quickly dismiss accusations or accounts of one's teaching that are less than glowing, but to begin to probe and reflect about why students may have viewed the teacher in such a way—to consider whether his actions may have been exclusionary to certain students and whether certain practices could be altered to provide more equity and inclusion.

The development of cultural competence and racial awareness is painful, difficult, and frequently avoided by many people in general, and practitioners in particular: It requires opening oneself up to critical inspection, harsh criticisms, and condemning opinions of others, and it entails having to listen to the unflattering assessment of one's own actions. This is especially painful when an individual believes firmly that she is fair to all students, equitable when it comes to providing learning opportunities, and committed to creating a just learning environment. Critical reflection is an ever-evolving task that it is never complete. Wilson (2002) notes the rigidity that can be part of the adaptive unconscious and explains that upon seeing new information that is inconsistent with the beliefs that we hold, there can be a reluctance or unwillingness to challenge previously held beliefs. Wilson states that individuals can be "slow to respond to new, contradictory information. In fact, we often unconsciously bend new information to fit our preconceptions, making it next to impossible to realize that our preconceptions are wrong" (p. 54). This reality speaks to the complexity and difficulty of critical reflection because it may require a concerted effort to dispel hardened beliefs, of which we may not even be aware, about people, groups, or certain situations.

If a teacher is truly interested in arriving at a space of equitable teaching, reflection, and analysis, a commitment to both racial awareness and cultural competence should be a lifelong process. This process consists of listening to the stories, experiences, histories, struggles, and setbacks of marginalized groups. It involves thinking about the possibility that the manner in which one may have viewed the world, and people's circumstances in it, may be grossly inaccurate or outright wrong. It may require readjusting and recreating perceptions. This process may also involve constructing new lenses and paradigms through which to view individuals and their experiences. Critical reflection can be tedious as a teacher builds new knowledge and reprograms age-old thoughts, replacing them with more informed data sets that can be used as a framework to guide transformative thoughts and behaviors.

One of the more painful parts of the critical reflection process entails acknowledging or recognizing one's own privilege as a member of a group that has received unearned opportunity and advantage (McIntosh, 1989). What is crucial about acknowledging privilege is that failure to begin dismantling these privileges once the individual becomes conscious of them is, in many ways, tantamount to acting in discriminatory ways. Therefore, it is not enough for the individual to say, "I have privilege because of my racial membership," but she must take active steps to ensure that future actions do not reinforce the remnants of that privilege. Perhaps the most important aspect of developing cultural competence, critical reflection, and the adaptive unconscious, and of dismantling privilege, is to recognize that neutrality is equivalent to acting against equity, fairness, and justice in the classroom. Ladson-Billings (1994) states that teaching is always a political act that is never neutral. Failure to recognize the complexities of action and neutrality can result in strained relationships between teachers and students from culturally diverse groups.

For many subordinated groups like African Americans, Latinos, Native Americans, and certain Asian Americans, the often sordid history of the United States has led to widespread distrust of those in positions in power—beliefs that undoubtedly can be and have been passed down through generations (Ogbu, 2003). Therefore, in the context of classrooms, it is not uncommon for students of color to have deep-seated mistrust or suspicion of teachers who come from racially privileged groups. Teachers have a tremendous responsibility and obligation to earn the trust of students from diverse backgrounds. It is vital for members of racially privileged groups to not merely provide lip service to the wrongs of racism and racial oppression and discrimination, but to consistently speak out against and raise objections to them, while continually acting in ways that move us toward racial and cultural equity. Within the context of schools, cultural competence and racial awareness may entail educators advocating on behalf of students if colleagues make disparaging comments about them, their families, or their intellectual abilities. Cultural practices that various students may express, such as religious traditions (e.g., Ramadan with fasting and prayer rituals or Jehovah's Witness practices of not pledging allegiance to the flag), should be acknowledged as different and not as deficient.

Issues of cultural competence and racial awareness are not restricted to the work of practitioners and school leaders, but have equal relevance to researchers engaged in documenting, describing, and evaluating the lived experiences of people of color. Milner (2007) urges researchers to look for dangers—seen, unseen, and unforeseen—when engaged in this important work. Milner also writes about the way people and communities of color and their experiences and histories become distorted and inaccurately portrayed, without careful concern and consideration for the positionality that comes with race and culture. He recommends that researchers examine their own racial and cultural identities, research themselves in relation to others, and engage in reflection and representation.

Any attempts to build cultural competence and racial awareness must be mindful of the dangers that may exist when certain cultural and racial paradigms go unchallenged. G. R. Howard (2006) speaks to this issue in relation to White teachers.

> Our frustration as educators flows from the fact that the dynamics of dominance are self-perpetuating. The luxury of ignorance, the assumption of rightness and the legacy of privilege have for centuries functioned together to support and legitimize White dominance. The interaction of these three dynamics has formed the "dominance paradigm," a pervasive and persistent worldview wherein White assumptions are held to be true and right, White ignorance of other groups is the norm, and the White privilege flourishes essentially unchallenged and unacknowledged. The dominance paradigm has allowed Whites to continue to benefit from past and present dominance, with or without our conscious intent and awareness. (p. 67)

G. R. Howard's (2006) notion that White ignorance is the norm is critical here because in most classrooms throughout the United States, White teachers are responsible for student learning. As noted in Chapter 2, the changing dynamics of the nation's schools indicate that many of the White teachers currently in classrooms will find themselves with learners who possess markedly different experiences than their own. Thus, an essential part of the work for teachers and teacher educators who work with preservice teachers is to require them to challenge the dominance paradigm.

RACIAL AWARENESS

In addition to having a clear sense of cultural competence, educators also should be aware of the importance of racial awareness. Racial awareness is a consciousness or framework that recognizes the historical, social, political, and economic consequences of being a member of a racially marginalized group in the United States (Bobo, Kluegel, & Smith, 1997; Bonilla-Silva, 1997; Tatum, 2007; W. J. Wilson, 2009). Racial awareness is more than just acknowledging individuals' racial classification, but consists of a consciousness of how race is manifested in the United States. As discussed in Chapter 5, educators must be willing to see how race shapes the way in which many young people understand their worlds and how the world shapes their understanding of themselves as racial beings. Racial awareness also entails having a working knowledge of how "Whiteness" permeates U.S. ideologies, culture, and practices (Roediger, 1994, 2005; Sleeter, 1996), where Whiteness typically is viewed as synonymous with being American and human, and understanding that derivations from being White are viewed through a lens of superiority. Bonilla-Silva (2003) describes Whiteness as "a social structure (a racialized social system) that awarded systemic privileges to Europeans" (p. 9) and suggests that attempts to dismantle Whiteness must be willing to uncover the social, political, economic, and ideological forces that reinforce White privilege. Roediger (1994) states that Whiteness creates and reinforces *White identities*, which create an ideological structure that promotes and accepts the oppression of non-Whites. He aligns this work with Baldwin's notion of the "lie of Whiteness," which seeks to eliminate or distort the realities, struggles, and contributions of non-Whites. Critical race theorist Cheryl Harris (1993) conceptualizes Whiteness as similar to property by stating that White privilege affords Whites the same benefits and opportunities that property owners possess—rights of disposition, rights to use and enjoyment, reputation and status, and the absolute right to exclude.

Another feature of racial awareness is mindfulness of the role of racism in the United States (Delgado & Stefancic, 1997; Gillborn, 2008). Issues that pertain to race and racism should not be taken lightly or overlooked, nor should they be dismissed as aberrant. Racial awareness is the willingness of educators to listen to students talk about their racialized experiences, to probe for deeper clarity about these experiences, and to seek ways to learn from them. The way in which young Black and Latino males frequently are criminalized in schools and society cannot be ignored, and requires a critical awareness of race and racism (Duncan, 2002; Ferguson, 2003). The same can be said for students of Latin descent and the political and social implications that accompany immigration in this country, and the racial ramifications associated with it. In addition, racial stereotypes exist for students from Asian backgrounds, as teachers assume that they fit a model minority classification (S. Lee, 1996). Each of the examples of racial essentializing and race-based classification of individuals is problematic and highly reductive because it centers on a belief that fails to reflect the complexities of race and how it is manifested, and is lacking in an awareness of racial context. An increasing number of scholars have encouraged White teachers to begin to rethink their racial privilege and to understand what it means for the experiences of non-White groups (G. R. Howard, 2006; Johnson, 2002).

A CASE STUDY OF CRITICAL REFLECTING: TEACHING TEACHERS TO REFLECT ON RACE

As a faculty member in a teacher education program that prepares teachers to teach in urban schools, I have been part of a team of faculty who have created a new mandatory course, "Identity and Teaching," for all preservice teachers. This course helps preservice teachers develop cultural competence and racial awareness that are vital for effectively teaching in diverse schools. The specific purpose of the course is to allow preservice teachers to interrogate various notions of their multiple identities, and to grapple with their racial, cultural, and gender identities. The most vexing challenge for students has been their examinations of their own racial identities. The course requires students to problematize the ways that race plays a role in their day-to-day realities. They wrestle with questions such as, "Who am I racially? What do I believe about other racial groups?" and "Does who I am and what I believe about race have ramifications for the students

I teach?" Students engage in readings and activities that pertain to their own racial identities. The reflections and revelations that emanate from the course are invaluable, and the emotional outpouring is a testament to how difficult it is for many individuals to come to grips with their own notions of racial privilege. Through the identity examination process, many of the students have come to realize the value of critical reflection and the role it can have for them as they teach in culturally diverse school settings.

Many of the students in the course explain how their discomfort is a result of race being a taboo topic for them (Tatum, 2007). They express concerns such as not wanting their comments to appear racially insensitive, racist, prejudiced, or politically incorrect. Yet, facilitators guiding race-related discussions cannot allow individuals' discomfort or ignorance about race to become an escape for not addressing and analyzing their own beliefs about race. Therefore, teacher educators should be willing to push students into the uncomfortable spaces where race is being discussed on an in-depth level. Students can be asked to think about why race was not a part of their upbringing, or challenged to think about why students of color believe that race and racism are real issues in their lives.

The process of examining identity also can mean taking students to task in a respectful manner when racially inappropriate comments are made within the context of a course, such as when a White student in one of my courses stated, "Why do we spend so much time on this race stuff; these people need to just get over it." The tone and tenor of such a comment suggest that race-related issues are insignificant and need not be discussed. However, hearing the stories, learning from the experiences, and hearing some of the painful episodes that people of color encounter, may help to enlighten those who want to avoid race-related topics. The process of critically delving into race-related topics is especially important for teachers in diverse school settings, because if teachers do not have experiential knowledge regarding issues of race, they may feel inadequately prepared and retreat to the safety net of practicing "colorblindness," the practice of not acknowledging the racial identities of their students (Schofield, 1986). With the best of intentions, colorblindness inadvertently renders students of color invisible.

Colorblindness can imply that there is something wrong with not being White, or that there is something embarrassing or insulting about acknowledging one's race or ethnicity (Delpit, 1995; Schofield, 1999). Williams (1997), a critical race theorist, asserts that colorblindness has pernicious effects for students of color in what is thought to be innocent and polite school discourse. She maintains that frequently attempts to dismiss or not see race pathologize students of color, and that Whiteness overtly and covertly becomes the norm. Thompson (1998) reinforces Williams's point by claiming that "politely pretending not to notice students' color makes no sense unless being of different colors is somehow shameful" (p. 524). Colorblind perspectives also may contribute to internalized racism, reinforce racial hierarchies, and contribute to the development of deficit models about students of color. Colorblind perspectives also may reproduce racial and cultural hegemony in school practices, such as curriculum choices, teacher expectations, testing procedures, instructional practices, and even more pedestrian tasks such as seating arrangements and opportunities provided for participation in learning. Because of the growing racial diversity in the United States, it is vital for teachers to understand and have the capacity to acknowledge racial diversity, and create safe, affirming, and supportive learning environments for their students to develop the knowledge, attitudes, and skills necessary to dialogue about race-related issues (Tatum, 2007).

The preservice teachers in our identity course are informed that as future teachers in urban schools, where many of their students will see their racial identities as important—and in some cases primary—facets of who they are, the ability to talk with students openly, honestly, and from an informed standpoint about race can be a huge asset. An inability to create a learning environment that recognizes the salience of race could place these novice teachers at an extreme disadvantage. Conversely, the ability to teach in a way that affirms students' racial identities, embraces and encourages discussions that pertain to race, and acknowledges the complexity of race in a multiracial society is an important asset in most urban schools.

While research on the topic is sparse, it remains clear that one of the pressing challenges in teacher education is the largely White population of former teachers who serve as teacher educators, many of whom have not problematized issues of race (Hollins & Guzman, 2005; Sleeter, 1996). Nevertheless, they are given the daunting task of helping preservice teachers to think critically about race-related issues. One can only begin to wonder what role this plays in the fact that so many novice teachers lack the capacity to engage students in dialogues about race (T.C. Howard & Aleman, 2007). Being able to effectively initiate and facilitate critical reflection about race and race-related issues requires the ability to critically examine one's own personal beliefs, opinions, and values about racial identity, and the race of others, as well as the ramifications of these intersecting and colliding values and beliefs.

With issues of race, culture, and diversity in mind, the reflective process in the identity course was enhanced by a 3-day workshop that each of the course instructors took before teaching the course. Each instructor engaged in a series of activities identical to the ones they would take their own students through—activities that required the students to come to grips with their own identities around race, ethnicity, social class, and gender. The willingness on the part of teacher educators to share their own lived experiences, expose their own human frailties, and reflect on their ever-evolving identities within a community of peers is important. The practice of reflecting on race in teacher education becomes superficial if facilitators of discussions are not clear and comfortable with both their own identities and those of others.

Whatever reflective mechanisms are put in place in teacher education programs must go beyond reflection just for the sake of thinking about issues related to teaching in racially diverse settings. Instead, they must actively engage preservice teachers in discourses about how race plays out in schools, how students make meaning of race, and to what degree race and race-related issues influence students' prospects for learning. Rist's (1970) research on labeling and teacher expectations revealed that teachers' preconceived notions about students and their academic potential frequently were influenced by race and consequently contributed to the salience of self-fulfilling prophecies wherein students question their own potential for academic success. Critical reflection on issues of race should inform all facets of teaching and learning and become an essential part of the preparation of teachers so that preservice teachers can begin to develop a conceptual understanding of and an effective framework for addressing racial issues when they arise in the context of teaching and learning. In order for critical reflection measures to have optimum effect and to help create useful strategies for racial awareness, a number of suggestions are offered to inform teacher educators, preservice teachers, inservice teachers, and school administrators about ways to translate critical reflection into greater racial awareness.

1. The development of teacher education faculty who are able to sufficiently address the complex nature of race, ethnicity, and culture. The task of developing racial awareness can prove difficult for novice teachers if there are not faculty members who are themselves willing to engage in critical reflection about racial awareness. Clinical educators, lecturers, or mentor teachers can be helpful in facilitating this critical racial awareness with preservice teachers. These individuals can share their own frustrations with, mistakes, and strategies for making meaning out of issues pertaining to race in diverse schools. For teacher educators who have never worked in racially diverse schools, the process of critical reflection is likely to be incredibly difficult. Consequently, it can be fruitful for teacher education programs to identify former classroom teachers who have experience working in racially diverse school settings to work with preservice teachers. If the teacher education program is not concerned with issues of equity and access and does not address the role of race and ethnicity in education, critical reflection will become a useless endeavor.

2. *The recognition of reflection as a never-ending process.* Schon (1987) describes reflection as a process that is tied to action and emphasizes the need for "reflection-in-action," an ongoing process predicated on continually thinking about one's actions and then modifying them accordingly. It is important to stress that critical reflection is never complete. Just as the very nature of teaching is built upon always revisiting curriculum, pedagogy, and assessment, the same holds true for critical self-reflection. Preservice teachers should realize that even the most seasoned and racially aware teachers are prone to mistakes, lapses in judgment, or other forms of missteps. However, they acknowledge their errors and improve their teaching accordingly.

3. *The understanding that teaching is not a neutral act. It is highly political, and issues such as race and class are always tied to teaching.* Ladson-Billings (1994) states that responsive teachers seek to instill political consciousness in students. Part of that consciousness entails being mindful of the complex nexus of race, class, gender, culture, and language. Each of these factors plays a notable role in the way in which students identify themselves and form their identities, both consciously and unconsciously. Consequently, teachers should be mindful of how their actions can contribute to or stifle the development of a healthy identity and sense of self among students. Teachers who refuse to monitor their own beliefs and classroom ethos can contribute to resistance on the part of students. Recognizing that all facets of teaching have explicit and implicit racial and cultural implications should result in ongoing reflection to clarify the educational agenda that is being promoted within a classroom setting. A growing number of works have begun to examine students' academic identity, and many of these works discuss the ways in which race plays a vital role, for students of color in particular, in shaping their images of themselves as learners (Flores-Gonzales, 1999; Welch & Hodges, 1997; Zirkel, 2002). These findings offer important implications for teachers in diverse schools.

4. The avoidance of reductive notions of race and culture. Racial aware-ness and cultural competence are based on the inclusion of cultural referents that students bring from home. Teachers should be careful not to allow racial classifications of students to be used as rigid and reductive cultural characteristics. A critical reflection process allows teachers to recognize the array of differences that exist within groups. Not all African American students work well in groups, not all Latino students are second language learners, and not all Asian American students are high achievers. While there may be central tendencies within groups, teachers must avoid creating stereotypical profiles of students that may do more harm than good (K. Gutierrez & Rogoff, 2003). Instead, teachers should develop individual profiles of students based on the students' own thoughts and behaviors. The more these points can be stressed to beginning teachers, the more likely they are to begin to conceptualize diversity in a comprehensive, yet individ-ualized, way that reflects the ways a specific student thinks, speaks, learns, and makes meaning of the world around him or her.

5. The explicit enumeration of issues to reflect on. There are a number of considerations that teachers should keep in mind in a critical re-flection process. Teachers should examine class data on an ongoing basis and ask challenging questions about equity in the classroom. For example, questions teachers might ask themselves as they reflect on these issues could include:

- What is the racial breakdown of students who are referred for special needs services?
- What is the racial breakdown of students referred for gifted education and recommended for AP/Honors classes?
- How frequently do I differentiate instruction?
- Do scoring rubrics give advantages for certain ways of knowing and expression?
- Do I allow culturally based differences in language, speech, reading, and writing to shape my perceptions about students' cognitive ability?
- Do I create a multitude of ways to evaluate students? Or do I rely solely on traditional and narrow means of paper, pencil, and oral responses?
- How often do I allow nontraditional means of assessment—such as role playing, skits, poetry, rap, or newspaper creations—to be a part of my class?

FINAL CONSIDERATIONS

Cultural competence and racial awareness offer important considerations for the way in which teaching and learning take place in multicultural and multiracial classrooms. The development of a critical consciousness about one's ideologies, beliefs, and attitudes about diverse
learners must always be interrogated for accuracy and for dispositions
that are ideal for all learners. The development of a critical consciousness should not be viewed as relevant only to White teachers, but
should be used by teachers of color as well. One of the mistakes that
can be made by teachers of color is assuming that being a member of
the same racial or ethnic group as one's students automatically gives
one a unique ability to connect to or effectively teach students of color.
The ways in which race, ethnicity, culture, language, and social class
are manifested in young people's lives is constantly in flux. Therefore,
it is important to recognize that while there may be experiences that
allow teachers of color to relate to certain realities of their students,
this is not necessarily a given, and it is therefore highly advisable for
teachers of color also to engage in the process of critical reflection.

CHAPTER 7

Examples of School Success for Culturally Diverse Students

The school performance of African American, Latino, certain Asian American, and low-income students has generated a plethora of discourse and research on the achievement gap since 2000 (Barton, 2004; Jencks & Phillips, 1998; Rothstein, 2004; Thernstrom & Thernstrom, 2003). Much of this work has centered on the disparate school outcomes for White and non-White students. While ongoing scrutiny has focused on underperforming students and schools, a growing number of schools have been able to turn the tide and improve the academic performance of culturally diverse and low-income students (Reeves, 2000). These schools, and their programs and practices, are important exemplars of where educational policy, practice, and research should be focused in an attempt to eliminate the achievement gap. A close investigation into the practices at high-performing schools with diverse and low-income student populations is important because it can go a long way in reversing the deficit tone that frequently is associated with the schooling of culturally diverse and low-income students. There must be a careful balance of bringing much-needed attention to the persistent and disproportionate underachievement of millions of culturally diverse and low-income students, while at the same time highlighting the success stories that are occurring. However, any analysis of the schooling experiences of diverse and low-income students must not frame the discussion in a way that suggests that *all* students from low-income and culturally diverse backgrounds are underperforming in schools and lack the capacity to be high-achieving students. The need to spotlight effective schools for students from diverse groups, the students in them, the role of their parents, and the work of school personnel has become increasingly critical.

One of the challenges for educational practitioners and researchers is to identify successful schools and to examine the practices that have

129

been vital to their success, and to describe where the achievement gap has been closed. This chapter will identify, highlight, and analyze the practices, programs, strategies, and solutions that have been effective in four different schools in eliminating academic disparities between African American, Native American, Latino, and certain Asian American students, and their higher-performing counterparts at other schools. The reason for highlighting these specific schools and the practices that educators use within them is to offer new directions, pose important research questions, examine the plausibility of the replication of these programs and practices, and offer a set of guiding principles for educators whose work is concerned with closing the achievement gap that has existed for too long in United States schools.

This chapter is divided into two sections. The first discusses four schools from across the country (two elementary, one middle, and one high school) that have been successful in helping culturally diverse and low-income students attain academic success despite factors such as poverty and race that typically work against their school performance. These schools were identified through a 3-year-long process of working with a plethora of educators to find schools that were defying the odds and closing the achievement gap. I will detail some of the emergent themes that were consistent across these schools and that contributed to their being as successful as they were in improving students' academic performance. A close examination of each of these schools revealed that there were five specific practices and ideological stances that appeared to be most critical in the success of these schools: (1) visionary leadership, (2) teachers' effective practices, (3) intensive academic support, (4) the acknowledgment of race, and (5) parental and community engagement.

The second section of the chapter will examine future considerations for the achievement gap, and look at the issues, differing roles, and much-needed questions that practitioners, researchers, policymakers, and parents should be aware of in the quest to create equitable schooling conditions for all students. This section describes some next steps or implications for future research, practice, and policy, and offers a set of challenges that exists for all stakeholders. Much of what this section will outline is what Dr. Martin Luther King, Jr. (1967) referred to as the "fierce urgency of now," that is necessary when it comes to transforming school outcomes for an increasingly low-income and diverse student population. Persistent underperformance of large and growing segments of the student population has critical short- and long-term implications for the economic, political, and social well-being of the nation. The failure on the part of concerned citizens in general, and educators more specifically, to act swiftly, to act effectively, and to act in an informed, authentic, and caring way to stem the tide of an increasingly fractured society, and to find meaningful ways to provide a way of thinking about the possibilities that education purports to provide in a democratic and egalitarian society, is incredibly serious. In many ways, young people are desperately crying for hope in what often seems like a hopeless world for many of them. Historically, education has been that beacon of hope for dozens of generations in this country to persevere and to struggle to create a better reality for themselves and their families (Anderson, 1988; Takaki, 1993). Unfortunately, the idea of education as a conduit for hope and improved life chances has dissipated for many of the descendants of those who fought tirelessly for educational access, equity, and opportunity. Viable interventions and transformative approaches to education are desperately needed to offer much-needed hope for millions of young people in U.S. society who often feel like hope is an elusive concept, a fleeting word that they are unable to grasp and apply in their own reality.

STORIES OF SCHOOL SUCCESS

Over the course of the past 3 years, I was able to spend time in four schools that made tremendous strides in closing the achievement gap. Each of these schools had populations that were predominantly African American or Latino, and each of these schools was situated in an urban community with a high free- and reduced-lunch population. All also were identified as Title I schools. These schools were selected based on a call that I put out for educators across the United States to nominate schools that were having proven success increasing the academic achievement of culturally and linguistically diverse and low-income students. To add more specificity to the identification of schools, four criteria were used: (1) student population had to be at least 50% non-White; (2) free and reduced-lunch population had to be at least 60%; (3) schools had to be public or public charter; and (4) Schools had to be able to show student improvement in core academic areas such as reading, math, science, or social studies for a minimum of 2 years.

Profile of the Schools

In order to provide additional context for each of the schools, I present brief profiles of each. The profiles are not intended to provide all of the information about these schools, but offer a snapshot of some of the salient features of the schools, in order to help situate the magnitude of the work that the administration and staff have done at the respective sites. Also, given that these schools were involved in this research project, I have used pseudonyms for all of the schools, and the individual teachers and administrators who participated in the informal interviews.

Promise Learning Center—Located in Los Angeles, CA, the Promise Learning Center (PLC) was established in 1997 as an independent K–5 elementary academy. The school serves approximately 250 students, all of whom live in the surrounding community. This community has been one of the more economically underserved communities in Los Angeles County for the past 5 decades since the aftermath of the Watts riots in 1965. The API ranking for PLC in 2000 was 577 and has increased steadily each of the past 8 years, reaching 824 in 2008, which contributed to its being named a California Distinguished School. The school classifies the majority of its students as Standard English learners. The school's population is 85% African American and 15% Latino. A Title I school, PLC refers to its location as a "Learning Community," where stakeholders include students, parents, teachers, support staff, volunteers, foster parents and grandparents, and concerned caregivers.

Duke Ellington Elementary School—Duke Ellington is a K–5 public school in Chicago with an enrollment of 337 students. The school was recently awarded the state's Academic Improvement Award, which honors schools for substantial gains in performance over a 3-year span. The award winners range across all levels, from schools where 32% of students are meeting the Illinois Learning Standards, to schools where 100% of students are meeting standards. Criteria for selecting these schools are rigorous. All recipients must be making adequate yearly progress. At least half of the students must come from low-income families and at least 60% must be passing the state achievement tests in reading and mathematics. The student population at Ellington is approximately 85% African American. The most notable gains at Ellington were present in the lower primary grades, where the majority (75%) of pre-K to 2nd graders were at or above grade level for reading proficiency.

Neighborhood Middle School—Located in Los Angeles County, Neighborhood Middle School (NMS) is another school that has made significant strides in closing the achievement gap. The school serves approximately 1,075 students in Grades 6–8, with a racial composition that is 60% Latino, 14.8% White, 11.8% Asian, and 11.6% African American. Approximately 66% of the students are classified as socioeconomically disadvantaged. NMS is a National Blue Ribbon School and ranks among the highest improving schools in the state of California. Over the past 9 years the school's API has increased by 235 points to its 2008 score of 812, which has earned the school the Dispelling the Myth Award, which is recognition in Standard & Poor's for closing the achievement gap, and the California Distinguished School Award. An examination of the student academic profile data shows that the school has made tremendous strides in increasing the academic performance of Latino and Asian students in particular, where API scores show dramatic decreases between these two student groups' performance and that of their White peers.

Sunnyside High School—Sunnyside High was discussed in greater depth in Chapter 4. Located in one of Los Angeles County's most economically depressed areas, this racially and ethnically diverse school has struggled with helping its students gain access to some of California's 4-year universities. Through the implementation of a UCLA Sunnyside GEAR UP plan, Sunnyside was able to experience a significant increase in the numbers of African American and Latino students who went to 4-year colleges after graduation.

Making a Difference

There were five attributes that were most common in these four schools. These characteristics were identified after spending a combined total of 1,000 hours at the schools. My time at these schools included observing professional development for staff, conducting professional development for staff, observing classrooms, interviewing over 25 teachers and 12 administrators, observing staff meetings, attending after-school programs, engaging in informal conversations with school staff, and observing many of the day-to-day operations of the schools during the 2007–08 and 2008–09 academic years. I asked respondents to offer their insights and perspectives on the major practices, strategies, and programs that contributed most to their school's academic success, and the challenges that they encountered in their quest to achieve high academic success for all students.

I will provide a brief glimpse into each of these characteristics and highlight several examples of how they were carried out in the school community, to offer insight into some of the practices that made these schools unique in their ability to produce high achievers in challenging circumstances. These characteristics, which do not offer new or radically different approaches to school success, are: (1) visionary leadership, (2) teachers' effective practices, (3) intensive academic intervention, (4) the explicit acknowledgment of race, and (5) engagement of parents and community. Scholars have described each of these characteristics and their ability to influence school outcomes (Dalton, 2008; T. C. Howard & Reynolds, 2009; Pine & Hilliard, 1990). In the following pages I will describe how each of these schools was able to incorporate these characteristics to transform school outcomes for culturally diverse and low-income students.

VISIONARY LEADERSHIP

One of the more critical features of each of these school sites was the vision that principals had for their school. The importance of effective leadership in school transformation has been studied and written about by a number of scholars (Crew, 2007; Leithwood et al., 2006; Leithwood & Reihl, 2003; National College for School Leadership, 2006). The vision of school transformation was clearly articulated to anyone inquiring about the mission of the schools, the goals for a given year, and in the school's top priority. Each of the principals at these schools set a tone and vision of high achievement, worked tirelessly to ensure academic success for all students, and was relentless in his or her efforts to get all stakeholders to buy into the vision for student learning and overall school success.

The leaders at each of these schools exhibited an intense and persistent effort to promote academic achievement. They appeared to be obsessed with different ways to maximize student learning and had energy that seemed to be infectious. The desire to transform school culture and improve student learning carried over to the faculty and staff at their schools. These principals' visions were continually conveyed to students, parents, teachers, and staff with a fervor that was palpable. During my visits to Neighborhood Middle School, conversations with the principal, Mrs. Sanchez, rarely ventured into a topic outside of student performance. She would make constant references to professional conferences that she had attended, research or practitioner-based articles that she had read and passed on to her staff, and principal colleagues of hers that she had talked to that offered insights on improving student learning. She described herself as "fixated on getting these kids to learn because I came from a community just like this one, and I know what is possible." During a visit to the school it was not uncommon to find her in classrooms, watching teachers teach, and on the school grounds ensuring that no student was out of class. She was clear about the fact that she viewed herself as an "instructional leader" and that she refused to be "holed up in my office pushing papers." She remained in perpetual motion and possessed a relentless vigor that was beyond words.

Mrs. Sanchez had a more personable approach to her work than Mrs. Shannon, who was the principal at Duke Ellington. A seasoned educator for more than 35 years, Mrs. Shannon frequently discussed "the urgency we face with our students." She possessed a passionate, no-nonsense approach with teachers, parents, staff, and students. Her stern yet caring approach was mentioned repeatedly by teachers when they were asked to explain the school's success with a high at-risk population. One teacher from Ellington stated, "If every school in America had a Mrs. Shannon, we wouldn't have an achievement gap." Mrs. Shannon refused to take any credit for her role in her school's unlikely success. She stated, "I learned a long time ago that as a school leader I give all the praise and credit to my staff, but accept the blame whenever something goes wrong." She stated that her selfless approach was rooted in her upbringing in the rural south during the 1960s when "we had real caring and connected communities, where you had no choice but to excel."

At the Promise Learning Center, Mrs. Gelson stressed that the reason her school witnessed unprecedented academic success had to do with the important roles that families and parents played in supporting the work of the school. Mrs. Gelson told me that she repeatedly tells her staff to not buy into the idea that working-class parents do not value their children's education. She said:

> I tell them [teachers] all the time, your students' parents value education just as much, if not more, than you do. They know what it is like to struggle, and these parents sometimes work two and three jobs trying to do the best they can. . . . Don't limit these parents . . . they just need the tools to show them how to maximize their children's potential.

Mrs. Gelson was adamant in her belief about the role that families play in building school community and achieving academic success. This was evident in the monthly family and community nights that were held at PLC and were designed to bring families and school staff together. I was amazed when visiting one of the events to find almost 80 parents on a Tuesday night who were attending to work with teachers and learn ways to help their children become better readers. The event, which lasted for 2 hours, included parents and teachers actively involved in a wide range of strategies that parents could use at home to help their young children. When I asked Mrs. Gelson how she was able to create a high level of parent participation, she said it was about "investing time to build the relationships with my parents . . . they are the key. If I don't have them on board, we [the school] don't go anywhere." Mrs. Gelson said that during her first year, she was hard-pressed to get more than a dozen parents to show up at these meetings because of the "distrust and anger" that parents had toward school officials. She then elaborated on the ways in which she began to establish a presence in the community. She talked about attending local churches, going to quinceneras, going to students' little league football and basketball games, and "just talking and learning about parents and what they go through." She said that she wanted parents to know that she was a part of their community and that she was there for them as a resource. Mrs. Gelson, like each of the other principals who were observed, had "contextual literacy" of her school and its surrounding community; that is, an understanding of the meta-messages, subtexts, local histories, and micropolitics that influence parents, students, schools, and their staff (Schein, 1985). She mentioned that PLC conducted food and clothing drives to help certain families. She also discussed several international trips on which they took students and the importance of "exposing students to the possibilities that the world has to offer."

The importance of visionary leaders in this study seems to be centered on an authentic and unyielding belief in students' success, engaging parents and family in the schooling process, and in many ways challenging nonbelievers who believed that students at the school could not be academically successful. As Mrs. Gelson stated during one of our conversations, "Some of the adults are the biggest problem . . . just getting them to believe what young people can do." Scheurich and Skrla (2003) talk about how removing the "barriers to believe" is vital for school leaders, and disrupting the negative and doubting beliefs that many teachers and administrators have toward the potential school success of students of color. These visionary leaders also seemed to work tirelessly to improve all aspects of the school, including organizational structure, physical appearance of the facilities, developing a family-type atmosphere among staff, and offering rewards and acknowledgment to those who helped make their schools successful.

EFFECTIVE INSTRUCTIONAL PRACTICES

In addition to visionary leadership, what was quite obvious in each of these schools were teachers who used effective instructional practices. Some researchers have suggested that effective teacher practice is the single most important variable in student achievement outcomes (Dalton, 2008; Darling-Hammond, 2004; Tharp & Gallimore, 1988). In many of the classrooms I visited at these schools, effective teacher practices were evident across a number of areas—teachers spent more time on task in classrooms; there were few interruptions, distractions, and disrupting of instructional time. The teachers had effective management practices, appeared to build classroom community, were able to multitask effortlessly, and had multiple ways of assessing students.

It was clear that students in most of the classrooms I studied were exposed to rigorous academic coursework. Extensive research has documented the role that rigorous teaching, critical thinking, and effective pedagogy have on students' academic outcomes (Abrami, et al., 2008; Barton, 2004; Ennis, 1989; Marzano, 2003). A visit to the classrooms at each of these schools revealed students who were actively involved in work and teachers who were engaged in teaching and challenging students in a multitude of ways. As a teacher from Neighborhood Middle School stated, "We believe in acceleration, not remediation." What was clear at each of these schools was that even though there were students who might not have been at grade level in some subjects, teachers refused to "teach down" to them. A number of previous studies on high-performing schools have documented the salience of rigorous coursework (Barton, 2004). While at Ellington Elementary School observing a preschool teacher working with a group of 22 students, I saw how students were being challenged on a level not common for students who are 5 and 6 years old. Here is an exchange between the teacher and a student.

TEACHER: We have 30 dots on the paper. How many ways can you regroup the dots?
STUDENT: I put six dots in this group, and then five in this group.
TEACHER: Can you put them in any other size groups?
STUDENT: So you mean I can group them in other ways?
TEACHER: Yes. Think about it. Look at the dots. Any other ways? Think some more.
STUDENT: Hmmm . . . let me see. Let me see. Oooh. I got it. I can

put 10 of the dots in a group, and then have three groups. Oh
yeah, and then I can keep thinking about other ways too.

This kind of exchange with a preschool student, showing complex
mathematical thinking about division and multiplication, was common in Ms. Neal's class. When I asked her how she was able to get
such young students to engage in such complex material, she said:

> A big part of it is using our time wisely. You see with us, no
> time is wasted. From the minute these students get here we
> are moving . . . plus I believe that these kids are a lot more ca-
> pable than people think. And that's what I tell them. You can
> do more, and I am going to help you do more. We spend a lot
> of time on the basics and then move to more advanced work.
> . . . Some struggle a bit, but a lot of them pick up the concepts
> easier than most people would think.

Mrs. Grayson at Sunnyside High School also kept her 10th-grade
English class on task. From the moment students entered her classroom there was a business-like atmosphere where students knew how
to get started on their independent work. Her lesson transitioned into
her brief lecture for the class period, to group discussion for the students, to independent writing, and then to peer editing, all within
a 50-minute period. I observed the class on several occasions. There
were few interruptions in class, minimal interruptions of the class
flow, and a level of seriousness about completing the work, engaging
in the content, and discussing the work in small groups and then in
the larger class setting. Mrs. Grayson said that she plans her classes
"to the minute, so there is no time lost. I have a lot I am trying to get
done and the students know that." When speaking with the teachers
from each of these schools, I noted four common themes that came
across in terms of what was most critical to their success. The themes
included rigor of the workload, students' time on task, building relationships with students, and displaying an authentic level of care that
was manifested in knowing them personally and challenging them
academically. To reiterate the importance of time spent on task, one of
the teachers from NMS discussed the priority that she gave to keeping
students going.

> If there is one thing I talk to new teachers about it is the im-
> portance of keeping students active and engaged; and the
> best way to do that is by being clear about every step of your

instructional process. Knowing what you are doing from the beginning of the day until the end. Time on task for me is important. When students are on task, you cut down on disruptions and behavior problems because you are moving students along constantly.

What was also obvious in these classrooms was that teacher collaboration was essential. At three of the schools, the teachers met regularly, either by grade level or by subject matter, to plan upcoming lessons and debrief on previous units and lessons. Most important, they frequently used student work and other data to drive their planning and instruction. At PLC, the fourth-grade teachers would bring various examples of students work to compare and contrast what they identified as common problems when students did not understand various concepts. Plans would be discussed to address these areas. At Sunnyside, math teachers examined data across grade levels to identify students who seemed to be in need of academic intervention. At Neighborhood Middle, Mrs. Sanchez made it mandatory for teachers to meet across grade levels and subject areas to analyze student work. She mentioned in one of our conversations, "I am big on data-driven instruction . . . if we don't know where students are, and what they need, we are teaching without context." One of the additional elements of teachers' practice that they believed contributed to higher levels of achievement was that teachers taught more depth than breadth. Despite increased pressures to move students along, a large number of the teachers in this study discussed the importance of going deeper with the teaching of content, rather than addressing it superficially and having students gain a superficial level of comprehension. A teacher from PLC said, "I may not be as far along as the [state] standard says I should be, but what I have covered, my students know and they know it well." Another teacher from PLC said:

> I don't believe in drive-by teaching . . . cover it with blinding speed, throw a bunch of new stuff at the kids . . . kids don't understand a thing, and then keep moving. No, I will re-teach, re-explain, have students give examples, work out problems on the board. I do not move until I know most of my students get it.

The teachers frequently discussed these different approaches during their collaboration meetings. At Ellington, the social studies and language arts teachers discussed the ways they would try to scaffold the various skills and concepts that they were covering in their respective classes. The teachers observed also seemed to teach in ways that recognized the importance of social interaction in teaching and learning (Vygotsky, 1978). In Mr. Dexter's sixth-grade class, students calculated decimals, percentages, and fractions by using coupons from a local grocery store and working in groups to compete to determine which group could save the most money purchasing a particular list of groceries. At Sunnyside, Mrs. St. Jacque taught the scientific process by allowing students to conduct their own hypotheses about the relationship between television watching, time spent on cell phones after school, and students' performance on class tests and quizzes. In one class at PLC, a second-grade teacher had students do intergenerational interviews to compare and contrast the differences in schooling experiences past and present. Students then wrote about these differences and gave a 1-minute informative speech about their findings. The ways in which teachers' practices were displayed, conveyed a sense of competence, confidence, and cultural context of the students, their homes, and the community; and an overall commitment of holding themselves responsible for their students' academic successes and failures.

INTENSIVE ACADEMIC INTERVENTION

Visionary leadership and effective teachers' practices were essential to the overall academic success at the four schools that were observed over a 2-year period. An additional area that was quite evident at each of these sites was the importance of intensive academic enrichment for struggling learners. Struggling students typically struggle because they do not have a firm conceptual understanding of new information. Moreover, the lack of cognitive structures to process new information and create meaning based on prior knowledge creates significant barriers to academic success (Garner, 2007). School personnel at these schools apparently recognized the cognitive disconnects that existed between students and their preferred ways of learning. Students at these sites typically were identified early in the year and then placed in particular programs or recommended for additional supports that were intended to assist them in "catching up," as one teacher at Ellington stated. At PLC, struggling students were encouraged to join the after-school Homework Club, which was focused on providing small-group teaching and learning sessions with three to four students and one teacher, usually around the areas of reading and math. The Homework Club met three times a week for 2 hours and typically had 40 to 45 students in attendance working intensely with teachers. At Sunnyside High School students were provided with after-school tutoring 5 days a week. The tutoring sessions were offered by university college students who provided support in algebra, English, chemistry, biology, and California High School Exit Exam preparation. Teachers and counselors advised particular students to access these services, with varying degrees of success. In several instances, the teachers asked tutors to approach particular students about accessing the tutoring services. A similar approach was in place at Neighborhood Middle. Its enrichment program was used to provide incoming seventh-grade students with academic assistance in algebra and English, with the goal being to help students reach proficiency in these areas by the end of the academic year. At each of these schools teachers discussed the importance of students who needed "extra help to get caught up," as one teacher stated, getting that help. All of the four principals attributed their overall school success to their targeted intervention with struggling students and to providing ongoing assistance to students. The principals also stressed the importance of maintaining these enrichment programs even as budget cuts threatened them. One principal stated:

> I just refuse to cut it. I will cut back staff hours, do fundraising, do whatever it takes to keep my enrichment program. It is so important to have a program that is ongoing that helps those kids. If we cannot help those learners, we cannot be proud of anything else we do.

The enrichment program at PLC was unique because it sought to help students feel proud about being part of the Homework Club. While the program was designed specifically for underperforming students, it was common for even higher achievers to attend daily, in order to receive additional help. Many of the teachers believed that having a wide range of students across the achievement spectrum helped to reduce the negative stigma that might have been associated with the after-school program. The staff talked about "not making academic difficulty a badge of embarrassment" and encouraging parents and students to take an active role in the enrichment programs.

In addition to enrichment programs, a number of teachers at these schools discussed specific steps that they took to assist students. Mrs. Williams, a first-grade teacher at PLC, described how she offered to tutor some of her students at their homes, free of charge, if their parents approved it. One teacher from Ellington said that she regularly kept several of her students in at lunch and recess to give them additional time on their reading proficiency. She stated, "I tell them they have to give up a little something to get better in other areas." At one of the recess sessions I observed, this teacher spent 20 minutes working with four students whom she identified as "not where they should be" in reading. During the session, students worked repeatedly on phonemic awareness, sound–symbol associations, blending, and vocabulary building. On another day, students worked on word attack and comprehension skills. While each of the schools had its own programs that targeted struggling learners, individual teachers also developed specific plans to assist students. There were dozens of teachers in each of the schools who devoted countless hours in their classrooms, in students' homes, in the school-sanctioned program, or at local community centers to provide extra academic support to students. At Ellington, one teacher talked about how she volunteered hours at a local Boys and Girls Club where many of the students went after school. She also coordinated a computer class with the site supervisor, in which students were involved in computer graphics, art, math and reading enrichment.

At Sunnyside, the university staff created a spoken word class that met every Friday for two hours after school. Every Friday, at least 20 to 24 students could be found in the classroom reading literary works, studying persuasive writing skills, and working on oral presentations to convey the rich meaning of texts they had developed during the class. One of the English teachers who was a frequent visitor to the spoken word class talked about the importance of this alternative space for learners.

> It's amazing. Some of the students here I could not get . . . [the students] to do a thing. I see them here [in the spoken word class], and they look like different students . . . they engage, they are excited . . . it's because they are able to use forms of expression that are different than what we usually use. . . . There is a lot about what happens here that we need to transport into the regular classroom.

The spoken word class became a space where students honed many of the skills and concepts that were taught in their English class. Students worked on organizing oral presentations on relevant and complex topics by breaking the topic into parts accessible to listeners, emphasizing key concepts or points, and closing with a recommendation or observation on the relevance of the subject to a wider context. The course content also stressed how students could provide a coherent and effective conclusion that reinforced the presentation in a powerful way or presented the topic in a new light (e.g., as a call to action, importance of intervention). In many ways, the spoken word class became a culturally responsive English course. Students covered many of the grade-level standards for high school English, such as comprehension, argument construction, literary analysis, analogies, metaphors, alliteration, rhetorical devices, thesis and main points of texts, parallelism, and hyperbole. However, they did so in ways that allowed them to talk about police brutality, male–female relationships, family issues, neighborhood concerns, poverty, race, gender, and a multitude of other social realities that students encountered on a daily basis, which made content meaningful, realistic, and pertinent to their own interests while they enhanced core academic skills.

Critical to closing achievement disparities is the building of core academic skills that students may not have developed. The students at the schools observed during this study were fortunate because the school staff recognized the importance of providing additional spaces and places for academic enrichment to occur. There seemed to be a concerted effort across the board to assist students academically, and once students showed progress, the efforts did not stop. What can be taken away from observing these practices and programs at the schools that I studied was a sense that given the demographics of the schools, traditional approaches and routines could not be expected to produce desired results. Transformative interventions were developed that sought to increase students' engagement in schools as well as their academic achievement.

EXPLICIT ACKNOWLEDGMENT OF RACE

As I stated in Chapter 5, the salience of race is always close to the teaching and learning process in U.S. schools. Race has always had a political effect on how people are treated (Marable, 1995). Moreover, education could be a primary example of how racial disparities have played out throughout U.S. history. S. J. Lee's (2005) work documents how issues such as identity formation and school structures create "racialized Americans," or individuals whose racial classification has a profound influence on how they experience schools, which for many of them is negatively. Despite the racial ramifications that influence U.S. schools and students, rarely are there explicit discussions among

school staff about how, when, and where, race and social and political constructions of race influence learning (Beauboeuf-Lafontant &
Smith Augustine, 1996; Tatum, 2007).

What was intriguing about each of these school sites was the ways
the school leaders and most of the staff were comfortable discussing
race, racism, and whether they influenced learning at these schools,
which were made up primarily of students of color. The principals of
these schools insisted that dialogues around race and ethnicity be an
integral part of the professional development that teachers received.
At a time when issues of race typically are excluded from school discourse, or discussed only in private circles, these school leaders were
explicit about addressing achievement, performance, and other school
matters, with race being a frequent subtext. In conversations with
teachers and principals matters pertaining to race were raised even
without being solicited. In one conversation, I asked the principal of
PLC what some of her most pressing concerns at the school were, and
she flatly replied, "My African American boys. I think we can do a better job reaching them. As a group, they are still not where they should
be, and that worries me. We lose so many of them, and I wonder what
more we can all do as educators to help them." She also talked about
how Black boys are "perceived negatively in general" and about how
she has to work hard to make sure that her staff did not harbor those
sentiments about Black males. At Ellington, the principal mentioned
that "this school is majority Black, so when we fail, we are not just failing students, but we are failing Black students, and that means something for the entire Black community."

At Neighborhood, one of the teachers observed that prior to the
current administration, "we never talked about who was learning, and
who was not learning in racial terms . . . but we all knew that it was
[the] Black and Hispanic kids . . . now we talk about it in the open,
which I think is a good thing." What became apparent in each of
these schools was a willingness to be comfortable around race-specific
dialogues. Moreover, it seemed that each principal set a tone to help
teachers become at ease discussing race. At Neighborhood, several
of the teachers mentioned that the recent change in demographics
had important implications for who they were teaching. One teacher
said:

> We are seeing a lot of Mexican students at the school now, and
> so our ELL population has exploded . . . we have to think dif-
> ferently about how we reach all students, but now language is
> a big part of our work.

Comments such as these seem to convey a real sense of how race, ethnicity, and language were part of school discourse, in ways that seemed comfortable and authentic. At Ellington, Mrs. Gooden stated that 3 years earlier she had decided that "my staff would not be afraid to talk about race." She elaborated about the manner in which race was discussed.

> We had this big discussion as a staff where we just put it [race] out there. What are we thinking about race and racism? There was a lot of emotion, a lot of soul searching, a lot of tension, but we kept discussing it over the course of the year, and it really helped us to become closer [as a staff], and now we deal with it.

At Sunnyside students created a club titled "Black and Brown," which was a coalition of Black and Latino students who were concerned about creating racial harmony. The principal said that she embraced the club because "the students deal with race every day . . . how could I not let them come together to stand up against prejudice?" In talking with several teachers at Neighborhood, all of whom were White, it was intriguing to hear them speak unabashedly about racist attitudes that were once part of school staff who are no longer at the school. Another teacher from Neighborhood talked about how teachers do not form racial cliques, but have more racially integrated groups, and stated that "we talk honestly and openly about race." At least two of the principals believed that their staff's willingness to engage in race-related dialogue contributed to the academic performance of the students at their schools. Mrs. Gelson, who is White, said that disaggregating data along racial lines was critical in seeing where certain students were falling short, and she engaged her staff in explicit dialogues about race in staff meetings. Mrs. Sanchez stated that she had meetings where she asked her teachers to offer explanations for the racial disparities in academic outcomes. She was encouraged to hear teachers talk about different expectation levels for different groups, and how they challenged themselves to work through prejudiced notions about groups of people and to put students first.

PARENTAL AND COMMUNITY ENGAGEMENT

Another critical element that was most apparent at each of these schools was the salience of parental engagement. Parents were not seen as opponents in a tug of war for what was in the best interests of children, but were viewed and treated as equal partners working in collaboration with school officials to create optimal learning environments for students at school and home. Research has shown that parental involvement has a significant influence on student achievement (Barnard, 2004; Fan & Chen, 2001). Becher's (1986) literature review on parental involvement revealed that there was "substantial evidence" showing that students whose parents are involved in their schooling have increased academic performance and overall cognitive development. Data from the National Assessment of Educational Progress reveals that parental levels of education and parental involvement in schools have a significant influence on student performance. The NAEP data report a difference of 30 scale points between students with parents who are involved and those without parental involvement (Dietel, 2006).

Researchers also have found that parental involvement is associated with a greater likelihood of their children aspiring to attend college and actually enrolling (Cabrera & Steven, 2000; Horn, 1998), as well as with higher grades (R. B. Lee, 1993; Muller & Kerbow, 1993), higher eighth grade mathematics and reading achievement (R. B. Lee, 1993; Sui-Chu & Douglas, 1996), lower rates of behavioral problems (R. B. Lee, 1993), and a lower likelihood of high school drop-out and truancy (McNeal, 1999). Sanders and Harvey (2002) conducted a case study of school–community partnerships and found that when schools were willing to structure authentic two-way communication with parents, levels of parental involvement increased considerably. Legislation has been passed to create more meaningful ways for parents to play a concerted and more active role in their children's education (Kasting, 1994; National Committee for Citizens in Education, 1987).

The ways in which parental engagement played out in these school sites varied. At PLC, parents frequently were seen on the school premises, volunteering in classrooms, and working with small groups of students, and in some cases were employed as school staff. At Ellington, parents were most visible in the Parent Center, which served as a meeting and resource room at the school for parents who were seeking information, assistance, or insight into the various resources that might be available for their children. The center was staffed by three parents who spent time in classrooms and worked with teachers, principals, and other school personnel to better understand ways to assist students. At Neighborhood Middle, school staff stated that they had a challenging time getting parents to be an integral part of the school community, but were successful in using students to recruit parents to become members of the PTA or School Site Council. At each of these schools teachers and administrators were quick to note that student success was a twofold accomplishment—their work and the commitment of parents. As one teacher from PLC stated, "Parents are these students' first teachers; without them doing their jobs, we could not do what we do." Another teacher from Neighborhood stated that closing the achievement gap required an acknowledgment of the role that schools play, but that "if we [teachers] blame parents when the students are not prepared, we have to give them credit when they are learning, so, yes, this school has parents who are committed." What was also evident were the ways in which school personnel acknowledged roles and actions by parents that were not necessarily visible to them. Mrs. Gelson, who had done a commendable job getting parents to play active roles in school functions, stated that she was not reluctant to "get on" parents about the roles that she expected them to play, and that their willingness to hold their children accountable "makes it easier for us to do our job." The parent presence at Sunnyside and Neighborhood was most intriguing because parental presence typically drops off at the secondary levels. Yet, at various functions that were sponsored by the school, the large numbers of parents in attendance seemed to speak to the ways that school staff worked to get them to attend college night symposium, high school exit exam forums, high school preparation sessions, and teacher–parent conferences. At PLC, parents played an active role in the students' trip to South Africa, were essential partners in fundraising efforts and publicity campaigns about the trip, and were useful in getting local business sponsorship for the event.

What was most apparent about observing parents and other concerned community members at each of these schools was the fact that they were valued. They seemed to be viewed as important stakeholders in the school's mission of academic success. At Ellington, it was rare to visit the school without seeing parents involved on the playground, in the cafeteria, working with teachers in the classroom, playing active roles in the PTA, and having a persistent presence in the building. As Mrs. Gooden said, "Every parent can contribute something . . . and it is my job to find out how they [parents] can help us." Parents' importance for student performance goes without saying. However, what became clear at these schools was that school personnel actively sought ways to include parents, made repeated efforts to get parents involved, and nurtured these relationships continually in ways that seemed to make parents feel wanted, welcomed, and valuable members of the school community. Some researchers have documented how schools can alienate parents and exclude them from playing active roles in schools (Reynolds, 2009). It is critical for school leaders and teachers to be proactive in their efforts to solicit parent involvement, engagement, and authentic partnership. Moreover, school officials must engage in reflective practices to ensure that they have not created hierarchical or exclusionary arrangements at their school sites that make parents feel unwelcome to become a core part of the school community.

FINAL THOUGHTS

Disparate school outcomes have been an integral part of the schooling experiences of nondominant students in the United States since the creation of public schools. Important strides have been made in indicating ways to create more equitable conditions for all students, despite ongoing challenges that have resisted such efforts for educational fairness and justice (C. D. Lee, 2007; Noguera, 2003; Reeves, 2000). Much of what the work in this book has tried to highlight is the complex, complicated, and constantly changing role that race and culture have played in American schooling historically, and how various attitudes, social constructions, identity politics, dispositions, and political, economic, and social conditions about "othered" groups continue to permeate school practices and educational opportunities today. The inability of school leaders, researchers, and policymakers to engage in meaningful work that is centered on school transformation, student empowerment, and community enhancement may dim the prospects for a democratic society and peaceful relations in the United States.

Much of what has to be examined in the debate on the achievement gap is how much a society that purports to be concerned about all of its citizens truly cares about closing the achievement gap and providing educational opportunities for all of its citizens, regardless of their race, class, culture, language, gender, sexual orientation, religious classification, or ability type. Social reproduction theorists posit that underachieving schools are not an accident, but reinforce existing social and economic structures that depend on low-wage, low-skill labor that continues to be a necessity in a capitalistic society (Apple, 1979, 2000; Giroux, 1992; MacLeod, 1995; McLaren, 1991, 2000). The persistent underperformance and disenfranchisement of countless low-income and diverse individuals give credence to these arguments. The plausibility of social reproduction theorists' argument seems even more credible when examining the plight of African American and Latino males, for example, whose educational prospects fare significantly worse than those of most of their White counterparts (Noguera, 2008). The ongoing disenfranchisement of groups such as Black males should cause major alarm. More than half of African American males do not graduate from high school, and they make up only small percentages of the students in AP, Honors, or GATE classrooms (T. C. Howard, 2008). Consequently, it should come as no surprise that Black and Latino males are the largest subgroups of individuals who are incarcerated, prompting some scholars to investigate the prevalence of a school-to-prison pipeline in the name of zero-tolerance policies (Skiba et al., 2003; Wald & Losen, 2003). Black and Latino males make up only 15% of the general population, but almost 70% of the prison population in the United States (Western, 2006). The fact that these numbers continue to be a normalized aspect of the United States without major outrage, probing, anger, or disruption of schooling experiences that might help to lower them adds credence to the claim that there is a lack of concern for certain populations. Duncan (2002) states that certain othered populations are often "beyond love" and calls for radical interventions in educational policy, research, and practice to help marginalized, racialized, and scrutinized populations. Again, the questions that must be posed in light of these tragic realities are, "Who really cares?" (T. C. Howard, 2008), and are we as a nation truly committed to providing all students a first-rate, rigorous, humanistic, culturally and socially responsive education that will allow them to compete in a technological age and global society?

The sense of urgency that is required for improving the educational opportunities and outcomes for students from culturally diverse and low-income backgrounds continues to gain importance as groups that once were considered "minority groups" collectively make up a growing segment of the nation's population. Hence, the future prosperity, safety, economic infrastructure, technological competitiveness, and political vitality of the country rely heavily on the manner in which we prepare all citizens, but have increased importance for those individuals who will make up the nation's core in the decades to come—culturally, racially, and linguistically diverse students. The fact that women, people of color, low-income individuals, and people born outside of the United States will make up an overwhelming majority of the nation's workforce in the next decade also underscores the need to create a manner of education that offers all students an opportunity for success. Anyon's (2005) insights into how the political economy will continue to shape labor and political opportunity in this technology-driven society cannot fall on deaf ears. Moreover, she calls for an analysis of the "proactive role of the federal government in maintaining poverty" (p. 17), which subsequently affects schools and harms the children who attend them. The increasing nature of globalization (Banks, 2009) will stress the value of highly trained, culturally competent, and globally literate citizens to engage in international trade and global relations that will help to sustain the United States as an economic, social, and political world leader. Where will that work-force come from? Where will the intellectual leadership and political acumen come from if we continue to neglect students from diverse groups and low-income backgrounds?

There is also a moral responsibility that has to be contemplated when examining disparate educational outcomes for growing num-bers of young people in the United States. Much of what has been lost for countless young people is any semblance of hope. Hope is a source of strength, an asset of possibility, and a tangible way of grasping for a reality that is not seen, but is believed to be within reach. Hope offers a response to the anxiety, stress, pain, suffering, misery, anger, and angst that seem to have become staples in urban, rural, and suburban communities across the nation. Duncan-Andrade (2009) makes a poi-gnant call for what he refers to as "critical hope," which "audaciously defies the dominant ideology of defense, entitlement, and preserva-tion of privileged bodies at the expense of the policing, disposal and dispossession of marginalized 'others'" (p. 9). Each of us has a moral responsibility to ponder what role we are taking to challenge injustice, what questions we are posing to eradicate discrimination, and what actions we are engaged in to end exclusion and oppression no mat-ter what shape or form it takes. How do we respond to the pain and suffering that young people experience in their homes, schools, and communities? As educators, whether we are practitioners, research-ers, or youth advocates, our work is important because it is centered squarely on the day-to-day possibilities of young people. Our work must operate from a paradigm of possibility, a stand of empowerment, a firm belief in the intellectual prowess of young people, and a stance that recognizes the unlimited potential that low-income students and students from diverse backgrounds bring from home to their schools every day. Much of the excitement and hope that young people bring from home are quickly extinguished by the institutions and people charged with developing and enhancing good feelings, academic and social development, and intellectual growth—schools and educators. Our work must help parents, students, teachers, and administrators to recognize and use the best strategies, skills, supportive practices and policies, reliable research, and ideological stances that provide trans-formative interventions for improved academic outcomes and life chances. Not only do the lives of young people depend on our work as transformative educators, but so do all of our collective fates.

References

Abrami, P. C., Bernard, R. M., Borokhovski, A. W., Surkes, M. A., Tamim, R., & Zhang, D. (2008). Instructional interventions affecting critical thinking skills and dispositions: A stage one meta-analysis. *Review of Educational Research, 78*(4), 1102–1134.

Academic English Mastery Program. Retrieved on March 23, 2008 from http://www.learnmedia.com/aemp/aempoverview.html.

Alexander, K., Entwisle, D.R., & Dauber, S. (1994) . *On the success of failure: A reassessment of the effects of retention in the primary grades.* New York: Cambridge University Press.

Alim, H. A., & Baugh, J. (2007). *Talkin Black talk: Language, education, and social change.* New York: Teachers College Press.

Anderson, J. D. (1988). *The education of Blacks in the south, 1860–1935.* Chapel Hill: University of North Carolina Press.

Anyon, J. (2005). *Radical possibilities: Public policy, urban education, and a new social movement.* New York: Routledge.

Apple, M. W. (1979). *Ideology and curriculum.* Boston: Routledge & Kegan Paul.

Apple, M. W. (2000). *Official knowledge: Democratic education in a conservative age.* New York: Routledge.

Aronson, E., Wilson, T. D., & Akert, R. M. (2002). *Social psychology* (4th ed.). Upper Saddle River, NJ: Prentice Hall.

Artiles, A. J. (1998). The dilemma of difference: Enriching disproportionality discourse with theory and context. *Journal of Special Education, 31,* 32–36.

Artiles, A. J., & Trent, S. C. (1994). Overrepresentation of minority students in special education: A continuing debate. *Journal of Special Education, 27,* 410–437.

Artiles, A. J., Trent, S. C., & Palmer, J. D. (2004). Culturally diverse students in special education: Legacies and prospects. In J. A. Banks & C. A. M. Banks (Eds.). The handbook of research on multicultural education (2nd Ed). (pp. 716–735). San Francisco: Jossey-Bass.

Au, K., & Jordan, C. (1981). Teaching reading to Hawaiian children: Finding a culturally appropriate solution. In H. Trueba, G. Guthrie, & K. Au (Eds.), *Culture and the bilingual classroom: Studies in classroom ethnography* (pp. 139–152). Rowley, MA: Newbury.

Au, K. (1993). *Literacy instruction in multicultural settings.* New York: Harcourt Brace.

Avery, P. G., & Walker, C. (1993). Prospective teachers' perceptions of ethnic and gender differences in academic achievement. *Journal of Teacher Education, 44*(1), 27–37.

Axtell, J. (1985). *The invasion within: The contest of cultures in colonial North America.* New York: Oxford University Press.

Baldwin, J. (1988). A talk to teachers. In R. Simonson & S. Walker (Eds.), *Multicultural literacy* (pp. 3–12). St. Paul, MN: Graywolf Press.

Balfour, L. (2001). The evidence of things not said: James Baldwin and the promise of American democracy. Ithaca: Cornell University Press.

Banks, J. A. (1989). Integrating the curriculum with ethnic content: Approaches and guidelines. In J. A. Banks & C. A. M. Banks (Eds.), *Multicultural education: Issues and perspectives* (pp. 189–207). Boston: Allyn & Bacon.

Banks, J. A. (1990). *Teaching strategies for the social studies: Inquiry, valuing, and decision making.* New York: Longman.

Banks, J. A. (1995). The historical reconstruction of knowledge about race: Implications for transformative teaching. *Educational Researcher, 24(2),* 15–25.

Banks, J. A. (1996). *Multicultural education, transformative knowledge, and action; Historical and contemporary perspectives.* New York: Teachers College Press.

Banks, J. A. (2002). Race, knowledge construction, and education in the USA: Lessons and history. *Race Ethnicity and Education, 5*(1), 7–27

Banks, J. A. (2004). Multicultural education: Historical development, dimensions, and practice. In J. A. Banks & C. A. M. Banks (Eds.), *Handbook of research in multicultural education* (2nd. Ed). (pp. 2–29). San Francisco: Jossey Bass.

Banks, J. A. (2006). *Race, culture, and education: The selected works of James A. Banks.* London & New York: Routledge.

Banks, J. A. (2009). *The Routledge international companion to multicultural education.* New York: Routledge.

Banks, J. A. & Banks, C. A. M. (2004). *Handbook of research on multicultural education.* (2nd edition). San Francisco: Jossey-Bass.

Barnard, W. M. (2004). Parent involvement in elementary school and educational attainment. *Children and Youth Services Review, 26,* 39–62.

Barnett, W. S. & Yarosz, D. (2004, August). *Who goes to preschool and why does it matter?* Preschool Policy Matters No. 8. New Brunswick, NJ: National Institute for Early Education research.

Barry, N. H., & Lechner, J. V. (1995). Preservice teachers' attitude about and awareness of multicultural teaching and learning. *Teaching and Teacher Education, 11*(2), 149–161.

Bartolome, L. I. (1994). Beyond the methods fetish: Toward a humanizing pedagogy. *Harvard Educational Review, 64*(2), 173–194.

Barton, P. (2004). Why does the gap persist? *Educational Leadership 62*(3), 3–12.

Beauboeuf-Lafontant, T. M. (1999). A movement against and beyond boundaries: "Politically relevant teaching" among African American teachers. *Teachers College Record, 100*(4), 702–723.

Beauboeuf-Lafontant, T., & Smith Augustine, D. (Eds.), (1996). *Facing racism in education* (2nd. Ed). Cambridge, MA: Harvard Education Review Press.

Becher, R. (1986). *Parents and schools*. ERIC Clearinghouse on Elementary and early childhood education No. ED269137. Retrieved May 16, 2008, from http://www.ericdigests.org/pre924/parents. htm

Bell, D. A. (1992). *Faces at the bottom of the well*. New York: Basic Books.

Bell, D. (2002). *Ethical ambition*. New York: Bloomsbury.

Bennett, D. H. (1988). The party of fear: From Nativists movement to the New right in American history. Chapel Hill: University of North Carolina Press.

Bernstein, B. (1961). Social class and linguistic development: A theory of social learning. In A. Halsey, J. Floud, & C. Anderson (Eds.), *Education, economy, and society* (pp. 288–314). New York: Free Press.

Berry, B. (1995). *Keeping talented teachers: Lessons learned from the North Carolina teaching fellows* (Report commissioned by North Carolina Teaching Fellow Commission). Raleigh, NC: Public School Forum.

Bloom, B., Davis, A., & Hess, R. (1965). *Compensatory education for cultural deprivation*. New York: Holt, Rinehart, and Winston.

Bobo, L., Kluegel, J. R., & Smith, R. A. (1997). Laissez faire racism: The crystallization of a 'kinder, gentler' anti-Black ideology. In S. Tuch & J. Martin (Eds.), *Racial attitudes in the 1990s: Continuity and change* (pp. 15–44). Westport, CT: Praeger

Boggs, S.T. (1985). The meaning of question and narrative to Hawaiian children. In C. B. Cazden, V. H. John, & D. Hymes (Eds.), *Function of language in the classroom* (pp. 299–327). Prospect Heights, IL: Waveland.

Bonilla-Silva, E. (1997). Rethinking racism: Toward a structural interpretation. *American Sociological Review, 62,* 465–480.

Bonilla-Silva, E. (2003). *Racism without racists: colorblind racism and the persistence of racial inequality in the United States*. Lanham, MD: Rowman & Littlefield.

Bourdieu, P. (1986). The forms of capital. In J. G. Richardson (Ed.), *The handbook of theory and research for the sociology of education* (pp. 241–258). Westport, CT: Greenwood Press.

Bowden, H. (1981). *American Indians and Christian missions*. Chicago: University of Chicago Press.

Bowles, S., & Gintis, H. (1976). *School in capitalist America*. New York: Basic Books.

Boykin, A. W. (1994). Harvesting culture and talent: African American children and educational reform. In R. Rossi (Ed.), *Educational reform and at-risk students* (pp. 116–138). New York: Teachers College Press.

Brooks-Gunn, J., & Duncan, G. J. (1997). The effects of poverty on children. *The Future of Children, 7*(2), 55–71.

Brown, J. S., Collins, A., & Duguid, S. (1989). Situated cognition and the culture of learning. *Educational Researcher, 18*(1), 32–42.

Brown, K., & Cole, M. (1997, Fall). Fifth dimension and 4-H: Complementary goals and strategies. *FOCUS: A monograph of the 4-H Center for Youth Development, 3*(4).

Bullivant, B. M. (1993). Culture: Its nature and meanings for educators. In J.A. Banks & C.A.M. Banks (Eds.). *Multicultural education: Issues and perspectives* (2nd ed., pp. 29–47). Boston: Allyn & Bacon.

Bullock, H. A. (1970). *A history of Negro education in the south: From 1619 to the present.* New York: Praeger.

Butchart. R. E. (1980). *Northern schools, southern Blacks, and Reconstruction: Freedmen's education, 1862–1875.* Westport, CT: Greenwood Press.

Cabrera, A. F., & Steven, M. (2000). Overcoming the tasks on the path to college for America's disadvantaged. *New Directions for Institutional Research, 27*(3), 31–43.

Caldwell, C. (1830). *Thoughts on the original unity of the human race.* Whitefish, MT: Kessinger Publishers.

California Department of Education (2006). Retrieved on June 1, 2008 from http://www.cde.gov/data quest.

Carter, P. L. (2005). *Keepin' it real: School success beyond Black and White.* New York: Oxford University Press.

Cazden, C. (2000). *Classroom discourse: The language of teaching and learning* (2nd ed.). Portsmouth, NH: Heinemann.

Chan, S. S. (1993). *Asian Americans: An interpretive history.* New York: Twayne.

Chernow, B.A., & Vallasi, G.A. (Eds.). (1993). *The Columbia encyclopedia* (5th ed.). New York: Columbia University Press.

Civil, M., & Khan, L. H. (2001). Mathematics instruction developed from a garden theme. *Teaching Children Mathematics, 7*(7), 400–405.

Cochran-Smith, M. (2003). The multiple meanings of multicultural teacher education. *Teacher Education Quarterly, 30*(2), 7–26.

Cole, J. B., & Guy-Scheftall, B. (2003). *Gender talk: The struggle for women's equality in African American communities.* New York: Ballantine.

Cole, M. (1996). *Cultural psychology: A once and future discipline.* Cambridge, MA: The Belknap Press.

Cole, M. (1997). Cultural mechanisms of cognitive development. In E. Amsel & K. A. Renninger (Eds.), *Change and development: Issues of theory, method, and application* (pp. 245–263). New Jersey: Erlbaum.

Cole, M. (1998). Can cultural psychology help us think about diversity? *Mind, Culture and Activity, 5*(4), 291–304.

Cole, M. (2000). Struggling with complexity: The handbook of child psychology at the millennium [Review of essay]. *Human Development, 43*(6), 369–375.

Cole, M. (2001). Remembering history in sociocultural research. Human Development. Special Issue: *Cultural Minds, 44* (2–3), 166–169.

Cole, M., & Engestrom, Y. (1993). A cultural historical approach to distributed cognition. In G. Salomon (Ed.), *Distributed cognitions* (pp. 1–46). Cambridge: Cambridge University Press.

Cole, M., & Engestrom, Y. (1995). Commentary. *Human Development, 38*(1), 9–24.

Coleman, J. S., Campbell, E. Q., Hobson, C. J., McPartland, J., Mood, A. M., Weinfeld, F. C., et al. (1966). *Equality of educational opportunity.* Washington, DC: Government Printing Office.

College Board. (1999). *Reaching the top: A report of the National Task force on minority high achievement.* New York: College Board.

Conchas, G. Q. (2006). *The color of success: Race and high achieving urban youth.* New York: Teachers College Press.

Cremin, L. A. (1970a). *American education: The colonial experience, 1607–1783.* New York: Harper & Row.

Cremin, L. A. (1970b). *American education: The national experience, 1783–1876.* New York; Harper & Row.

Cremin, L. A. (1988). *American education: The metropolitan experience, 1876–1980.* New York: Harper & Row.

Crenshaw, K. W. (1997). Color-blind dreams and racial nightmares; Reconfiguring racism in the post-civil rights era. In T. Morrison & C. B. Lacour (Eds.), *Birth of a nation'hood* (pp. 97–168). New York: Pantheon Books.

Crew, R. (2007). *Only connect: The way to save our schools.* New York: Crichton Books.

Cross, T., Bazron, B., Dennis, K. & Isaacs, M. (1989). *Towards a culturally competent system of care: A monograph on effective services for minority children who are severely emotionally disturbed* (Vol. I). Washington, DC: Georgetown University Center for Child and Human Development.

Cunningham, P. M. (2005). *Phonics they use: Words for reading and writing* (4th ed.). New York: Pearson.

Dalton, B., Sable, J., & Hoffman, L. (2006). *Characteristics of the 100 largest public-elementary and secondary school districts in the United States: 2003-04++* (INCES 2006-329). Washington, DC: National Center for Education Statistics.

Dalton, S. S. (2008). *Five standards for effective teaching: How to succeed with all learners.* San Francisco, CA: Wiley & Sons.

Damen, L. (1987). *Culture learning: The fifth dimension on the language classroom.* Reading, MA: Addison-Wesley.

Darder, A. (1991). *Culture and power in the classroom: A critical foundation for bicultural education.* Westport, CT: Bergin & Garvey.

Darder, A., & Torres, R. (2004). *After race: Racism after multiculturalism.* New York: New York University Press.

Darling-Hammond, L. (1997). *The right to learn.* San Francisco: Jossey-Bass.

Darling-Hammond, L. (2004). What happens to a dream deferred? The continuing quest for equal educational opportunity. In J. A. Banks & C. A. M. Banks (Eds.), *Handbook of research on multicultural education.* (2nd ed.) (pp. 607–630). San Francisco: Jossey-Bass.

Darling-Hammond, L. (2007). The flat earth and education: How America's commitment to equity will determine our future. *Educational Researcher, 36*(6), 318–334.

Darling-Hammond, L., & Sykes, G. (2003). Wanted: A national teacher supply policy for education: The right way to meet the "high qualified teacher" challenge. *Educational Policy Analysis Archives, 11*(3). Retrieved June 30, 2007, from http: //epaa.asu.edu/epaa/v11n33/

Davis, K. (1997). *Exploring the intersection between cultural competency and managed behavioral health care policy: Implications for state and county mental health agencies.* Alexandria, VA: National Technical Assistance Center for State Mental Health Planning.

Delgado, R. (Ed.). (1995). *Critical race theory: The cutting edge.* Philadelphia: Temple University Press.

Delgado, R., & Stefancic, J. (1997). (Eds.), *Critical White studies: Looking behind the mirror.* Philadelphia, PA: Temple University Press.

Delgado, R., & Stefancic, J. (2001). *Critical race theory.* New York: New York University Press.

Delpit, L. D. (1995). *Other people's children: Cultural conflict in the classroom.* New York: New Press.

DeNavas-Walt, C., Proctor, B. D. & Smith, J. (2007). *Income, poverty, and health insurance coverage in the United States: 2006* (U.S. Census Bureau current population report, pp. 60–233). Washington, DC: U.S. Government Printing Office. Retrieved January 29, 2008, from http://www.census.govprod/2007pubs/p60-233.pdf

Derman-Sparks, L., Phillips, C. B., & Hilliard, A. G. (1997). *Teaching/learning anti-racism: A developmental approach.* New York: Teachers College Press.

Dietel, R. (2006). *Get smart: Nine ways to help your child succeed in school.* San Francisco: Jossey-Bass.

Dixson, A. D. & Rousseau, C. K. (2006). *Critical race theory in education.* New York: Routledge.

Donato, R. (1997). *The other struggle for equal schools: Mexican Americans during the civil rights era.* Albany: State University New York Press.

Dreeben, R. (1987). Closing the divide: What teachers and administrators can do to help Black students reach their reading potential. *American Educator, 11*(4), 28–35.

D'Souza, D. (1995). *The end of racism: Principles for a multiracial society.* New York: Free Press.

DuBois, W. E. B. (1903). *Souls of Black folk*: New York: Heron Press.

Duncan, G. A. (2002). Beyond love: A critical race ethnography of the schooling of adolescent Black males. *Equity and Excellence, 35*(2), 131–142.

Duncan-Andrade, J. M. R. (2008). Visions of teachers leaving no more children behind. In K. M. Teel & J. E. Obidah (Eds.), *Building racial and cultural competence in the classroom* (pp. 111–126). New York: Teachers College Press.

Duncan-Andrade, J. M. R. (2009). Note to educators: Hope required when growing roses in concrete. *Harvard Educational Review, 79*(2), 1–13.

Dunn, R., & Dunn, K. (1992). *Teaching elementary students through their individual learning styles.* Boston: Allyn & Bacon.

Easter, L. M., Shultz, E. L., Neyhar, T. K., & Reck, U. M. (1999). Weighty perceptions: A study of the attitudes and beliefs of preservice teacher education students regarding diversity and urban education. *The Urban Review, 31*(2), 205–220.

Edelman, M. W. (2008). *The sea is so wide and my boat is so small.* New York: Hyperion.

Eisenmann, L. (2001). Creating a framework for interpreting US women's educational history: lessons from historical lexicography. *History of Education, 30*(5), 453–470. Retrieved July 16, 2009, from http://www.informaworld.com/smpp/title~content=t713599897~db=all~tab=issueslist~branches=30 - v30

El Nasser, H. (2004, March 18). Census projects growing diversity: By 2050 Population burst, societal shifts. *USA Today*, p. 1A.

Engestrom, Y. (1987). *Learning by expanding: An activity-theoretical approach to developmental research*. Helsinki: Orienta-Konsultit.

Engestrom, Y. (1990). *Learning, working, imagining: Twelve studies in activity theory*. Helsinki, Finland: Orienta-Konsultit.

Engestrom, Y. (1999). Activity theory and individual and social transformation. In Y. Engestrom, R. Miettinen, & R. Punamaki (Eds.), *Perspectives on activity theory* (19–38). New York: Cambridge University Press.

Ennis, R. H. (1989). Critical thinking and subject specificity: Clarification and needed research. *Educational Researcher, 18*(3), 4–10.

Ensign, J. (2003). Including culturally relevant math in an urban school. *Educational Studies, 34*, 414–423.

Erickson, F. E. (1986). Cultural difference and science education. *The Urban Review, 18*(2), 117–124

Erickson, F. (2002). Culture and human development. *Human Development, 45*(4), 299–306.

Erickson, F., & Mohatt, G. (1982). Cultural organization of participation practices in two classrooms of Indian students. In G. Spindler (Ed.), *Doing the ethnography of schooling* (pp. 132–174). New York: Holt, Rinehart & Winston.

Fan, X. T., & Chen, M. (2001). Parental involvement and students' academic achievement: A growth modeling analysis. *Journal of Experimental Education, 70*, 27–61.

Ferguson, A. A. (2003). *Bad boys: Public schools in the making of Black masculinity*. Ann Arbor: University of Michigan Press.

Ferguson, R. E. (1991). Paying for public education: New evidence on how and why money matters. *Harvard Journal on Legislation, 28*(2), 465–498.

Ferguson, R. (2000). *A diagnostic analysis of Black-White SAT disparities in Shaker Heights, Ohio*. Washington, DC: Brookings Institute.

Flores-Gonzales, N. (1999). Puerto Rican high achievers: An example of ethnic and academic identity. *Anthropology and Education Quarterly, 30*(3), 343–362.

Ford, D. Y. (1996). *Reversing the underachievement among gifted Black students: Promising practices and programs*. New York: Teachers College Press.

Fordham, S. (1991). Racelessness in private schools: Should we deconstruct the racial and cultural identity of African American adolescents? *Teachers College Record, 92*, 470–484.

Fordham, S. (1998). Racelessness as a factor in Black students' school success: Pragmatic strategy or Pyrrhic victory? *Harvard Educational Review, 58*, 54–84.

Fordham, S., & Ogbu, J. (1986). Black students' school success: Coping with the burden of "acting White." *The Urban Review, 18*(3), 176–206.

Foster, M. (1989). "It's cookin' now": A performance analysis of the speech events of a Black teacher in an urban community college. *Language in Society, 18*(1), 1–29.

Foster, M. (1993). Educating for competence in community and culture. *Urban Education, 27*(4), 370–394.

Foster, M. (1997). *Black teachers on teaching*. New York: The New Press.

Franklin, J. H. (1988). *From slavery to freedom: A history of the Negro American*. New York: Knopf.

Fraser, J. W. (2001). *The school in the United States: A documented history*. New York: McGraw-Hill.

Freire, P. (1970). Cultural action for freedom. *Harvard Educational Review, VIII*, 26–39.

Freire, P. (1973). *Pedagogy of the oppressed*. New York: Continuum Press.

Gardner, H. (1993). *Frames of mind: The theory of multiple intelligences*. New York: Basic Books.

Gardner, H. (1995). Cracking open the IQ box. In S. Fraser (Ed.), *The bell curve wars: Race, intelligence, and the future of America* (pp. 23–35). New York: Basic Books.

Garner, B. K. (2007). *Getting to got it*. Alexandria, VA: Association for Supervision and Curriculum Development.

Gay, G. (1995). Mirror images on community issues. In C. Sleeter & P. McLaren (Eds.), *Multicultural education, critical pedagogy and the politics of difference* (pp. 155–190). Albany, NY: State University of New York Press.

Gay, G. (2000). *Culturally responsive teaching: Theory, research, and practice*. New York: Teachers College Press.

Gay, G. & Howard, T. C. (2000). Multicultural education for the 21st century. *The Teacher Educator, 36*(1), 1–16.

Gay, G., & Kirkland, K. (2003). Developing cultural critical consciousness and self-reflection in pre-service teacher education. *Theory Into Practice, 42*(3), 181–187.

Genesse, F., Leary, K., Sounder, W., & Christian, D. (2005). English language learners in U.S. schools: An overview of research findings. *Journal of Education for Students Placed At Risk,10*(4), 363–385.

Gillborn, D. (2008). *Racism and education: Coincidence or conspiracy?* New York: Routledge.

Giroux, H.A. (1992). Post-colonial ruptures and democratic possibilities: Multiculturalism as anti-racist pedagogy. *Cultural Critique, 21*, 5–40.

Glazer, N. & Moynihan, D.P. (1963). *Beyond the melting pot: the Negroes, Puerto Ricans, Jews, Italians, and Irish of New York City*. Cambridge, MA: M.I.T. Press.

Goldschmidt, P., & Wang, J. (1999). When can school affect dropout behavior? A longitudinal multilevel analysis. *American Educational Research Journal, 36*, 715–738.

Gonzales, G. (1990). *Chicano education in the segregation era: 1915–1945*. Philadelphia: Balch Institute.

Gonzales, M.G. (1999). *Mexicanos: A history of Mexicans in the U.S.* Bloomington, IN: Indiana University Press.

Gotanda, N. (1991). A critique of "Our constitution is color-blind: *Stanford Law Review, 44*, 1–68.

Gould, S. J. (1981). *The mismeasure of man*. New York: Norton.

Grant, C. A., & Sleeter, C. E. (2007). *Doing multicultural education for achieve-*

ment and equity. New York: Routledge.

Green, J. E., & Weaver, R. A. (1992). Who aspires to teach? A descriptive study of pre-service teachers. *Contemporary Education, 63*(3), 234–238.

Grisson, J. B. & Shepard, L. A. (1989). Repeating and dropping out of school. In L. A. Sheppard & M. L. Smith (Eds.), *Flunking grades: Research and policies on retention* (pp. 34–63). New York: Falmer Press.

Gutierrez, K. D. (2002). Studying cultural practices in urban learning communities. *Human Development, 45,* 312–321.

Gutierrez, K., Baquedano-López, P. & Tejeda, C. (1999). Rethinking diversity: Hybridity and hybrid language practices in the third space. *Mind, Culture, & Activity 6*(4), 286–303.

Gutierrez, K., & Rogoff, B. (2003). Cultural ways of learning: Individual traits or repertoires of practice. *Educational Researcher, 32*(5), 19–25.

Gutierrez, R. A. (2004). Ethnic Mexicans in historical and social science scholarship. In In J. A. Banks & C. A. M. Banks (Eds.), *Handbook of research on multicultural education* (2nd. ed., pp. 261–287). San Francisco: Jossey-Bass.

Gutstein, E., Lipman, P., Hernandez, P., & de los Reyes, R. (1997). Culturally relevant mathematics teaching in a Mexican American context. *Journal for Research in Mathematics Education, 28*(6), 709–737.

Haberman, M. (1991). The pedagogy of poverty versus good teaching. *Phi Delta Kappan, 73*(4), 290–294.

Hadaway, N. L., & Florez, V. (1987–1988). Diversity in the classroom: Are our teachers prepared? *Teacher Education & Practice, 4*(1), 25–30.

Hale, J. E. (2001). *Learning while Black: Creating educational excellence for African American children*. Baltimore: Johns Hopkins Press.

Hale-Benson, J. (1986). *Black children: Their roots, culture, and learning styles*. Baltimore, MD: Johns Hopkins University Press.

Hall, S., & Moats, L. (1999). *Straight talk about reading: How parents can make a difference in the early years*. Lincolnwood, IN: Contemporary Books.

Haney-Lopez, I. (1996). White by law. In R. Delgado (Ed.), *Critical race theory: The cutting edge* (pp. 542–550). Philadelphia: Temple University Press.

Harris, C. (1993). Whiteness as property. *Harvard Law Review, CVI,* 1701–1791.

Harry, B., & Anderson, M. G. (1999). The social construction of high-incidence disabilities: The effect on African American males. In V. C. Polite & J. E. Davis (Eds.) *African American Males in School and society* (pp. 34–50). New York: Teachers College Press.

Harry, B., & Klingner, J. (2006). *Why are so many minority students in special education?* New York: Teachers College Press.

Heath, S. B. (1983). *Ways with words: Language, life, and work in communities and classrooms*. New York: Cambridge University Press.

Herrnstein, R., & Murray, C. (1994). *The bell curve: Intelligence and class structure in American life*. New York: Free Press.

Hess, D. E. (2009). *Controversy in the classroom: The democratic power of discussion*. New York: Routledge.

Hickson, J., Land, A. J., & Aikman, G. (1994). Learning style differences in middle school pupils from four ethnic backgrounds. *School Psychology International, 15,* 349–359.

Higham, J. (1972). *Strangers in the land: Patterns of American nativism 1860–1925*. New York: Atheneum.

Hilfiker, D. (2002). *Urban injustice: How ghettos happen*. New York: Seven Stories Press.

Hill, P., & Roza, M. (2004). *How within-district spending inequalities help some schools fail*. Washington, DC: Brookings Institute.

Hirsch, E. D. (1987). *Cultural literacy: What every American needs to know*. Boston: Houghton Mifflin.

Hobbs, F., & Stoops, N. (2002). *Demographic trends in the 20th century* (U.S. Census 2000 Special Reports, Series CENSR-4). Washington, DC: U.S. Government Printing Office.

Hodgkinson, H. (2001). Educational demographics: What teachers need to know. *Educational Leadership, 58*(4), 6–11

Hollie, S. (2001). Acknowledging the language of African American students: Instructional strategies. *The English Journal, 90*, 54–59.

Hollins, E. R., & Guzman, M. T. (2005). Research on preparing teachers for diverse populations. In M. Cochran-Smith & K. M. Zeichner (Eds.), *Studying teacher education: The report of the AERA panel on research and teacher education* (pp. 477–548). Mahwah, NJ: Erlbaum.

Holzman, M., (2006) *Public education and Black male students: The 2006 State Report Card*. Schott Educational Inequity Index, Cambridge, MA: The Schott Foundation for Public Education.

hooks, b. (1995). *Killing rage*. New York: Holt.

Horn, J. G. (1998). Stakeholders' evaluation of rural/small schools. *Rural Educator, 20*(1), 5–11.

Horsman, R. (1981). *Race and manifest destiny: The origins of American racial Anglo-Saxonism*. Cambridge, MA: Harvard University Press.

Howard, G. R. (2006). *We can't teach what we don't know: White teachers, multiracial schools* (2nd ed). New York: Teachers College Press.

Howard, T. C. (2001a). Powerful pedagogy for African American students: Conceptions of culturally relevant pedagogy. *Journal of Urban Education, 36*(2), 179–202.

Howard, T. C. (2001b). Telling their side of the story: African American students' perceptions of culturally relevant teaching. *The Urban Review, 33*(2) 131–149.

Howard, T. C. (2003a). Culturally relevant pedagogy: Ingredients for critical teacher reflection. *Theory Into Practice, 42*(3), 195–202.

Howard, T. C. (2003b) "A tug of war for our minds": African American high school students' perceptions of their academic identities and college aspirations. *The High School Journal, 87*(1), 4–17.

Howard, T. C. (2008). "Who really cares?" The disenfranchisement of African American males in preK–12 schools: A critical race theory perspective. *Teachers College Record, 110*(5), 954–985.

Howard, T. C. & Aleman, G. R. (2007). Teacher capacity for diverse learners: What do teachers need to know? In M. C. Smith, S. Feiman-Nemser, D. J. McIntyre & K. E. Demers (Eds.), *Handbook of research on teacher education.* (pp. 157–174). New York: Routledge.

Howard, T. C. & Reynolds, R.E. (2009). Examining parent involvement in reversing the underachievement of African American students in middle-class schools. *Educational Foundations, 22*(1–2), 79–88.

Huber, L. P., Johnson, R. N., & Kohli, R. (2006). Naming racism: A conceptual look at internalized racism in U.S. schools. *Chicano-Latino Law Review. 26,* 183–200.

Ingold, T. (1994). Introduction to culture. In T. Ingold (Ed.), *Companion encyclopedia of anthropology: Humanity, culture, and social life* (pp. 329–349). London: Routledge.

Institute of Industrial Engineers. (2009). *What is change?* Retrieved December 2, 2008, from http://www.iienet2.org/Details.aspx?id=3290

Irvine, J. J. (1990). *Black students and school failure.* Westport, CT: Greenwood Press.

Irvine, J. J. (2003). *Educating teachers for diversity: Seeing with a cultural eye.* New York: Teachers College Press.

Irvine, J. J., & Armento, B. (2001). *Culturally responsive teaching: Lesson planning for the elementary and middle grades.* New York: McGraw-Hill.

Irvine, J. J. & Irvine, R. W. (1983). The impact of the desegregation process on the education of Black students. *Journal of Negro Education, 52*(4), 410–422.

Irvine, J. J. & York, D. E. (1993). Teacher perspectives: Why do African-American, Hispanic, and Vietnamese students fail? In S. W. Rothstein (Ed.), *Handbook of schooling in urban America* (pp. 161–173). Westport, CT: Greenwood Press.

Isaacs, M., & Benjamin, M. (1991). *Towards a culturally competent system of care. Programs which utilize culturally competent principles.* (Vol. II). Washington, DC: Georgetown University Child Development Center.

Jacobson, M. F. (1999). *Whiteness of a different color: European immigrants and the alchemy of race.* Cambridge, MA: Harvard University Press.

Jaschik, S. (2008, August 27). The SAT's growing gaps. *Inside Higher Ed.* Retrieved November 30, 2009, from http://www.insidehighered.com/news/2008/08/27/sat

Jencks, C. (1972). *Inequality: A reassessment of the effect of family and schooling in America.* New York: Basic Books.

Jencks, C. & Phillips, M. (Eds.). (1998). *The Black–White test score gap.* Washington DC: Brookings Institute.

Jensen, A. R. (1969). How much can we boost IQ and scholastic achievement? *Harvard Educational Review, 39*(1), 1–123.

Jimerson, S. R. (1999). On the failure of failure: Examining the association between early grade retention and education and employment outcomes during late adolescence. *Journal of School Psychology, 37,* 243–272.

Johnson, L. (2002). "My eyes have been opened": White teachers and racial awareness. *Journal of Teacher Education, 53*(2), 153–167.

Kaestle, C. F. (1983). *Pillars of the republic: Common schools and American society, 1780–1860.* New York: Hill and Wang.

Kasting, A. (1994). Respect, responsibility, and reciprocity: The 3 Rs of parent involvement. *Childhood Education, 70*(3), 146–150.

Kellow, T. J., & Jones, B. D. (2005). Stereotype threat in African American high school students: An initial investigation. *Current Issues in Education [Online], 8*(15). Retrieved July 15, 2008, from http://cie.ed.asu.edu/volume8/number 20

KewalRamani, A., Gilbertson, L., Fox, M., & Provasnik, S. (2007). *Status and trends in the education of racial and ethnic minorities* (NCES, 2007-039). Washington, DC: National Center for Education Statistics. Institute of Education Sciences. U.S. Department of Education.

King, J. E. (1991). Dysconscious racism: Ideology, identity, and the miseducation of teachers. *The Journal of Negro Education, 60*(2), 133–146.

King, M. L. (1967). Beyond Vietnam: A time to break silence. (Speech given by Dr. Martin Luther King to the assembled "Clergy and Laymen Concerned About Vietnam," at Riverside Church in New York City on April 4, 1967.)

Knapp, M., & Wolverton, S. (2004). Social class and schooling. In J. A. Banks & C. A. M. Banks (Eds.), *Handbook of research on multicultural education* (2nd ed, pp. 656–681). San Francisco, CA: Jossey-Bass.

Kochman, T. (1981). *Black and white styles in conflict.* Chicago: University of Chicago Press.

Kohl, H. (1995). *I won't learn from you: And other thoughts on creative maladjustment.* New York: The New Press.

Kornhaber, M. L. (2004). Assessment, standards, equity. In In J.A. Banks & C. A. M. Banks (Eds.), *Handbook of research on multicultural education* (2nd ed., pp. 91–109). San Francisco: Jossey Bass.

Kozol, J. (1991). *Savage inequalities.* New York: Crown Books.

Kozol, J. (2005). *The shame of a nation.* New York: Crown Books.

Kroeber, A. L., & Kluckhohn, C. (1952). *Culture: A critical review of concepts and definitions.* Paper 47. Cambridge, MA: Harvard University Peabody Museum of American Archeology and Ethnology.

Labov, W. (1970). *A study of non-standard English.* Washington, DC: ERIC Clearinghouse for Linguistics.

Ladson-Billings, G. (1994). *The Dreamkeepers: Successful teaching for African-American students.* San Francisco: Jossey-Bass.

Ladson-Billings. G. (1995). Toward a theory of culturally relevant pedagogy. *American Educational Research Journal, 32*(3), 465–491.

Ladson-Billings, G. (2000). Racialized discourses and ethnic epistemologies. In N. Denzin & Y. Lincoln (Eds.), *Handbook of qualitative research* (2nd ed., pp. 257–277). Thousand Oaks, CA: Sage.

Ladson-Billings, G. (2006). From the achievement gap to the education debt: Understanding achievement in U.S. schools. *Educational Researcher, 35*(7), 3–12.

Lareau, A. (2007). Invisible inequality: Social class and childrearing in Black families and White families. In A. R. Sadovnik (Ed.), *Sociology of education: A critical reader* (pp. 325–354). New York: Taylor & Francis.

Lave, J. (1988). *Cognition in Practice: Mind, mathematics, and culture in everyday life.* Cambridge: Cambridge University Press.

Lee, C. D. (1995). Signifying as a scaffold for literary interpretation. *Journal of Black Psychology, 21*(4), 357–381.

Lee, C. D. (1998). Culturally responsive pedagogy and performance-based assessment. *The Journal of Negro Education, 67*(3), 268–279.

Lee, C. D. (2002). Interrogating race and ethnicity as constructs in the examination of cultural processes in developmental research. *Human Development 45*, 282–290.

Lee, C. D. (2004). Double-voiced discourse: African American vernacular English as resource in cultural modeling classrooms. In A. Ball and S. Freedman (Eds.), *Bakhtinian perspectives on language, literacy, and learning* (pp. 129–147). Cambridge: Cambridge University Press.

Lee, C. D. (2007). *Culture, literacy, and learning: Blooming in the midst of the whirlwind.* New York: Teachers College Press.

Lee, R. B. (1993). *A comprehensive review of the literature and research on the Black male.* New York: City University of New York, Medgar Evers College, Ralph J. Bunche Center for Public Policy.

Lee, S. (1996). *Unraveling the "model minority" stereotype: Listening to Asian American youth.* New York: Teachers College Press.

Lee, S. J. (2005). *Up against whiteness: Race, school and immigrant youth.* Teachers College Press: New York.

Leithwood, K., Day, C., Sammons, P., Harris, A., & Hopkins, D. (2006). *Seven strong claims about successful school leadership,* Nottingham, England: National College for School Leadership.

Leithwood, R., & Reihl, C. (2003). *What we know about successful school leadership.* Philadelphia: Temple University Press.

Lewis, A. E. (2006). *Race in the schoolyard: Negotiating the color line in classrooms and communities.* New Brunswick, NJ: Rutgers University Press.

Lipman, P. (1995). "Bringing out the best in them": The contribution of culturally relevant teachers to education. *Theory Into Practice, 34*(3), 203–208.

Lomawaima, K. T., & McCarty, T. L. (1999). The un-natural history of American Indian education. In K. G. Swisher & J. W. Tippeconnic, III (Eds.), *Next steps: Research and practice to advance American Indian education* (pp. 13–31). Charleston, WV: ERIC Clearinghouse on Rural Education and Small Schools.

Lorde, A. (1984). *Sister outsiders: Essays and speeches by Audre Lorde.* Berkeley, CA: Crossing Press.

Lorde, A. (1999). Age, race, class, and sex: Women redefining difference. In A. Kesselman, L. D. McNair, & N. Schniedewind (Eds.), *Women: Images and realities, a multicultural anthology* (pp. 361–366). Mountain View, CA: Mayfield.

Low, V. (1982). *The unimpressible race: A century of educational struggle by the Chinese in San Francisco.* San Francisco: East/ West Publishing.

Lynn, M. (1999). Toward a critical race pedagogy: A research note. *Urban Education, 33*(5), 606–626.

Lynn, M. (2006). Education for the community: Exploring the culturally relevant practices of Black male teachers. *Teachers College Record, 108*(12), 2497–2522.

MacLeod, J. (1995). *Ain't no makin' it: Aspirations and attainment in a low-income neighborhood.* Boulder, CO: Westview Press.

Marable, M. (1992). *Black America*. Westfield, NJ: Open Media.

Marable, M. (1995). *Beyond black and white: Transforming African American politics*. New York: Verso.

Marable, M. (1997). *The crisis of color and democracy: Essays on race, class, and power*. Monroe, ME: Common Courage Press.

Marable, M. (2002). *The great walls of democracy: The meaning of race in American life*. New York: Basic Civitas Books.

Martin, D. B. (2000). *Mathematics success and failure among African-American youth: The roles of sociohistorical context, community forces, school influence and individual agency*. Mahwah, NJ: Erlbaum.

Marzano, R. J. (2003). *What works in schools: Translating research into action*. Alexandria, VA: Association for Supervision and Curriculum Development.

Marzano. R. J., Waters, T., & McNulty, B. A. (2005). *School leadership that works*. Alexandria, VA: Association for Supervision and Curriculum Development.

Matsuda, M. J. (1993). Public response to racist speech: Considering the victim's story. In M. J. Matsuda, C. R. Lawrence III, R. Delgado, & K. Williams Crenshaw (Eds.). *Words that wound: Critical race theory, assaultive speech, and the first amendment* (pp. 17–52). San Francisco: Westview Press.

McCarthy, C. (1988). Rethinking liberal and racial perspectives on racial inequality in schooling: Making the case for nonsynchrony. *Harvard Educational Review, 58*(3), 265–279.

McClain, C. J. (1994). *In search of equality: The Chinese struggle against discrimination in nineteenth-century America*. Berkeley: University of California Press.

McDermott, R. P. (1977). Social relations as contexts for learning in school. *Harvard Educational Review, 47*(2), 198–213.

McIntosh, P. (1989, July/August). White privilege: Unpacking the invisible knapsack. *Peace and Freedom*, 10–12.

McLaren, P. (1988). Culture or canon? Critical pedagogy and the politics of literacy. *Harvard Educational Review, 58*(2), 213–234.

McLaren, P. (1991). Critical pedagogy: Constructing ans arch of social dreaming and a doorway to hope. *Journal of Education, 173*(1), 9–34.

McLaren, P. (2000). *Che Guevara, Paulo Freire, and the pedagogy of revolution*. Boulder, CO: Rowman & Littlefield.

McNeal, R. B. (1999). Parental involvement as social capital: Differential effectiveness on science achievement, truancy, and dropping out. *Social Forces, 78*, 117–144.

McWhorter, J. (2000). *Losing the race*. New York: Free Press.

Mercer, J. R. (1989). Alternative paradigms for assessment in a pluralistic society. In J. A. Banks & C. A. M. Banks (Eds.), *Multicultural education: Issues and perspectives* (pp. 289–304). Boston: Allyn & Bacon.

Milner, H. R. (2003). Reflection, racial competence, and critical pedagogy: How do we prepare pre-service teachers to pose tough questions? *Race Ethnicity and Education, 6*(2),193–208

Milner, H. R. (2007). Race, culture, and researcher positionality: Working through dangers seen, unseen, and unforeseen. *Educational Researcher, 36*(7), 388–400.

Min, P. G. (2004). Social science research on Asian Americans. In J. A. Banks & C. A. M. Banks (Eds.). *The handbook of research on multicultural education* (2nd ed., pp. 332–348). San Francisco: Jossey-Bass.

Moll, L. C. (1992). Literacy research in community and classrooms: A sociocultural approach. In R. Reach, J. Green, M. Kamil & T. Shannahan (Eds.), *Multidisciplinary perspectives in literacy research* (pp. 211–244). Urbana, IL: National Conference on Research in English.

Moll, L. (2000). Inspired by Vygotsky: Ethnographic experiments in education. In C. D. Lee & P. Smagorinsky (Eds.), *Vygotskian perspectives on literacy research: Constsructing meaning through collaborative inquiry* (pp. 256–268). New York: Cambridge University Press.

Moll, L., & Gonzales, N. (2004). Engaging life: A funds-of-knowledge approach to multicultural education. In J. A. Banks & C. A. M. Banks (Eds.), *Handbook of research on multicultural education* (2nd ed., pp. 699–715). San Francisco: Jossey Bass.

Montagu, M. F. A. (1942). *Man's most dangerous myth: The fallacy of race.* New York: Columbia University Press.

Morrell, E., & Duncan-Andrade, J. (2005). Toward a critical classroom discourse: Promoting academic literacy through engraining hip hop culture with urban youth. *English Journal, 91*(6), 88–94.

Morrison, T. (1987). *Beloved.* New York: Knopf.

Moynihan, D. P. (1965). *The Negro family: The case for national action.* Washington, DC: U.S. Government Printing Office.

Muller, C., & Kerbow, D. (1993). Parent involvement in the home, school, and community. In B. Schneider & J. S. Coleman (Eds.), *Parents, their children, and schools* (pp. 13–42). Boulder, CO: Westview Press.

Myrdal, G. (1944). *An American dilemma: The Negro problem and modern democracy.* New York: Harper Brothers.

Nasir, N. (2000). Points ain't everything: Emergent goals and average, and percent understanding in the play of basketball among African American students. *Anthropology and Educational Quarterly, 31*(3), 283–305.

Nasir, N. (2002). Identity, goals, and learning: Mathematics in cultural practice. *Mathematical Thinking and Learning, 4*(2 &3), 213–247.

Nasir, N., & Cobb, P. (2002) Diversity, equity, and mathematical learning. *Mathematical Thinking, and Learning, 4*(2 &3), 91–102

Nasir, N. S., & Cobb, P. (2006). *Improving access to mathematics: Diversity and equity in the classroom.* New York: Teachers College Press.

National Center for Cultural Competence. (2008). *Developing cultural competence.* Washington, DC: Georgetown University Center for Child and Human Development.

National Center for Education Statistics. (2001). *The condition of education 2000.* Washington, DC: U.S. Department of Education.

National Center for Education Statistics. (2003). *School and staffing survey, 1999–2000.* Washington, DC: National Education Association.

National Center for Education Statistics. (2004). *National assessment of educational progress: 2004 long-term trend assessment results.* Retrieved August 5, 2007, from http://nces.ed.gov/nationsreportcard

National Center for Education Statistics. (2005). *The condition of education 2005* (NCES 2005-094). Washington, DC: U.S. Department of Education.

National Center for Education Statistics. (2006). *National assessment of educational progress: 2006 long-term trend assessment results.* Retrieved August 5, 2007, from http://nces.ed.gov/nationsreportcard

National Center for Education Statistics (2007a). *The condition of education 2007.* Washington, DC: U.S. Department of Education.

National Center for Education Statistics. (2007b). *The nation's report card: Achievement gaps: How Black and White students perform on NAEP.* Washington, DC: Institute of Education Sciences, U.S. Department of Education. Available from http://nces.ed.gov/nationsreportcard/

National Center for Education Statistics. (2008). *The condition of education 2008.* Washington, DC: U.S. Department of Education.

National Center for Homeless Education. (2007). *Education for homeless children and youth program: Analysis of 2005–2006 federal data collection and three year comparison.* Retrieved on July 11, 2008 from http:www.serve.org/nche

National Collaborative on Diversity in the Teaching Force. (2004). *Assessment of diversity in America's teaching force: A call to action.* Washington, DC: Author.

National College for School Leadership. (2006). Leadership succession: An overview—securing the next generation of school leaders. Nottingham, England: Author. Available from www.ncsl.org.uk/publications

National Committee for Citizens in Education. (1987). Helping parents help their kids: Parent involvement improves student performance. In National School Public Relations Association (Ed.), *The evidence continues to grow . . . Parent involvement improves student achievement.* Arlington, VA: National School Public Relations Association.

National Endowment for the Arts (2007). To read or not to read: A question of national consequence. Research Report #47. Retrieved on April 26, 2008 from http://www. nea.gov/research/toread.pdf.

Natriello, G., McDill, E. L., & Pallas, A. M. (1990). *Schooling disadvantaged children: Racing against catastrophe.* Westport, CT: Praeger.

Nelson-Barber, S., & Estrin, E. T. (1995). Bringing Native American perspectives to mathematics and science teaching. *Theory Into Practice, 34*(3), 174–185.

Neuman, S. B. (2009). *Changing the odds: Breaking the cycle of poverty and disadvantage for children at risk.* New York: Guilford Press.

Nieto, S. (2000). *Affirming diversity: The sociopolitical context of multicultural education.* (3rd ed.). New York: Longman.

Nieto, S. (2003). *What keeps teachers going?* New York: Teachers College Press.

Noddings, N. (2005). *The challenge to care in schools: An alternative approach to education.* (2nd. ed). New York: Teachers College Press.

Noguera, P. (2003). *City schools and the American dream.* New York: Teachers College Presss.

Noguera, P. (2008). *The trouble with Black boys . . . and other reflections on race, equity, and the future of public education.* San Francisco: Jossey-Bass.

Oakes, J. (2005). *Keeping track: How schools structure inequality* (2nd ed.). New Haven, CT: Yale University Press.

Oakes, J., Rogers, J., Silver, D., Valladares, S., Terriquez, V., McDonough, P., Renée, M., & Lipton. M. (2006). *Removing the roadblocks: Fair college opportunities for all California students.* University of California/All Campus Consortium for Research Diversity & UCLA Institute for Democracy, Education and Access. Retrieved October 26, 2008, from http://www.ucla-idea. org

Obidah, J. E., & Teel, K. M. (2001). *Because of the kids: Facing racial and cultural differences in schools.* New York: Teachers College Press.

O'Connor, C., & DeLuca Fernandez, S. (2006). Race, class, and disproportionality: Reevaluating the relationship between poverty and special education placement. *Educational Researcher, 35*(6), 6–11.

Ogbu, J. (1987). Opportunity structure, cultural boundaries, and literacy. In J. Langer (Ed.), *Language, literacy, and culture: Issues of society and schooling* (pp. 149–177). Norwood, NJ: Ablex Press.

Ogbu, J. (2003). *Black American students in an affluent suburb: A study of academic disengagement.* Mahwah, NJ: Erlbaum.

Oliver, M. L., & Shapiro, T. M. (1997). *Black wealth, white wealth: A new perspective on racial inequity.* New York; Routledge.

Olson, L. (1997). *Made in America: Immigrant students in public schools.* New York: New Press.

Omi, M., & Winant, H. (1994). *Racial formation in the United States: From the 1960s to the 1990s.* New York: Routledge.

Orfield, G. (2004). *Dropouts in America: Confronting the graduation crisis.* Cambridge, MA: Harvard Education Press.

Orfield, G., & Losen, D. (2002). *Racial inequity in special education.* Cambridge, MA: Harvard Education Publishing Group.

Orfield, G., Losen, D., Wald, J., & Swanson, C. B. (Eds.). (2004). *Losing our future: How minority youth are being left behind by the graduation rate crisis.* Cambridge, MA: Civil Rights Project, Harvard University.

Pak, Y. K. (2002). *"Wherever I go I will always be a loyal American": Schooling Seattle's Japanese Americans during World War II.* New York: Routledge.

Palmer, P. (1998). *The courage to teach.* San Francisco: Jossey-Bass.

Pang, V. O., Kiang, P. N., & Pak, Y. K. (2004). Asian Pacific American students: Challenging a biased educational system. In J. A. Banks & C. A. M. Banks (Eds.), *Handbook of research on multicultural education* (2nd ed., pp. 542–563). San Francisco: Jossey-Bass.

Parham, T. A. (2002). *Counseling persons of African descent: Raising the bar of practitioner competence.* Thousand Oaks, CA: Sage.

Parker, L., & Lynn, M. (2002). What's race got to do with it? Critical race theory's conflicts with and connections to qualitative research methodology and epistemology. *Qualitative Inquiry, 8*(1), 7–22.

Parsons, T. (1949). *Essays in sociological theory.* New York: Free Press.

Parsons, E. C. (2005). From caring as a relation to culturally relevant caring: A White teacher's bridge to Black students. *Equity and Excellence, 38,* 25–34.

Passel, J. S., & Cohn, D. (2008). *U.S. population projections 2005–2050.* Washington, DC: Pew Research Center.

Pearl, A. (1970). The poverty of psychology—an indictment. In V. L. Allen (Ed.), *Psychological factors in poverty* (pp. 348–364). Chicago: Markham.

Perry, T. (2003). Up from the parched earth: Toward a theory of African American achievement. In T. Perry, C. Steele, & A. Hilliard III (Eds.), *Young, gifted and Black* (pp. 1–10). New York: Beacon Press.

Pierce, C. (1974). Psychiatric problems of the Black minority. In S. Arieti (Ed.), *American handbook of psychiatry* (pp. 512–523). New York: Basic Books.

Pierce, C. (1995). Stress analogs of racism and sexism: Terrorism, torture, and disaster. In C. Willie, P. Rieker, B. Kramer, & B. Brown (Eds.), *Mental health, racism and sexism* (pp. 277–293). Pittsburgh, PA: University of Pittsburgh Press.

Pierce, E. (2005). Culturally relevant teaching: A teacher's journey to "get it right." *Multicultural Education, 12,* 1–6.

Pine, G. J., & Hilliard, A. G. (1990, April). Rx for racism: Imperatives for America's schools. *Phi Delta Kappan, 71*(8), 593–600.

Planty, M., Hussar, W., Snyder, T., Kena, G., KewalRamani, A., Kemp, J., Bianco, K., & Dinkes, R. (2009). *The condition of education 2009* (NCES 2009-081). National Center for Education Statistics, Institute of Education Sciences, U.S. Department of Education: Washington, DC.

Pollock, M. (2004). *Colormute: Race talk dilemmas in an American school.* Princeton, NJ: Princeton University Press.

Popham, W.J. (2001). *The truth about testing: An educator's call to action.* Alexandria, VA: Association for Supervision and Curriculum Development.

Powell, R. (1997). Then the beauty emerges: A longitudinal case study of culturally relevant teaching. *Teaching and Teacher Education, 13*(5), 467–484.

Ramírez, M. & Casteñada, A. (1974). *Cultural democracy, bicognitive development, and education.* New York: Academic Press.

Ravitch, D. (2003). *The language police.* New York: Knopf.

Reeves, D. B. (2000). *Accountability in action: A blueprint for learning organizations.* Denver, CO: Advanced Learning Press.

Reimer, E. (1971). *School is dead.* New York: Doubleday.

Reynolds, A. (1992). Grade retention and school adjustment: An explanatory analysis. *Educational Evaluation and Policy Analysis 14*(2), 101–121.

Reynolds, R. E. (2009). *Holla if you hear me: Giving voice to those we have missed. A qualitative examination of Black middle-class parent engagement in public secondary schools.* Unpublished dissertation, University of California, Los Angeles.

Riessman, F. (1962). *The culturally deprived child.* New York: Harper.

Rist, R. C. (1970). Student social class and teachers' expectations: The self-fulfilling prophecy in ghetto education. *Harvard Educational Review, 40,* 411–450.

Roderick, M. (1994). Grade retention and school dropout: Investigating the association. *American Educational Research Journal, 31*(4) 729–759.

Roediger, D. R. (1994). *Towards the abolition of Whiteness: Essays of race, politics and working class history.* London: Verso.

Roediger, D. R. (2005). *Working toward Whiteness: How America's immigrants became White. The strange journey from Ellis Island to the suburbs.* New York: Pegasus.

Rogoff, B. (2003). *The cultural nature of human development.* New York: Oxford University Press.

Rogoff, B., & Angelillo, C. (2002). Investigating the coordinated functioning of multifaceted cultural practices in human development. *Human Development, 45,* 211–225.

Rose, M. (1988). Narrowing the mind and page: Remediating writers and cognitive reductionism. *College Composition and Communication, 39*(3), 267–301.

Rothstein, R. (2004). *Class and schools: Using social, economic, and educational reform to close the Black–White achievement gap.* New York: Teachers College Press.

Rousseau, C., & Tate, W. (2003). No time like the present: Reflecting on equity in school mathematics. *Theory Into Practice, 42,* 211–216.

Ryan, W. (1971). *Blaming the victim.* New York: Random House.

Sanders, M. G., & Harvey, A. (2002). Beyond the school walls: A case study of principal leadership for school–community collaboration. *Teachers College Record 104*(7), 1345–1368.

Schein, E. (1985). *Organizational culture and leadership.* San Francisco: Jossey-Bass.

Scheurich, J. J., & Skrla, L. (2003). *Leadership for equity and excellence.* Thousand Oaks, CA: Corwin Press.

Schofield, J. W. (1986). Causes and consequences of the colorblind perspective. In S. Gaertner & J. Dovidio (Eds.), *Prejudice, discrimination and racism: Theory and practice.* (pp. 231–253). New York: Academic Press.

Schofield, J. W. (1999). The colorblind perspective in school: Causes and consequences. In J. A. Banks & C. A. M Banks (Eds.), *Multicultural education: Issues and perspectives* (4th ed., pp. 247–267). Boston: Allyn & Bacon.

Schon, D. (1983). *The reflective practitioner: How professionals think in action.* New York: Basic Books.

Schon, D. (1987). *Educating the reflective practitioner: Toward a new design for teaching and learning in the professions.* San Francisco: Jossey-Bass.

The Schott Foundation for Public Education (2008). *Given half a chance: The Schott report on public education and Black males.* Retrieved on January 23, 2009 from http://blackboysreport.org/node/13

Selden, S. (1999). *Inheriting shame: The story of eugenics and racism in America.* New York: Teachers College Press.

Shade, B. J. (1997). *Culture, style and the educative process: Making schools work for racially diverse students.* Springfield, IL: Thomas.

Sheets, R. H. (1995). From remedial to gifted: Effects of culturally centered pedagogy. *Theory Into Practice, 34*(3), 186–193.

Shepard, L. A. & Smith, M. L. (1990) Synthesis of research on grade retention. *Educational Leadership 47*(8), 84–88.

Shulman, L. J. (1987). Knowledge and teaching: Foundations of the new reform. *Harvard Educational Review, 57,* 1–22.

Siddle Walker, V. (1996). *Their highest potential: An African American community in the segregated south.* Chapel Hill: University of North Carolina Press.

Singleton, G. E & Linton, C. (2006). *Courageous conversations about race.* Thousand Oaks, CA: Corwin Press.

Skiba, R. J., Simmons, A., Staudinger, L., Rausch, M., Dow, G., & Feggins, R. (2003, May). *Consistent removal: Contributions of school discipline to the school-prison pipeline.* Paper presented at the School to Prison Pipeline Conference, Boston, MA.

Sleeter, C. E. (1996). *Multicultural education as social activism.* Albany: State University of New York Press.

Sleeter, C. E., & Bernal, D. D. (2004). Critical pedagogy, critical race theory, and anti-racist education: Implications for multicultural education. In J.A. Banks & C.A.M. Banks (Eds.), *Handbook of research on multicultural education* (2nd ed.) Jossey-Bass.

Sleeter, C. E. (2008) Preparing white teachers for diverse students. In M. Cochran-Smith, S. Feiman-Nemser, & J. McIntyre (Eds.). *Handbook of research in teacher education: Enduring issues in changing contexts.* (3rd ed., pp. 559–582). New York: Routledge.

Sleeter, C. E., & Grant, C. A. (2009). *Making choices for multicultural education: Five approaches to race, class, and gender* (6th ed.). New York: Wiley.

Smith, R., Mollem, M., & Sherrill, D. (1997). How preservice teachers think about cultural diversity. *Educational Foundations, 11*(2), 41–62.

Smith-Maddox, R., & Solorzano, D. G. (2002). Using critical race theory, Paulo Freire's problem-posing method, and case study research to confront race and racism in education. *Qualitative Inquiry, 8*(1), 66–84. Retrieved January 13, 2008, from resources/ed_articles2002/Black_Boys.html

Smitherman, G. (1977). *Talkin' and testifyin': The language of Black America.* Boston: Houghton Mifflin.

Smitherman, G. (1994). *Black talk: Words and phrases from the hood to the amen corner.* Boston: Houghton Mifflin.

Snow, C. E., Burns, M. S., & Griffin, P. (1998). *Preventing reading difficulties in young children.* Washington, DC: National Academy Press.

Snyder, T. (1998). *Digest of educational statistics.* Washington, DC: National Center for Education Statistics.

Solorzano, D. (1997). Images and words that wound: Critical race theory, racial stereotyping, and teacher education. *Teacher Education Quarterly, 24,* 4–16.

Solorzano, D. G. (1998). Critical race theory, race and gender microaggressions, and the experience of Chicana and Chicano scholars. *International Journal of Qualitative Studies in Education, 11*(1), 121–136.

Solorzano, D., Allen, W. R., & Carroll, D. (2002). Keeping race in place: Racial microaggressions and campus racial climate at the University of California, Berkeley. *Chicago-Latino Law Review, 23,* 15–112.

Solorzano, D. G., & Delgado Bernal, D. (2001). Examining transformational resistance through a critical race and latcrit theory framework. Chicana and Chicano students in an urban context. *Urban Education, 36*(3), 308–342.

Solorzano, D., & Yosso, T. (2001). Critical race and LatCrit theory and method: Counterstorytelling, Chicana and Chicano graduate school experiences. *International Journal of Qualitative Studies in Education, 14*(4), 471–495.

Solorzano, D., & Yosso, T. (2002). Critical race methodology: Counterstorytelling as an analytical framework for educational research. *Qualitative Inquiry, 8*(1), 23–44

Spring, J. (2006). Deculturalization and the struggle for equality (5th ed.). New York: McGraw-Hill.

Steele, C. M. (1992, April). Race and the schooling of Black Americans. *The Atlantic Monthly, 269,* 67–78.

Steele, C. M. (1995). Stereotype threat and the intellectual test performance of African Americans. *Journal of Personality and Social Psychology, 69*(5), 797–811.

Steele, C. M. (1997). A threat in the air: How stereotypes shape intellectual identity and performance. *American Psychologist,* 52(6), 613–629.

Steele, C. M. & Aronson, J. (1995). Stereotype threat and the intellectual test performance of African-Americans. *Journal of Personality and Social Psychology, 69*(5), 797–811.

Steele, C. M., & Aronson, J. (1998). How stereotypes influence the standardized test performance of talented African American students. In C. Jencks & M. Phillips (Eds.), *The Black–White test score gap* (pp. 401–427). Washington, D C: Brookings Institute

Steele, S. (1990). *The content of our character.* New York: St. Martin's Press.

Sternberg, R. J. (1985). *Beyond IQ: A triarchic theory of human intelligence.* Cambridge: Cambridge University Press.

Sui-Chu, E. H., &. Douglas, W. J. (1996). Effects of parental involvement on eighth-grade achievement. *Sociology of Education, 69*(2), 126–141.

Takaki, R. (1989). *Strangers from a different shore: A history of Asian Americans.* New York: Little, Brown.

Takaki, R. (1993). *A different mirror: A history of multicultural America.* New York: Little, Brown.

Tate, W. (1995). Returning to the root: A culturally relevant approach to mathematics pedagogy. *Theory Into Practice, 34*(3), 166–173.

Tate, W. (1997). Race-ethnicity, SES, gender, and language proficiency in mathematics achievement: An update. *Journal for Research in Mathematics Education, 28,* 652–679.

Tatum, B. D. (2007). *Can we talk about race? And other conversations in an era of school resegregation.* Boston: Beacon Press.

Taylor, E., Ladson-Billings, G., & Gilborn, D. (2009). *Foundations of critical race theory in education.* New York: Routledge.

Teel, K. M. & Obidah, J. E. (Eds.). (2008). *Building racial and cultural competence in the classroom.* New York: Teachers College Press.

Terrel, M., & Marck, D. L. H. (2000). Preservice teachers' expectations for schools with children of color and second-language learners. *Journal of Teacher Education, 51*(2), 149–155.

Tettagah, S. (1996). The racial consciousness attitudes of White prospective teachers and their perceptions of the teachability of students from different racial/ethnic backgrounds: Findings from a California study. *Journal of Negro Education, 65*(2), 151–163.

Tharp, R. G., & Gallimore, R. (1991). *Rousing minds to life.* Cambridge: Cambridge University Press.

Thernstrom, A., & Thernstrom, S. (2003). *No excuses: Closing the racial gap in learning.* New York: Simon & Schuster.

Thompson, A. (1998). Not the color purple: Black feminist lessons for educational caring. *Harvard Educational Review, 68*, 522–554.

Thornton, R. (1987). *American Indian holocaust and survival*. Norman: University of Oklahoma Press.

Tough, P. (2008). *Whatever it takes: Geoffrey Canada's quest to change Harlem*. New York: Houghton Mifflin.

Trumbull, E. (2001). *Bridging cultures between home and school*. Mahwah, NJ: Erlbaum.

Tyack, D. B. (1974). *The one best system*. Cambridge, MA: Harvard University Press.

Tyack, D. (2004). *Seeking common ground: Public schools in a diverse society*. Cambridge, MA: Harvard University Press.

U.S. Census Bureau (2006). *An older and more diverse nation by midcentury*. Retrieved on December 14, 2008 from http://www.census.gov/Press-Release/www/releases/archives/population/012496.html

U.S. Census Bureau (2007). American fact finder. Available from *http://www.census.gov/*

Urban, W., & Wagoner, J. (2000). *American education: A history*. New York: McGraw-Hill.

Valencia, R. R. (1997). *The evolution of deficit thinking: Educational thought and practice*. Washington, DC: Falmer Press.

Valencia, S. W., & Buly, M. R. (2004). Behind test scores: What struggling readers really need. *The Reading Teacher, 57*, 520–530.

Valenzuela, A. (1999). *Subtractive schooling: U.S.-Mexican youth and the politics of caring*. New York: State University New York Press.

VanTassel-Baska, J. (1992). *Planning effective curriculum for gifted learners*. Denver, CO: Love.

Villegas, A. M. & Lucas, T. (2002). Preparing culturally responsive teachers. *Journal of Teacher Education, 53*(1), 20–32

Vygotsky, L. S. (1978). *Mind and society*. (M. Cole, V. John-Steiner, S. Scribner, & E. Souberman, Eds.). Cambridge, MA: Harvard University Press.

Wald, J., & Losen, D. J. (2003). *Deconstructing the school-to-prison pipeline*. San Francisco: Jossey-Bass.

Warren, J. R., & Halpern-Manners, A. (2007). Is the glass emptying or filling up? Reconciling divergent trends in high school completion and dropout. *Educational Researchers, 36*(6), 335–343.

Wartfosky, M. (1973). *Models*. Dordrecht: D. Reidel.

Webb-Johnson, W., & Larke, P. J. (2002). Case XX tracking: Two teachers respond. In N. Quisenberry, J. McIntyre, & G. Duhon, (Eds.), *Racism in the classroom: Case studies* (pp 138–143). Alney, MD: Association of Teacher Educators & Association for Childhood Education International.

Weinberg, M. (1997). *Asian American education: Historical background and current realities*. Mahwah, NJ: Erlbaum.

Welch, O. M., & Hodges, C. R. (1997). *Standing outside on the inside: Black adolescence and the construction of academic identity*. New York: State University of New York Press.

West, C. (1993). *Race matters*. Boston: Beacon Press.

Western, B. (2006). *Punishment and inequality in America*. New York: Sage Foundation.

Wideman, J. E. (1998). *Damballah*. New York: Mariner Books.

Williams, P. (1997). Vampires anonymous and critical race practice. *Michigan Law Review, 95*, 741–765.

Wilson, T. D. (2002). *Strangers to ourselves*. Cambridge, MA: Harvard University Press.

Wilson, T. D., & Dunn, D. S. (1986). Effects of introspection on attitude-behavior consistency: Analyzing reasons versus focus on feelings. *Journal of Experimental Social Psychology, 22*, 249–263

Wilson, T. D. & D. T. Gilbert (2003). "Affective forecasting." In Mark P. Zanna, *Advances in experimental social psychology* (pp. 345–411). San Diego, CA: Academic Press.

Wilson, W. J. (2009). *More than just race: Being Black and poor in the inner city*. New York: Norton.

Woodson, C. G. (1968). *The education of the Negro prior to 1861*. New York: Arno Press. (Original work published 1919)

Wortham, S. (2002). Struggling toward culturally relevant pedagogy in the Latino diaspora. *Journal of Latinos and Education, 1*(2), 133–144.

Wright, S. P., Horn, S. P., & Sanders, W. L. (1997). Teacher and classroom context effects on student achievement: Implications for teacher evaluation. *Journal of Personnel Evaluation in Education, 11*, 57–67.

Yopp, H. K. (1992). Developing phonemic awareness in young children. *The Reading Teacher, 45*, 696–703.

Yosso, T. J. (2005). Whose culture has capital? A critical race theory discussion of community cultural wealth. *Race Ethnicity and Education, 8*(1), 69–91.

Zirkel, S. (2002). Is there a place for me? Role models and academic identity among White students and students of color. *Teachers College Record, 104*(2), 357–376.

Zumwalt, K., & Craig, E. (2005). Teachers' characteristics: Research on the indicators of quality. In M. Cochran-Smith & K. M. Zeichner (Eds.), *Studying teacher education* (pp. 157–260). New York: Routledge.

Index

About the Author

Tyrone C. Howard is Associate Professor of Education in the Division of Urban Schooling, and Director of Center X in the Graduate School of Education & Information Studies at UCLA. His research interests are primarily concerned with academic achievement of youth in urban schools. His work has centered on the achievement gap facing African American and other culturally diverse students, and the importance of reversing persistent underachievement. Dr. Howard also has done research and writing on the influence of culture on learning, critical race theory, social studies, and multicultural and urban education. Professor Howard's research has been published in journals such as *Teachers College Record*, *The Journal of Higher Education*, *Urban Education*, *The Journal of Teacher Education*, *Theory and Research in Social Education*, and *The Journal of Negro Education*. Dr. Howard recently was recognized by the American Educational Research Association's Committee on Scholars of Color with an Early Career Contribution Award for his research and scholarship. In 2007, Professor Howard received the Graduate School of Education and Information Studies Distinguished Teaching Award.